D0393451

BORN RED

BORN RED

A Chronicle of
the Cultural Revolution

GAO YUAN

Stanford University Press
Stanford, California
1987

Stanford University Press
Stanford, California

© 1987 by the Board of Trustees of the
Leland Stanford Junior University

Printed in the United States of America

CIP data appear at the end of the book

To my son Nathaniel Taihang Gao,
with the hope that
his generation will be wiser than mine

Contents

Contents

viii

Foreword

Gao Yuan's chronicle takes us through the first violent years of China's Great Proletarian Cultural Revolution. Like Anne Frank's diary of the Holocaust closing in around her or the story of Dith Pran's journey through the killing fields of Cambodia, it offers a voice that speaks to us of the human anguish of inhuman events.

The immediacy of Gao's account of his experiences as a Red Guard in the Cultural Revolution brings us as close as we are likely to get to the political vortex that turned millions of teenagers into the agents of national madness. His description of how the movement gripped him and his schoolmates reveals, as no scholarly analysis can, the fury that brought China to the brink of civil war. Through his eyes we see how ideological expletives gave way to deadly explosives as the weapons of revolutionary conflict. His witness to the unspeakable violence that the young rebels inflicted on one another and their teachers evokes images of the children run amok in *Lord of the Flies*. The graphic depictions of brutalities committed in the name of idealism may at times shock us—yet they are also needed reminders that noble rhetoric can often be a mask for ignoble deeds.

But *Born Red* is so much more than the recollection of a political nightmare. It is a deeply personal narrative of an adolescent torn by conflicting loyalties as he is called upon to join in the destruction of the world that has nurtured him.

Some of the book's most powerful moments tell of family ties and friendships sundered by class struggle; yet it is just such bonds that ultimately provide the only safe harbor as the storm of the Cultural Revolution rages beyond reason. Gao's saga also provides tribute to the durability of cultural traditions at a time when nihilism appeared triumphant: we can almost smell the dumplings cooking and hear the firecrackers popping as Lunar New Year festivities unfold even while Red Guards desecrate ancient artifacts in the name of revolutionary purity.

For readers already familiar with the Cultural Revolution, Gao Yuan's memoirs need no further introduction. But for those who come to this book with less background in contemporary Chinese history, it is helpful to set more fully the context of events that Gao describes.

The origins of the Cultural Revolution are to be found in Mao Zedong's perception that the People's Republic of China (PRC) in the mid-1960's was drifting away from the road to socialism down which the country had embarked after its founding in 1949. Mao had been the preeminent leader of the Chinese revolution since the 1930's, when he had become the principal architect of the strategy of peasant insurrection that had brought the Communists to power. Since Liberation he had not only retained his leading position as Chairman of the Chinese Communist Party (CCP), but had also come to see himself as the guardian of the ideals for which the revolution had been fought.

As Mao surveyed the situation in China in the 1960's he saw much that clashed with his notions of what a revolutionary society should be: a tracked educational system that provided better opportunities for the children of intellectuals and officials than for the offspring of the working classes; a cultural life dominated by traditional themes and forms rather than revolutionary content; economic policies emphasizing individual prosperity instead of the collective good; and a Communist Party that had transformed itself from a servant of the people into an elite organization managing society in a bureaucratic manner. He was alarmed by corruption and self-seeking among cadres, a bias in social programs that favored urban dwellers and neglected the welfare of the peasantry—the very class that had been the lifeblood of the Chinese revolution—and the ideological softness of China's young people, who had grown up in relatively good times and knew of the hardships of life before Liberation only through books and the tales of their elders. If such trends continued, Mao thought, China would experience a return to the dark days of the past—a "restoration of capitalism"—and all the sacrifices and struggles of the past would have come to naught.

How had the PRC reached such a juncture? Mao concluded that many Chinese Communists had succumbed to the ideological disease of "revisionism," that is, they were revising the fundamental principles of Marxism-Leninism, retaining the shell of doctrine to justify their continuing political domination and to preserve the special status and perquisites that they and their families enjoyed. The Chairman had a long-standing fear that the CCP would lose its revolutionary spirit once it had come to power and settled down to the mundane tasks of governance and modernization. In the mid-1950's he dissented from the view of some of his senior colleagues that with the completion of land reform, the collectivization of agriculture, and the nationalization of the country's major industries the Party could shift its attention from radical change to economic development.

Mao came to believe that even though landlords and capitalists had been eliminated as functioning social classes, the influence of their feudal and bourgeois ways still permeated Chinese society; unless "class struggle" continued against the remnants of reaction, the revolution would be lost, defeated not by the invading armies of imperialism or by a counterrevolution of the defeated classes of the past, but by the political degeneration of "capitalist roaders" lurking in the body and the soul of the Party. This conviction would later take the form of the "theory of continuing the revolution under the dictatorship of the proletariat," the guiding doctrine of the Cultural Revolution, which encapsulated Mao's view that only by persisting in the ideological battle against the new bourgeoisie and by constantly remaking social institutions and human values could socialism in China survive.

Gao Yuan's family bore the practical brunt of Mao's theories of revisionism: his father, veteran Communist Gao Shangui, came under brutal Red Guard attack at the start of the Cultural Revolution for paying too much attention to economic matters while ignoring class struggle and revolutionary politics in carrying out his duties as head of a county government.

Mao's fears about the threat posed to socialism by internal enemies found political expression at several points before the Cultural Revolution. In 1957, the CCP waged a fierce "anti-Rightist campaign" against intellectuals and others judged to have revealed their diehard opposition to socialism during the Hundred Flowers period, when they took too literally the Party's invitation to offer professional advice and constructive criticism as an aid to national development. Millions were adversely affected: some were sent to prison, others were put to work in factories or on farms to remold their bourgeois thoughts through hard labor, and still others had their career prospects—and those of close relatives—ruined by being branded as "Rightists," conservatives who had to be closely monitored to prevent their corrosive influence from diverting the course of the revolution.

In the midst of the Great Leap Forward (1958–60)—Mao's grand design to achieve rapid economic growth through the mobilization of China's enormous reservoir of human labor and attain true communism through radical social engineering—the Chairman wrathfully rejected the warnings of Defense Minister Peng Dehuai that the movement's extravagant targets and precipitous methods were courting calamity. Mao accused Peng and several other prominent leaders of attempting to sabotage the Great Leap by denigrating the revolutionary spirit of the masses. A vituperative media campaign against "Right opportunism" accompanied a purge of Party cadres deemed to have been less than completely enthusiastic about the Leap. A resurgence of radicalism (along with abysmal weather conditions and the withdrawal of Soviet aid) did, indeed, undo the economy, plunging China into an industrial depression and rural famine now believed to have claimed as many as 30 million lives.

And again in the early 1960's, when China was just beginning to recover from the agonies of the Great Leap Forward, Mao, although somewhat chastened by the disaster, still pressed his claim that class struggle against the enemies of socialism should remain the Party's first priority. A "Socialist Education Movement" was launched in 1963 to ferret out bourgeois tendencies among lower-level cadres, and the less-than-thorough manner in which the campaign was conducted fed Mao's growing suspicion that the poison of revisionism had infested the highest ranks of the country's leadership.

The Soviet Union also figured prominently in the genesis of

Mao's concern about the rightward drift of China's development, a concern that would eventually culminate in the Cultural Revolution. The Sino-Soviet alliance began to unravel in the late 1950's as the two major Communist powers diverged sharply in their positions on a number of important issues. China bristled at what it considered the heavy-handed way in which Moscow sought to maintain control of the socialist bloc and at the compromises the Soviets were willing to make with imperialism simply for the sake of peaceful coexistence. The Russians, for their part, were appalled by what they saw as the PRC's reckless foreign policy and were increasingly skeptical of Mao's unorthodox brand of communism, manifested most clearly in the Great Leap Forward. (Such conflicts echoed the tensions of the 1920's and 1930's when the Russians, as proponents of the doctrine that Communist movements by definition had to be based in the cities among the industrial proletariat, were dismayed to see the Chinese revolution under Mao's direction turning to the countryside and the peasantry.)

Ultimately, Mao deduced that Soviet deviance in foreign policy matters could only be traced to even more profound deviance in ideology and domestic politics: under Khrushchev the Soviet Union had forsaken socialism for a brand of capitalism in which the Communist Party had become a new ruling class. For Mao the question was, Would China follow a similar political trajectory?

Thus, by the mid-1960's, events both at home and abroad had led Mao to the conclusion that without decisive remedial action, socialist revolutions inevitably degenerated into revisionism. There was little he could do about Soviet revisionism other than to orchestrate an international propaganda campaign against "Khrushchev's phony communism" and the "great power chauvinism" of the Russians—an endeavor in which he was enthusiastically joined by his closest comrades in the CCP leadership. Within China, though, Mao still commanded the power and the prestige to stem the tide of revisionism. His solution was the Great Proletarian Cultural Revolution—but, in this case, some of his closest comrades would eventually become his targets. Only when the revisionists had been removed from power, Mao believed, could the PRC resume its march toward socialism and communism.

The Cultural Revolution, then, was intended to clear the way for a more egalitarian and participatory society. Through mass political struggle and ideological transformation, bourgeois bureaucracy would give way to proletarian democracy, self-interest to self-sacrifice, and cultural elitism to populism in the arts. Radical organizational changes would redistribute power, while adjustments in the flow of resources would greatly reduce individual and group income inequalities, regional economic disparities, and the gap between city and countryside. Such a revolution would, it was promised, unfetter the productivity of the masses and open the door to a new era of abundance for all. These ideals, hammered home at every opportunity, were instrumental in attracting adherents to the early stages of the Cultural Revolution, both within China and among many foreign observers who were fascinated by the "Maoist" model of development.

Mao had two other motivations for launching the Cultural Revolution. First was a concern about the youth of China. Mao believed that they could become worthy successors to the revolution only if they themselves participated in making revolution. This perception was critical to the decision to fight the early rounds of the Cultural Revolution in the schools and to the emergence of the Red Guards as one of Mao's main allies in his struggle against the Party bureaucracy.

Second, although the Cultural Revolution was a battle of ideas, it was also a power struggle. In the aftermath of the Great Leap Forward, Mao had voluntarily stepped back from day-to-day decision-making within the Party hierarchy, choosing instead to concentrate on ideological questions and broader policy matters. But by 1965 he felt slighted by other top leaders: they paid him lip service as Chairman of the Party and proclaimed symbolic allegiance to his theories as their guiding philosophy, but they ignored his counsel and circumvented his authority. Mao saw the Cultural Revolution, then, as an instrument through which he would reestablish his personal dominance in Chinese politics.

Both of these underlying motives for the Cultural Revolution themselves derived from Mao's preoccupation with revisionism: an untempered youth would provide a breeding ground for the spread of bourgeois ideology, while the same leaders Mao perceived as snubbing him were also those whom he believed were leading China down the road to capitalism.

The Cultural Revolution itself was an enormously complex event—or, more precisely, series of events. Although some argue that the movement ended with the demobilization of the Red Guards and the reassertion of political order by the army in 1968–69, the official Chinese assessment now considers the Cultural Revolution to have lasted for an entire decade, 1966–76. There is merit to this view since it took the full ten years to work out all the contradictions unleashed by Mao's campaign, although the event said to mark the formal end of the Cultural Revolution—the arrest of the Gang of Four in

October 1976—ironically paved the way for a complete repudiation of the movement by those now in power in Beijing.

The first tremor of what was to become the political earthquake of the Cultural Revolution was felt in the fall of 1965, when Mao sanctioned a scathing press denunciation of revisionist trends in Chinese culture. This attack initially appeared to be only another installment in the Party's periodic upbraiding of intellectuals seen to have taken liberalization too far. But Mao quickly became disgruntled by the efforts of officials charged with overseeing cultural policy to define the critique as merely an academic debate and to obscure the deeper ideological and political implications of deviant trends among China's intelligentsia.

This evasiveness on the part of high-ranking cadres hardened Mao's view that the Party could not cleanse itself. Instead, he would have to turn to the people to bring the Party back into line with its own ideals. Nothing short of a mobilization of the masses against the organizationally strong but ideologically rotten bulwark of the Communist Party would put an end to revisionism. It would be a "revolution from below," although one inspired by and ultimately subservient to the man who stood at the pinnacle of power.

By the spring of 1966, the Cultural Revolution was a full-scale national movement in which counterrevolutionaries within the Party, along with "representatives of the bourgeoisie" in academic and cultural circles, had been identified as the targets of attack. This was the beginning of the mass phase of the Cultural Revolution—and the beginning point of Gao's narrative—in which power at the center passed into the hands of radical ideologues and anarchy prevailed below as the institutions of order were either paralyzed by the hunt for revisionists or stood by in tacit support of local rebels.

Foreword

The centerpiece of this period was, of course, the emergence of the Red Guards, a generic label for the vast array of student groups that took up Mao's call to battle against the enemies of socialism. The Red Guards first appeared spontaneously on Beijing campuses to resist the efforts of school authorities (acting in accordance with the instructions of high Party officials) to limit the scope of the burgeoning Cultural Revolution to criticism of a few scholars and academic bureaucrats. As word of the rebellion by Beijing students spread, Red Guard organizations quickly sprang up all over China.

A major Party meeting in August 1966 sanctioned the mass uprisings that were becoming the main thrust of the Cultural Revolution (a nice piece of historical irony, since many of the leaders present at that meeting would later come under attack by the very masses they had authorized to rebel). The Red Guards received Mao's personal blessing to continue their efforts to expose revisionism at eight dramatic rallies attended by some thirteen million youths in the capital between August and November of that year. Thus, the Red Guards became one of the pillars of the Maoist alliance in the first phase of the Cultural Revolution. They were joined by elements of the People's Liberation Army (PLA), which, under the command of Lin Biao, had been fashioned into what Mao considered the only remaining repository of revolutionary virtue among the established institutions of society, and by a coterie of radical ideologues that included Mao's wife, Jiang Qing, and Mao's long-time personal secretary, Chen Boda, who is one of the few national leaders to figure prominently in the events described by Gao Yuan.

The rapid expansion of the Red Guard movement revealed that Mao's call to make revolution had struck responsive chords among China's youth. Some responded out of blind faith in the man they had been indoctrinated to love since childhood. Others saw the movement as a chance to vent simmering frustrations about inequities in the educational system or about clogged channels of mobility after graduation. Still others used the Red Guards as an instrument of vengeance against teachers they disliked or classmates they envied. And many, intoxicated with power and uninhibited by authority of any kind, simply went along for the thrill. As *Born Red* tells so dramatically, few of the youthful participants really understood the ideological meaning of the Cultural Revolution, and in their hands the struggle between the proletariat and the bourgeoisie degenerated into gang wars, joyrides, souvenir hunts, and orgies of destruction.

Among the issues that propelled the Red Guard movement into the violent factionalism that ultimately proved its undoing was the question of class origin. Children from "bad" classes (e.g., former landlord or capitalist families), regardless of their own political credentials, were definitively excluded from joining the Red Guards, and indeed often became targets of attack; the sons and daughters of intellectuals also frequently suffered ostracism or physical abuse, especially if their parents had been denounced. Rebel groups were themselves divided by the family backgrounds of their respective memberships. The offspring of workers, cadres, and soldiers were pitted against one another as each faction claimed that only its class status was pure enough to embody Chairman Mao's sacred cause. They fractured and fought over who were the true rebels and who were merely "royalists" out to protect their parents and their parents' patrons from the rightful wrath of the revolutionary masses.

During all of 1967 and the first part of 1968, the conflagration of local rebellion spread throughout China, burning with ever-greater intensity as internecine Red Guard warfare responded to the leadership struggles in Beijing. Factions of factory workers and military units also joined the fray, thereby greatly escalating the tempo of violence. "Power seizures" rooted out suspected revisionists of both large and petty stripe, and left authority in the hands of rebels who often had little in mind except vengeance against their opponents. Efforts to restore order proved abortive as Mao's political whirlwind took on a momentum of its own.

By mid-1968, Mao became frustrated by the persistence of turmoil and discord, and he ordered the PLA to restore peace in China's cities. (The violence of this phase of the Cultural Revolution was largely an urban affair, barely touching the countryside.) In any case, the Red Guards had largely served one of his purposes in the Cultural Revolution. They had helped immobilize the Party establishment, allowing Mao to reassert his personal power and depose his chief rivals—the President of the PRC, Liu Shaoqi, and Deng Xiaoping, Secretary-General of the CCP. The "capitalist-roaders" at the top had been toppled.

The army took control of schools, factories, government offices—wherever authority had broken down. PLA units disarmed the rebels and set about rebuilding the political system in the form of "revolutionary committees" composed of representatives of the military, the masses, and cadres who had weathered the tempest of the Cultural Revolution. Millions of Red Guards were dispatched to the countryside, where they were expected to continue their revolutionary tempering, but this time through hard physical labor under peasant supervision. Others, like Gao Yuan, were demobilized as Red Guards and remobilized into the army as China's military manpower needs expanded in response to escalating border hostilities with the Soviet Union.

In April 1969, the convening of the Ninth Congress of the CCP (the first full Party Congress since 1956) brought to a close the first stage of the Cultural Revolution. The keynote speech lauded the routing of the bourgeoisie in the ranks of the Party and the reaffirmation of proletarian power. Delegates waved the "Little Red Book" of quotations from Mao's writings that had become the bible of the campaign. Lin Biao was named as the CCP's only Vice-Chairman and enshrined in the new Party constitution as Chairman Mao's "close comrade-in-arms and successor." The radicals who had shaped the ideology of the Cultural Revolution and who had been the patrons of the Red Guards were also strongly represented in the leadership lineup, as were central and regional military commanders charged with maintaining civil peace while a new political order was put in place. The Ninth Party Congress was a celebration of all that the destruction of the previous three years had achieved. But it also planted the seeds of the political conflict that would mark the next stage of the Cultural Revolution.

It is here that the main body of Gao Yuan's book leaves off, although his Postscript provides a concise overview of the major events in China through the mid-1980's and an update on the lives of the many personalities we come to know so well in the pages of *Born Red*. But the Cultural Revolution continued to dominate the Chinese political scene for several years after Gao and his schoolmates ceased to be active participants, albeit in a form very different from that of the Red Guard era.

The period from April 1969 through the summer of 1971

was a time of military ascendancy in Chinese politics. Army officers held a preponderance of power in the upper echelons of the Party under Mao and in the revolutionary committees that were the main organs of government beneath the center. However, the political role of the People's Liberation Army began to be curtailed drastically following a showdown between Mao and Lin Biao that reached fateful proportions during the years 1970–71.

The Chairman and his designated successor clashed over a number of issues, including Lin's desire for even greater power and his resistance to the restoration of civilian Party authority. Lin also opposed Mao's decision to begin a diplomatic rapprochement with the United States as a counterweight to the perceived threat from the Soviet Union, whose conflict with China had broken out in military hostilities in the late 1960's. The radicals in the leadership also bore a grudge toward Lin as the commander of the forces that had suppressed their beloved Red Guards and kept the rebels from playing a major role in the revolutionary committees.

The factional struggles within the top leadership escalated to the point that, in September 1971, Lin and a number of his close associates attempted to stage a coup. Their plan was to assassinate Mao, blame the deed on the radicals, and seize power in the name of national security. The plan was exposed prematurely, and Lin, along with several of his co-conspirators, allegedly perished in a plane crash in Outer Mongolia while fleeing to the Soviet Union.

Although Lin's demise removed one of the prime movers of the Cultural Revolution, the tumult was by no means over. The next stage of the Cultural Revolution (roughly early 1972 to mid-1973) was the heyday of the ideologues. It was a period when Jiang Qing and other radicals used their grip on the PRC's media and propaganda organs to stoke the embers of class struggle. The physical persecutions that had marked the first phase of the movement subsided, but the climate of intimidation persisted as intellectuals and others suspected of being tainted with bourgeois ideology were forced to work in degrading circumstances.

In policy matters where the radicals exerted strong influence, reforms meant to give substance to the ideals of the Cultural Revolution were implemented. For example, new school admissions criteria stressed political activism and gave preference to the children of the working masses, while curricula were revamped to emphasize their revolutionary content and encourage participation in productive labor. In economic policy, radical rhetoric persisted, yet was unable to undermine the moderating influence of surviving veteran cadres like Premier Zhou Enlai.

The Tenth Party Congress, in August 1973, ushered in the final stage of the Cultural Revolution. This meeting put in place a leadership sharply divided between radicals committed to pursuing the goals of the Cultural Revolution and moderates who wanted to turn down the political heat, refocus the nation's energies on modernization, and reinstate some of the Party officials overthrown in the earlier phases of the movement. The ideological schism at the top was reflected dramatically in two personnel decisions endorsed by the Congress (though obviously initiated by Mao): the appointment as a Party Vice-Chairman of Wang Hongwen, a young factory worker who had been among the rebel leaders in Shanghai, and the rehabilitation of Deng Xiaoping, who six years earlier had been purged as China's second-most-notorious revisionist.

The next three years can be characterized as a tug-of-war

within the Chinese elite over concrete policy and abstract ideology; but the critical issue that lurked behind the debate was the succession to Mao. All the players (including Mao) were increasingly aware of the aged and ailing Chairman's mortality. Radicals and moderates became locked in a struggle for positions that they hoped would give them the power to determine China's direction in the post-Mao era.

Mao, despite his increasing infirmity, seemed to play a balancing act between the contending groups. For instance, he approved plans spearheaded by Zhou Enlai and Deng Xiaoping in 1974–75 to speed up China's economic development, including a more tolerant attitude toward scientists and a more open attitude toward foreign involvement in the economy; he also is known to have warned Jiang Qing and her associates to cease their factional maneuverings. On the other hand, he allowed the radicals to use his mantle in a series of propaganda campaigns—aimed indirectly at Zhou and Deng—intended to revive the spirit of the Cultural Revolution and to stand as a warning that attention to modernization was no excuse for a resurgence of revisionism.

Zhou Enlai's death in January 1976 ignited a furious final round in the battle of the titans of Chinese politics. Zhou was succeeded as Premier by Hua Guofeng, a relative political neophyte at the center of power who emerged with Mao's endorsement as a compromise candidate between the radicals and the moderates. The radicals were able to engineer yet another purge of Deng Xiaoping the following April, accusing him of masterminding a betrayal of the Cultural Revolution and once again plotting to lead China down the capitalist road.

In the summer of 1976, the radicals seemed to be riding high: their two main nemeses, Zhou and Deng, were gone;

Mao appeared to be backing their side; a pliable Premier stood astride the machinery of government; and their control of the media allowed them to project an image of enormous strength while loudly touting the themes of class struggle and proletarian dictatorship that had been the ideological fuel of the Cultural Revolution. When Mao died on September 9, the radicals had good reason to believe that they had indeed won the war to succeed him.

But the Cultural Revolution had one more twist in store. Less than a month after Mao died, Hua Guofeng, acting with the support of veteran cadres and key PLA officers, ordered the arrest of the top radical leaders, the so-called Gang of Four: Mao's widow Jiang Qing, the worker-rebel Wang Hongwen, and two propagandists, Yao Wenyuan and Zhang Chunqiao, who had been at the forefront of the Cultural Revolution since its inception. Hua was named Party Chairman and moved quickly to undercut the radicals' bases of support, especially in the para-military people's militia and propaganda organs.

Although the final scenes in the decade-long drama of the Great Proletarian Cultural Revolution took several more months to play out, the ouster of the Gang of Four signified the virtual end of the movement. The radical rhetoric continued for a while, and Hua Guofeng's efforts to shroud himself in Mao's memory raised doubts about whether there would really be an ideological turnabout.

But the second political resurrection of Deng Xiaoping, in August 1977, set in motion the chain of events that, over the next few years, put to rest all such doubts: the removal of leaders who preferred to cling to some of the symbolism and substance of the Cultural Revolution; the replacement of Hua Guofeng in the posts of state Premier and Party Chairman by close Deng protégés (Zhao Ziyang and Hu Yaobang); the reinstatement of a multitude of veteran cadres pushed aside by rebel upstarts; the posthumous exoneration of those who had been denounced as counterrevolutionary revisionists and had lost their lives during the radical storm; a reevaluation of Mao's record that affirmed his contributions yet forthrightly blamed him for serious political mistakes; the dramatic trial of the Gang of Four, in which detailed testimony about their misdeeds during the Cultural Revolution served as the major evidence to justify long prison sentences.

Perhaps the most important indication of how much post-Mao China has turned its back on Mao's Cultural Revolution lies in the package of remarkable economic and social reforms implemented under Deng's aegis. Whether it be the blatant appeal to material self-interest that is the essence of the shift from collectivized to household-based agriculture (and that accounts for the astounding growth in China's rural production in recent years) or the restructuring of Chinese education along strictly meritocratic and professional lines, Deng's reforms are, in many ways, reminiscent of the policies of the early 1960's that so incurred Mao's ideological indignation and predisposed him toward the launching of the Cultural Revolution.

The Deng Xiaoping era in China represents a victory of the victims of the Cultural Revolution. The movement that was hailed at its outset as a profound effort to transform the very soul of the nation and as the only way to ensure that China would continue to march along the road to socialism is now depicted as the darkest period in the PRC's history. The Cultural Revolution is said to have been a time of political chaos that ripped apart the fabric of Chinese society, of cultural repression that maimed the country's intelligentsia, and of economic stagnation that seriously jeopardized the people's livelihood.

Mao's allies in the great campaign have met unforeseen fates. His chief lieutenants have perished in disgrace or been imprisoned for their crimes against the Chinese nation. Even the Chairman's mortal remains, which lie embalmed in Beijing's Tiananmen Square, have been made to confront the inversion of all that was held sacred during the Cultural Revolution: in late 1983 Mao's mausoleum was remodeled to incorporate a memorial to other deceased Party luminaries, including Liu Shaoqi, the arch-villain of the assault on revisionism.

In the immediate aftermath of the Cultural Revolution, former Red Guards were written off as a "lost generation," scorned for their acts of rebellion and often consigned to inferior jobs because of inadequate education. Several million still languish in the countryside, where they have remained since being abandoned by their radical patrons at the top; "representatives" of this group occasionally make their way to Beijing or other cities to demand resettlement in the urban areas. But the open economic environment in China today has provided many of these ex-rebels (now in their thirties and forties) with new opportunities to put their pasts behind them. Some are moving into positions of responsibility commensurate with their abilities and age, while others are enriching themselves by taking utmost advantage of private commerce, free markets, and other "sprouts of capitalism" attacked vehemently during the Cultural Revolution but now greatly encouraged in the current climate of reform. Mao's children have become Deng's heirs.

What legacy has the Cultural Revolution bequeathed China? On the one hand, there are deep psychological scars that individual Chinese will bear for life and social wounds that will not heal for generations. There is pervasive political apathy and ideological cynicism that is a welcome retreat from the frantic politics of recent decades, yet is worrisome to a regime still committed to socialist principles. And there is fear, based on the vagaries that have seized the Party in the past when its leadership or priorities have been challenged, that another such movement could erupt: witness the widespread nervousness (especially among older intellectuals) when a short-lived campaign against the "spiritual pollution" of bourgeois ideology in 1983–84 was heartily endorsed by leaders who felt that Deng's reforms were going too far too fast.

On the other hand, some good might be born of the tragedy. Past excesses have created an environment conducive to change. The urgent need to revive production after the disruption of the Cultural Revolution has provided an important impetus for the creative rethinking of economic policy. The discrediting of radical ideas about the relationship between politics and production, which are widely seen as having been a recipe for national weakness and personal poverty, has immeasurably increased both popular enthusiasm and ideological leeway for a reform of the economy.

The lessons of the Cultural Revolution may also yield political fruit. There is a growing recognition in China that the roots of the decade of chaos go deeper than one man's fantasies or the fanaticism of his followers, and must ultimately be traced to the nature of the political system constructed under Mao's command. Weak institutions proved susceptible to usurpation by individuals and factions; and inadequate constraints on power and a lack of legal safeguards provided fertile soil for autocracy and repression. Many believe only political reform that brings the nation a true measure of democracy can prevent the recurrence of a nightmare like the Cultural Revolution.

There is great interest at all levels of society in finding forms of democracy suited to Chinese conditions and traditions. Some of the most urgent and eloquent demands for such political reform come from former Red Guards, especially those fortunate enough to piece together a decent education, who are now in the forefront of movements based both in China and abroad to champion the cause of Chinese democracy. They share the political skepticism of many of their generation, but they have chosen activism over apathy. Once again they call for a profound remaking of China's polity, but now their call is for the likes of a separation of powers, checks and balances, contested elections, the rule of law, freedom of the press—principles and procedures they once repudiated as merely the political trappings of capitalism, but which they today know must, in some manner, lie at the heart of any democracy, be it bourgeois or socialist, Western or Chinese.

Many of China's leaders also talk of the necessity for political change, and, despite noticeable opposition from conservatives who feel threatened by a more open political system, some meaningful steps have been taken in that direction. Recent policies have provided for greater accountability of public officials, limited tenure in office, prohibitions against the adulation of individual leaders, and laws that give some degree of protection for the rights of citizens against arbitrary incursions by the state. While such measures do little to undermine the ultimate authority of the Communist Party, they are hopeful signs. The abuses of power that caused so much misery during the Cultural Revolution have heightened present sensitivities to political malfeasance and have generated some momentum toward democratic reform. How far this momentum proceeds is one of the most vital questions facing China as it heads toward the twenty-first century.

During the Cultural Revolution, Mao often said that there could be "no construction without destruction," and, indeed, that destruction had to precede construction. This dictum became the rationale for an assault on Chinese culture and the persecution of countless men and women. But the Cultural Revolution, which destroyed so much, could not construct: its ideals were overwhelmed by the violence that became its motive force, its claim to be a moral cause was belied by the hatred on which it was built. That the new order emerging in the movement's wake bears so little resemblance to all Mao hoped might rise from the ashes of his crusade against revisionism is but the Cultural Revolution's final irony.

William A. Joseph

Wellesley College

Preface

One of the casualties of the Chinese Cultural Revolution was my diary. Sometime during the factional battles at my middle school, amidst the advances and retreats, the victories and defeats, it disappeared. So the best chronicle of what I saw, heard, thought, and felt at the time has been lost. This book is an attempt to recover that loss, to recapture an experience that shaped the lives of millions of young Chinese like myself.

Everything in these pages is essentially true; virtually every scene remains vivid in my memory, although I necessarily had to reconstruct much of the dialogue. I have changed some local place names—the reader will not find Shimen, Yizhen, Lingzhi, or Shuiyuan on the map of Hebei province. I also have disguised the names of my schoolmates, in the recognition that all, innocent or guilty, were caught up in a movement beyond anyone's ability to control.

As for my own name, the reader will notice that I am called one thing as narrator and another as author. I gave up Gao Jianhua in favor of Gao Yuan after the Cultural Revolution. I considered Jianhua, "construct China," too common a given name, and my grandfather had long before thought up an alternative. He called me Gao Yuan after Qu Yuan, a poet of the Warring States period. Gao Yuan also suits me because it means "highland," describing the area where I was born, on the edge of North China's loess plateau.

This book owes its existence to those who went through the political storm of the Cultural Revolution with me—fellow students, teachers and administrators, and family members. My first debt of gratitude as an author is to them.

I am also grateful to numerous people who helped me transform my memories into print, including a certain University of California professor whose harsh critique of my writing prompted me to throw out my first attempt at autobiography and start afresh.

Many other people helped me in less painful ways. Those whose enthusiasm for earlier drafts of this book encouraged me to press on include Thomas Leonard, Marilyn Young, Peter Collier, Orville Schell, and Carolyn Wakeman, and my friends Nancy Jervis, James Caldwell, and Pat and Jerry Werthimer. I owe special thanks to Barbara Chan, who lent me her home in the Berkeley hills while she was on vacation, providing me with an ideal environment at a key stage in the writing process.

I am also thankful to Beata Grant, who introduced my memoirs to Stanford University Press; Vikram Seth, my first editor at the Press; and Muriel Bell, who took over where Vikram left off with an equally high degree of enthusiasm and care.

Nyna and Ted Polumbaum gave me much encouragement and advice during the three years that I worked on this book. But my greatest thanks go to my closest comrade-in-arms, Judy Polumbaum, who helped me rework my prose in the course of three major revisions. Her sensitivity to Chinese experience combined with her vantage point as an American reader and her skill as an editor are in large part responsible for the form in which my story comes to you.

G.Y.

Preface

BORN RED

The Hold of History

Early one morning in the spring of 1966, I awoke to a rocking sensation. I opened my eyes to see the bare bulb that lit my dormitory room at Yizhen Number One Middle School swinging like a pendulum. My roommates and I scrambled out of our quilts and spilled outdoors in our underwear. Little Mihu knocked over the urine-filled chamber pot on the way out.

At this time of year, it was still cold on the North China plain. Little Mihu began to shiver. I assumed an earthquake had roused us, but the buildings on campus appeared intact and no cracks had opened up in the ground. After milling around for a while, students began to disappear back into their dormitories. I went back to my room to put on the long-sleeved knit shirt and thick, cotton-padded pants and jacket that I wore from late October to early April.

Later in the day, with schoolmates clustered around me, I tuned in a Beijing news broadcast on my homemade transistor radio. A quake measuring 6.7 on the Richter Scale had struck a county a hundred kilometers to the south, killing thousands of people and leaving thousands more injured and homeless. The People's Liberation Army was conducting relief and rescue operations, and Premier Zhou Enlai himself had flown in by helicopter to comfort the survivors.

We officially learned of the earthquake at an outdoor assembly after dinner. Vice-Principal Lin Sheng, speaking from a podium set up between two red pillars on the porch of the Teachers' Building, called on us to donate clothes and bedding for the victims, and instructed us to form stretcher-bearing teams to meet injured people who were coming by train and helicopter to the Army Hospital in Yizhen. I brought my buckwheat-husk pillow to the collection station set up at the school's main gate and helped chop branches from trees to make stretcher poles. My classmate Yuanchao, whose father ran the Army Hospital, had brought a real stretcher to school for first-aid training, so he and I paired up to carry it. Most of the stretcher teams set out in a torchlit procession to the railroad station. Yuanchao and I went with a smaller group to a flat area behind the hospital. Guided by campfire light, five helicopters landed in succession, the wind from their rotors raising dust and scattering embers. Medics passed an old woman with a crushed leg onto our stretcher, and we carried her into a ward.

Students had almost stopped talking about the earthquake when the aftershocks came a couple of weeks later. For one night, we were advised to sleep in our clothes with our feet toward the door. The next day, Vice-Principal Lin announced that a regional earthquake alert was in force. Every class set to work building wooden shacks to sleep in. As a precaution, we carried our desks, chairs, and blackboards out of our classrooms and had classes outside.

As far as we students were concerned, all this was an exciting diversion. Some of the townsfolk of Yizhen took the earthquake more seriously. Although most of Yizhen was untouched, the quake had snapped off the tip of the Wooden Pagoda, one of four ancient pagodas in town. Local people saw this as an evil omen.

One of the superstitious diehards, as we called them, was

the white-bearded man who climbed our school bell tower every morning to ring the wake-up bell. He claimed that history already had proved that earthquakes portended disaster. For instance, he said, after a strong quake in the year 8 A.D., General Wang Mang usurped the throne of the Western Han dynasty and wreaked havoc throughout China. Not until seventeen years later did a relative of the Han emperors, Liu Xiu, kill Wang Mang and set up the Eastern Han dynasty to carry on Han rule.

If you had the slightest doubt about the truth of this story, the old man would remind you that Liu Xiu had stopped in Yizhen on his way to fight Wang Mang. The head of Yizhen county, recognizing a bright young man, convinced Liu Xiu to marry his niece Guo. After Liu Xiu's victory, Guo became empress. If you still were dubious, the old bell-ringer would add that, at their wedding, Liu Xiu and Guo had cut a gourd in two and each had drunk wine from one half to express their love and loyalty. And where did they buy the wine? At the very tavern now called the Empress Guo Wineshop, on Four Harmonies Street downtown. By this time, how could you not believe the old man?

Just to be sure, I went to the school library to look up the old man's stories in the county chronicles. I found accounts of everything he had said. He had failed to mention one important fact, however. Empress Guo's good luck did not last very long. Soon after Liu Xiu set up his dynasty, he took a fancy to another beautiful woman, demoted Guo to concubine, and made the other woman empress.

Such tales were common in Yizhen, a town more than twenty-five centuries old. Civilizations had risen and fallen here so many times that you could dig up broken bricks three meters deep in the ground. Yizhen was still surrounded by an

The Hold of History

old city wall, now collapsing and overgrown with bushes and shrubs. A stream circled the wall on three sides like a silver belt. The Hutuo River lay to the south. To the west ran the highway, still unpaved, and next to it the tracks of the Beijing–Guangzhou railway. The town itself was a blend of ancient cultures. Besides the quartet of traditional Chinese pagodas, there was a Gothic-style cathedral, once presided over by a powerful Catholic bishop and now used by the Army Hospital as an auditorium, and an onion-domed mosque where local Moslems still worshipped. A favorite playground was Dafo Temple, a walled compound near the town's east gate. Its scores of shrines and halls included the hall of the Goddess of Mercy, whose statue was 22 meters tall and had 42 arms.

In recent centuries, Yizhen had attracted all kinds of people, from Jewish merchants to American missionaries to Japanese invaders. In 1900, the allied troops of the eight Western powers had come all the way here in pursuit of people who had burned churches during the Boxer Rebellion. The town had changed hands nobody knew how many times. When I happened on a rusty spearhead or arrow point in the fields outside the city wall, I could almost imagine ancient soldiers swarming over the battlements. The last fighting in the area had been in 1947, when the People's Liberation Army had stormed the town and wiped out a whole Kuomintang division.

Yizhen carried on many ancient customs and trades. Virtually everybody knew how to make firecrackers from scratch. The townspeople even made their own nitrate, scraping soil from the surface of local reed ponds and then boiling and filtering it. They mixed the homemade nitrate with sulfur and charcoal to make gunpowder. The men liked to hunt

The Hold of History

4

hares, and peddlers plied the alleys at night selling pot-stewed hare meat. It was said that the base of the sauce they used for stewing had been handed on since the days of Liu Xiu. Each time the sauce got low in the pot, they added to it, but they never threw it out.

Every household in Yizhen contained treasures centuries old, from Shang tripods to Ming vases to the eighteen types of ancient weapons. And the old folks, like the man who rang our school bell, were full of tales. They talked about the prime minister the town had produced for the Ming dynasty and the various native sons who had become ministers in the Qing court. But the favorite figure of all was the heroic general Zhao Yun. Armed only with spear and sword, Zhao Yun had broken the siege of an entire army to save the son of Liu Bei, a descendent of Liu Xiu, who later became emperor of the state of Shu, one of the Three Kingdoms.

Yizhen was Zhao Yun's hometown. His birthplace was thought to be a mansion on Perpetual Victory Street. One of the girls in my class lived on that street. Her surname was Zhao and she claimed to be Zhao Yun's descendant. I accepted her claim readily. People said Zhao Yun had watered his war-horse and sharpened his Green Iron Sword at the stone trough in Dafo Temple. I believed that, too, until workmen who turned the trough over to repair a crack discovered an inscription from the Tang dynasty on its bottom. The inscription showed the trough was thirteen hundred years old, four centuries too young for Zhao Yun to have used it.

Yizhen was not my hometown. My three brothers, one of my two sisters, and I had all been born in Shuiyuan, a town in the Taihang Mountains just inside the Great Wall. My older brother, Weihua, had arrived at the beginning of the Korean War, and his name meant "safeguard China." I was

The Hold of History

born two years later, in 1952. My name, Jianhua, meant "construct China." My first younger brother was Zhihua, "command China," and my second, Xinghua, "make China flourish." These were all common names for the time. My younger sister Meiyuan's name suggested refinement and beauty. Our littlest sister, the only native of Yizhen among us, was named Yiyuan after the town.

My father, Gao Shangui, whose given name meant "mountain laurel," had led a guerrilla unit against the Japanese aggressors in the Taihang Mountains. After the Japanese surrender in 1945, he was named head of Shuiyuan county, already a Communist base area. In 1955, the Hebei provincial government assigned him to head the criminal division of the province's high court. He preferred discussing farming with peasants to reading legal documents, so before long he asked for a transfer back to a county post. In 1957, he was appointed head of Yizhen county, which then had a population of 350,000 people, and he and Mama moved to the county seat.

We children stayed in Shuiyuan with Mama's father for another two years. That was the time of the Great Leap Forward. To me, Chairman Mao's dream of entering the industrial age overnight was personified by a man astride a rocket, the man I saw in billboards captioned, "Surpass England in Fifteen Years!" I spent several days helping Grandpa smash the family's iron pots and strip the front door of its handsome brass fittings to provide scrap metal for the homemade neighborhood steel furnace. Swept up in the mass mobilization, Grandpa went to work as a cook in some neighboring houses that had been turned into a public dining hall. All the villages around Shuiyuan were merging into the new people's communes. People were saying that true communism was just around the corner.

Grandpa and the five of us rode to Yizhen in the back of a pickup truck late in 1959. We brought along our rice bowls and chopsticks. Grandpa got another job as a neighborhood cook. We quickly discovered who the town hero was, and every night we begged Grandpa to tell us stories from the classic *Romance of the Three Kingdoms*, especially the parts about Zhao Yun.

One day, the neighborhood dining hall suddenly closed, and we had to buy new pots to do our own cooking in. Soon, everything began to run short. For the first time, we were issued ration coupons to buy such daily necessities as grain, oil, cloth, coal, even matches. As the economic difficulties spread, townsfolk and peasants from the surrounding countryside began to dismantle Yizhen's city wall. People pried the bricks off the rammed-earth core and sold them or used them to build pigsties and privies. Papa became very concerned about the destruction. For one thing, the wall was one of the best-preserved city walls in the province, and Papa wanted to maintain it as a historic artifact. For another, he knew the wall was important for flood control. Sometimes during the rainy season, the Hutuo River overflowed its banks, but so far the wall had kept the water out of the town itself. Papa issued a directive forbidding any further vandalism to the wall. The notice was posted on buildings all around the town, with Papa's bold, rough signature at the bottom.

The directive halted the destruction, but it also got Papa in trouble. At the next meeting of the Yizhen County Party Committee, the Party secretary, Han Rong, accused him of issuing a decree without approval of the Party leadership.

Papa, also a member of the Party Committee, argued that he had acted within the scope of his responsibilities as county head. Other members of the committee supported him. But Han Rong did not give up there. He sent a letter to the Provincial Party Committee charging Papa with forming an anti-Party clique. Papa had criticized Han Rong in the past for being autocratic. In private, Papa also complained about his womanizing. Now Han Rong was getting back at him. The provincial leaders removed Papa as county head, decreased both his official rank and his salary, and had him transferred to work as an ordinary laborer in a steel plant in the prefectural capital, Shimen.

Our family continued to live in a quiet neighborhood of Yizhen. Yiyuan, the sixth child, had just been born. Mama cut short her maternity leave to return to work as an accountant for the local tax bureau. Grandpa took care of the household. We five older children attended Democracy Street Primary School.

The years 1960–62 later came to be called the "Three Difficult Years." During that period, I often came home from school so hungry that I could no longer stand. I would lie down on the stone steps in front of the house. At mealtime, Grandpa would dish out thin gruel and distribute steamed bread made of cornmeal and sweet-potato flour among the six of us, with portions determined by age. Weihua and I each got two buns; Zhihua, Xinghua, and Meiyuan one-and-a-half; and Yiyuan one. Grandpa would remind us that "Kong Rong gives big pears to his elder brothers." Kong Rong, a descendant of Confucius, had lived during the Three Kingdoms. One story about him said that as a child, he chose the smallest pear because he was the youngest in his family.

Grandpa's tales made meals as pleasant as possible under the circumstances, and we never fought over food, even though we rarely finished a meal with full stomachs. Zhihua would lick his bowl several times to make sure he got every drop of gruel. Sometimes we went foraging for wild plants for the table. We added boiled willow and poplar leaves to our bread dough. We peeled elm bark and chewed it ragged. We tried a recipe whose main ingredient was ground corncobs, which resembled meat in texture but not in taste. We grew algae in jars of water set out in the sun; this was supposed to be a good way to manufacture protein, but we abandoned it after one batch because it tasted so awful. We ate insects whenever we had the energy to catch them. We would tie a female dragonfly to a string and flaunt it around the reed ponds, enticing the males and then catching them as they were mating. We also caught cicadas on the tip of a pole primed with glue.

Sometimes we went scavenging for cooking fuel. When our coal rations ran out in the spring, Grandpa would take us to the cotton fields in the southwest part of town to dig roots out of the thawing, muddy ground. In autumn, we put dry leaves and grass into the stove. As for clothing, it was not exactly as Radio Moscow claimed—"one pair of pants for every two Chinese"—but we were in rags, and even our patches were patched.

Because of his demotion, Papa's income had dropped from 130 *yuan* a month to less than a hundred. Mama's salary was 42 yuan a month, the same as it had been for a dozen years. Inflation during the Three Difficult Years was so bad that the price of a persimmon soared from less than three *fen* before 1960 to 50 fen (or half a yuan) by 1962. So the family's total income was worth only 280 persimmons a month. Luckily, the government had kept the price of rationed grain stable.

Meanwhile, the cost of just about anything that was not edible went down. People sold incense burners, porcelain, figurines, jewelry, and other family heirlooms on the street at ridiculously low prices. You could buy museum-quality antiques for a couple of yuan. Even such bargains moved slowly, for there were far more sellers than buyers in the market. One day when Grandpa was out buying food, he saw a Ming dynasty porcelain bowl at a peddler's stand. The dappled brown bowl was in perfect condition, just big enough to cup comfortably in the hands. An imprint on the bottom testified that it had been made during the reign of Emperor Xuande, in the early fifteenth century. The price was 50 fen, the cost of a persimmon. Grandpa bought it without even bothering to haggle.

My big brother Weihua was intrigued by street-corner salesmanship and decided to try his hand at it. He took a camelhair sweater to the marketplace and stood there for a day, refusing to budge from his price of fifteen yuan. He came home with the sweater. He went to the railway station the next day and again failed to find anyone who would meet his price. Grandpa recommended that he abandon the effort; after all, if people would not buy a two-thousand-year-old bronze tripod for two yuan, how could you expect them to buy a used sweater for seven times that much?

Papa had never spent much time with us children because of the demands of his work. Now, even though he was no longer an official, we still saw little of him. When he came home from the steel factory, he would lock himself into a rundown little shrine near our house. The place belonged to Old Liu, a retired army officer who supplemented his pension by

The author's father,
Gao Shangui, early 1960's

growing corn on a vacant lot on the western edge of town. Old Liu felt Papa had been wrongly dismissed and let him use the dilapidated shrine whenever he wished. We finally learned what Papa had been doing in that shrine one day in early 1963, when a messenger arrived with a piece of paper saying that County Head Gao Shangui had been rehabilitated. Papa had been writing petitions to the Provincial Party Committee and the Central Committee, and they had reexamined his case.

Papa had been a very popular county head, and his dismissal had provoked a flood of complaints to the provincial authorities. People even compared him to Hai Rui, a county head in the Ming dynasty famed for his integrity and fairness. Hai Rui had once carried a coffin to the court and criticized

The Hold of History

11

the emperor to his face. He had been dismissed and reappointed several times during his life. Papa was to be reassigned to government work. He was not totally vindicated, however. It soon became apparent that his partial rehabilitation was the outcome of a deal between Han Rong and the provincial Party leaders to placate the public. Han Rong escaped without punishment, or even criticism. On the contrary, he was promoted to the post of Party secretary of Shimen municipality.

Papa was named head of the neighboring county of Lingzhi, which had a population of a quarter of a million. He and Mama, Grandpa, and the four youngest children moved there on a rainy day in August 1963, which turned out to be the start of a week of torrential rains. The Hutuo River overflowed its banks, and Yizhen's city wall kept the floodwaters out. Papa's prestige in the county he had just left rose another notch. Afterward, the people of Yizhen continued to think of him as a kind of county head emeritus. Unfortunately, they also resumed dismantling the city wall.

Learning to Be Red
and Expert

After Papa's reassignment to Lingzhi, my big brother Weihua and I stayed in Yizhen. Weihua had finished primary school and passed the entrance examinations for the Yizhen Number One Middle School, better known as Yizhong. I did not want to switch schools in my sixth and last year of primary school, so I stayed on at Democracy Street Primary School as a boarder. With Papa's name cleared and the general economic situation starting to improve, I felt a new sense of confidence. My teachers, knowing I was the son of the man whose foresight had saved the town from flooding, were especially kind to me. My homeroom teacher helped me wash and resew my quilt before winter set in, and made me a new pair of cloth shoes. The food in the school cafeteria was not abundant, but it was adequate and tasty, and I could feel my energy growing by the day.

That was the year my concentration shifted from the next meal to my studies. My favorite class was Chinese, taught by Teacher Ji, an emotional man who often got angry with us and then left apologies on the blackboard in flowing, classical-style poems. Like the other teachers, Ji gave me special attention, including monthly haircuts. But he was strict with me when it came to schoolwork. I became a prolific writer, completing 24 compositions during winter vacation alone. I was especially proud when he gave me a grade of 100 percent on an essay about a snowball fight. I also was learning the basics of poetry. By the end of the school year, several of my poems were accepted for broadcast on a provincial children's radio program.

I passed the entrance exams to Yizhong and joined Weihua in the fall of 1964. I was twelve, quiet and studious. Weihua, now fourteen, had established himself as a natural leader and something of a prankster. Nonetheless, he studied hard and was especially good at Russian. I began to learn English.

Yizhong was a fairly new school. It had been founded in 1946 as a "guerrilla school" in territory where control was seesawing between the People's Liberation Army and the Kuomintang. In 1964, there were 1,200 students in six grades. After the first three grades, you crossed the divide from junior middle school to senior middle school. Each grade was further divided into classes of 50 students. Each class had a number—Weihua was in class 79, the 79th group to enter the school since its founding, and I was in class 85.

Our walled campus sat on the northernmost side of town; part of the north side of the city wall formed our rear wall. We slept, ate, and went to classes in gray brick buildings with tiled roofs and upturned eaves. Almost all the campus architecture was Chinese, except the Principal's Residence, a three-story building with arches, pillars, and balustrades, and the South Gate, a triple marble arch that framed the main entrance to the school. These two Western-style structures dated from the days of a missionary school set up in the early 1900's. Before that, a Daoist monastery had occupied the site; the school's templelike reading room and bell tower were legacies of that period.

At the back of the campus was a lake, a product of the Great Leap Forward. The school originally had planned to build a spring-fed swimming pool there. Enthusiastic students had dug a hole three times Olympic size. But the cement to line the pool never arrived, owing to a shortage of building materials. During the Three Difficult Years, fish were raised in what came to be called Rear Lake. It became the focus of a school tradition, a marathon fish-catch and feast held on the first day of June, the anniversary of the founding of the school.

Between Rear Lake and the north wall was a communal vegetable garden. From spring until autumn, classes took turns growing everything from turnips and cabbage to eggplant and cucumber. We also grew experimental plots of wheat for our botany classes.

The 25 boys in class 85 lived in two adjoining dormitory rooms. The 25 girls lived in the area we called Vatican City, from which boys were strictly barred. Every morning, the girls would meet us under the willow trees on the path outside our dormitory. The boys never got around to washing up until later, but the girls always started the day with their faces scrubbed and their hair combed or braided. Our class monitor, Caolan, whose name meant "orchid," had two pigtails that stood stiffly off her shoulders.

All 50 of us would fall into line by height and file out the South Gate to the sports ground for our morning jog and calisthenics. Our commander for this daily routine was the class sports manager, Shuanggen, a stocky boy with a square, bronzed face. Shuanggen's name meant "double roots"—he was expected to carry on the family line for both his father and his childless uncle. If anyone was capable of such an arduous task, it was the seemingly inexhaustible Shuanggen. He never seemed short of breath as he ran alongside our formation shouting, "One, two, three, four . . . " Panting, we would chorus back, "One, two, three, four . . . " After five laps around the track, my heart would be pounding. By this time, the whole school was out exercising. When the loudspeakers over the field emitted the scratchy prelude to the worn calisthenics recording, everybody stopped jogging and spread out at arm's length. In unison, we stretched, bent, twisted, kicked, and jumped, first to one side, then to the other. The recorded voice barked instructions over the stirring music, but nobody needed to listen. Every schoolchild in the nation knew this set of exercises by heart.

After the final set of jumping jacks and marching in place, many students raced to the far end of the field for a turn on the obstacle course, 200 meters of walls, planks, trenches, and barbed wire that had been built so we could supplement our militia training. We had militia drill with wooden rifles several times a week to prepare for war against the imperialists and hegemonists. I was learning about imperialism and hegemonism in politics class, and also from my big brother. "We're besieged from all sides," Weihua would remind me from time to time. "To the north is the Soviet bear. Southwest are the Indian reactionaries. The Japanese devils still harbor secret desires against us. Chiang Kai-shek on Taiwan talks about recovering the mainland. To the south, the American imperialist wolves are trampling over Vietnam."

We got to breakfast with a good appetite. I looked forward to every meal in our dining hall, simple as the food was. Grains were the staple, with salted turnips at breakfast and one or two vegetable dishes flavored with bits of meat at lunch and dinner. Extra meat would appear on holidays or when people from the Provincial Education Department arrived for an inspection.

Because of rationing, the grain distribution system was carefully worked out. Students from the countryside were the luckiest: they got as much grain as their families could afford to give them. Before each term, the village kids swapped some of their grain for coupons at their local ration offices, and in the school dining hall they traded back the coupons for grain. Some also brought their own rice and millet to school. In autumn, many returned from weekend visits home with sacks of sweet potatoes over their shoulders or tied to their bicycle racks.

Students from towns were limited to a set amount of grain, starting at 30 *jin* a month for boys and a bit less for girls in the first grade, and increasing with each grade. Just over half our coupons were for "coarse grain"—usually *wotou* (steamed cornbread), but sometimes millet, soybeans, or sweet potatoes. The rest were for "fine grain," rice or wheat. We carefully figured out how many ounces of what kind of grain to order at each meal so as not to use up our rations too early or finish up our fine grain first. I once made the mistake of using up my fine grain coupons in two weeks. For the next two weeks, I ate a steady diet of wotou, which sat like lumps of clay in my stomach, while my schoolmates savored their rice gruel, noodles, and wheatcakes.

Not that coarse grain was bad. I especially liked the corn porridge served at breakfast, with its little flecks of seaweed and soy bits. The only student in our class who almost never ate coarse grain was Yuanchao, whose father was head of the Army Hospital. Yuanchao was proud of the fact that his father was a Long March veteran. He was proud of his name, which meant "aid Korea," and his younger sister's name, Kangmei, "resist America." He also was proud of his privileges, which he seldom shared. He often brought food from the hospital kitchen to school and ate salted eggs with real oven-baked bread in his room instead of coming to the dining hall.

Mealtimes were chaotic and noisy. We rinsed our tin bowls, spoons, and chopsticks at a long sink and jostled for a place in line before the serving windows. If you were early enough, you could grab a stool. Otherwise you stood at one of the square wooden tables that we called "tables of the eight immortals" because you could fit two people at each side. I usually ate with the other boys in my class. Often we were joined by the class tomboy, Huantian, whose name meant "changing heaven." We liked to tease Huantian about her habit of talking with her mouth full so that little bits of food and saliva flew out. Sometimes she got angry and traded earthy curses with Sanxi, "triple happiness." I was shocked the first time I heard Huantian say, "Fuck your mother!" because girls did not say such things. But I soon got used to her language and almost forgot she was a girl.

Class 85 was a tight-knit group by the time we got to the second year of middle school, united by a common stock of jokes, insults, and nicknames. Nobody called Little Mihu by his real name; he was "little muddle" to us, a timid, accident-prone boy who was forever tripping over the chamber pot. Little Bawang, "little overlord," had earned the title of a capricious general of the Three Kingdoms period with his overbearing manner. Erchou, "two foul odors," was notorious for his farts. He claimed sweet potatoes were to blame. His noxious smell aside, Erchou was a dependable fellow. Our homeroom teacher, Wen Xiu, appointed him daily-life manager of the class, which meant he was responsible for such things as grain rations and coal for the dormitory stoves in winter. In the campaign to learn from the model soldier Lei Feng, when we pooled money to buy ourselves shears and cut one another's hair, Erchou emerged as the best barber.

Little Bawang was our manual-labor manager. This manual labor, to which we devoted two afternoons a week, involved such tasks as cleaning latrines and planting vegetables. Teacher Wen introduced each work session by reminding us of Chairman Mao's observation that peasants might have cow dung on their feet, but their minds were purer than the intellectuals'. I especially disliked latrine duty because I ended up with nightsoil on my clothes, which I could not take off to wash since I had only one winter and one summer outfit. I kept my bourgeois thoughts to myself as we trooped off to the work site armed with oversized ladles, buckets, brooms, and powdered lime. Little Bawang strutted ahead giving directions. Inside the latrine, the girls ladled the nightsoil from the brick-lined trench into the buckets and then sprinkled lime into the trench. The boys carried the buckets outside and emptied them into a wooden tank cart. I would stagger with my bucket, trying to hold it away from my body.

Yuanchao usually wore a surgical mask, which the rest of us considered prissy. "Oh, you're wearing your muzzle again," Sanxi would taunt him. "Shut your mouth, you country bumpkin!" Yuanchao would retort. The rest of us would take a break to watch the skirmish.

"What's wrong with country bumpkins?" Sanxi would say. "Your father was a country bumpkin before he went on the Long March."

"Who are you to insult my father? He climbed snow-topped peaks and crossed dangerous marshlands to help make the revolution, and what was your father doing? Your father was quaking in his mud hut!"

Yuanchao would be quaking with anger, but the easygoing Sanxi would merely shrug and resume heaving buckets. When the cart was full, Sanxi would position himself between the shafts like a donkey and lift them from the ground. The rest of us pushed and pulled to help him haul the load to the manure pit by the vegetable garden behind Rear Lake.

When we worked in the girls' side, Sanxi would go through a repertoire of crude peasant jokes. "What are the Four Big Reds?" he would ask. "The rose, the tomato, the evening glow, and the horse-riding cloth." The last was a euphemism for a sanitary napkin. "What are the Four Big Exhaustions? Cleaning the pigsty, making bricks, pulling wheat, and fucking." He did not care that the girls were there too. Yuling, our class study manager, always blushed bright red and looked down at her feet.

Learning to Be Red and Expert

Yuling had become my best friend, although I could never admit it because she was a girl. She had been my classmate at Democracy Street Primary School. Like most primary school pupils, we both belonged to the Young Pioneers. But I was just an ordinary member, whereas she was a brigade leader. Every year, she made the list of "three-good" students—those who exemplified good schoolwork, good ideology, and good health. When we entered Yizhong, we were assigned to share a desk. At first, we drew a chalk line down the middle of the desktop, dubbed the McMahon Line by our classmates after the boundary that had been in dispute during the 1962 border war between India and China. At first, Yuling and I rarely talked. Gradually, as the line rubbed off, I began asking her for help with English, and she asked me for help with math.

I regarded Yuling almost as a big sister; she was taller and stronger and more grown-up than I. Once when I snagged my padded pants on the barbed wire of the obstacle course, she mended the tear while I lay on my stomach. I went to her first with all my new discoveries—like the time I discovered that Chairman Mao was staring at me. His gaze from the portrait over the blackboard at the front of our classroom followed me wherever I went. When I told Yuling, she laughed and told me not to be neurotic. She said every portrait was painted that way.

Yuling's mother taught music at a nearby normal school. Her father was a professor at a medical college in Shimen. He had studied in the United States in the 1940's and had returned to China in 1950 to help build socialism. He had tutored Yuling in English from the time she began learning Chinese characters. Yuling hoped to join the Youth League but worried that her intellectual background would work against her. Youth League members were the aristocracy of Yizhong. Applicants had to prove themselves worthy of carrying on the glorious tradition of the Chinese Communist Party. Good grades, good character, and correct political views were required. Your chances were better if you came from a revolutionary family. And everybody knew that it helped if you acted obedient and never offended anybody.

I learned how fierce the competition to join the Youth League could be during my first year at Yizhong. A senior student was under great pressure from his father, a county security official, to advance politically. He became desperate after his application for Youth League membership was rejected several times. He stole his father's pistol and shot at the Youth League secretary of his class as she was walking across campus. Because he was nervous, he missed and hit a tree. The boy fled from the campus, and all of us were alerted to look out for him. A few nights later, under a full moon, he climbed over the school wall and fired a shot through his dormitory window, wounding a classmate he suspected of blackballing him. Other students chased him to Rear Lake. My roommates and I, roused by the commotion, ran to the lake to see a crowd of angry seniors pelting him with turnips as he floundered in the water. He had jumped in, hoping to commit suicide, but the lake was too shallow. Finally, he came ashore. Later he was sentenced to twenty years in jail.

Class 85 had four Youth League members. Ten of us still belonged to the Young Pioneers, but as a children's organization, that group was not taken very seriously in middle school. The rest were known as the "masses," though some called themselves the "democrats" or "Bolsheviks outside the Party."

My most revolutionary friend was an older boy, the thin,

pale, bespectacled Fangpu. He was in his last year and I in my second when we got to know each other. Fangpu was a Youth League member and a good orator who often gave speeches at school assemblies. We had read each other's poetry on the literary bulletin board on the porch of the Teachers' Building. His poems, elegant and full of imagery, always had political themes, perhaps because his father was a revolutionary martyr, having died in the civil war between the Communists and the Kuomintang after the defeat of Japan.

One day at lunch, Fangpu noticed me eating "horse greens," a wild vegetable I had discovered during the Three Difficult Years. I still ate them because my ten-yuan monthly allowance from home did not buy as much food in the dining hall as I would have wished. Horse greens grew free for the plucking along the base of the city wall. I cooked them on the steamers provided for common use. They were rather tasteless but had a nice crunchy texture.

Fangpu felt sorry for me because he thought I was eating weeds. "Can't you afford to buy cabbage?" he asked me. "What's your family status?" I introduced myself and told him that my father was Gao Shangui, head of Lingzhi county. Fangpu recognized my name from the literary bulletin board. He patted me on the shoulder and said, "Nowadays, not even peasant kids eat weeds, but the son of a county head still does. If your father had been a Kuomintang magistrate before Liberation, you'd have lived a luxurious life. But a Communist official and his whole family sacrifice for the sake of the people." Fangpu was not rich either; his mother lived on the revolutionary martyr's pension. But relatives in the countryside supplied him with good vegetables. He insisted on sharing his cabbage and onions with me.

At lunch the next day, he gave me a poem he had written

Learning to Be Red and Expert

in my honor. It referred to me as "little brother" and praised my revolutionary spirit of "hard work and plain living." I wrote a poem with the same rhyme scheme in response, thanking him for his encouragement. That was the start of our friendship. We usually discussed poetry. Fangpu delighted in modern poets who put revolutionary sentiments into time-honored classical forms. One of his favorite examples was a poem by scholar Zhao Puchu called "Weeping Over the Three Ni's." Written in ancient style, it used a pun on the Chinese names for John F. Kennedy, Nikita Khrushchev, and Jawaharlal Nehru—all contained the character *ni*—to ridicule the misfortunes of imperialism, revisionism, and reaction.

Imperialism, revisionism, and reaction were also the themes of our politics class. Unfortunately, our politics teacher, Guo Pei, was not as interesting as Zhao Puchu. When Weihua first pointed out Teacher Guo to me, I was struck by her smallness: she looked like a fragile doll, with a small nose, small mouth, and delicate limbs. Her small eyes glinted behind thick glasses. Weihua told me that, first, she never smiled; second, she never talked about anything but politics; and third, she was boring. I was prepared for the worst.

My first conversation with Teacher Guo did nothing to disabuse me of my preconceptions. She told me that, as a middle-school student, I would have to pay more attention to politics than I had in primary school. Without thinking, I blurted out, "Politics is boring!" Teacher Guo looked shocked. "Who told you that?" she asked. "My big brother," I answered. Her glinty eyes bored into me as she said, "You and Weihua both need to heighten your political consciousness."

A few days later, my homeroom teacher, Wen Xiu, called me to her office. She spoke gently. "Jianhua, I invited you here to tell you that what you told Teacher Guo was wrong. You should know better. You're not the son of uneducated peasants; your parents are both veteran revolutionary cadres." If I planned to go on to college, I would have to be both red and expert, she said. The only way to become red was through ideological remolding. "Examine yourself. Perhaps you feel superior because of your family's good political status. That is all the more reason to work hard to remold yourself." Periodically, Teacher Wen would call me back for another gentle reprimand. I began to feel that my family's revolutionary credentials were a burden. Maybe being "born red" was not such an advantage after all.

I became even more certain of this when the School Party Committee launched an ideological campaign aimed at students from revolutionary families. It started with the case of the senior student who had failed to get into the Youth League. After he was sent to jail, our school Party secretary, Ding Yi, called an assembly. "This case is a vivid example of how the son of a veteran cadre can degenerate into a criminal!" he declared.

The campaign intensified after a senior student drowned during a school outing to the Hutuo River. The boy had gone outside the swimming area and been caught in the current. Lifeguards recovered his body a kilometer downstream. This boy had been at the top of his grade in both English and Russian. His father was an official in the provincial government. Everyone had been sure the son would get a high-status job, perhaps as translator for the Foreign Ministry in Beijing. When he drowned, his body was hastily buried at an unmarked grave outside the north side of the city wall. There was not even a memorial meeting. Instead, Ding Yi called another assembly, at which he criticized the dead boy for violating discipline.

In politics class, Teacher Guo instructed us to search our hearts for inner contradictions. Family origin was important: those of us from good backgrounds had to be certain not to stray from the path, and those from bad backgrounds had to struggle against their inferior inheritance. Yizhong had only a handful of students of "high" antecedents, which included capitalists, landlords, rich peasants, counterrevolutionaries, rightists, and bad elements. Most students were of "low" origin, meaning their parents were poor or lower-middle peasants, farmhands, workers, or revolutionary cadres. In between were middle and upper-middle peasants, petty proprietors, and intellectuals.

I did not know any real capitalists or even landlords. The "highest" students in class 85 were three from upper-middle-peasant background. The "lowest" was Yuanchao, whose background was both poor peasant and revolutionary cadre. I had once been the same combination. Papa had always told me not to claim revolutionary-cadre status when I was filling in forms because it might bring me privileges I did not deserve, so I would write in only "poor peasant." However, Papa's home village had reclassified his origin to lower-middle peasant not long after I enrolled in Yizhong. The reclassification was part of a movement going on in the countryside, the Four Cleanups. I was upset to lose my "poor peasant" designation. Mama, who came from middle-peasant stock, tried to comfort me by saying poor and lower-middle were about the same. But I knew there was a difference. Now I had a double burden: living up to my revolutionary father and living down his lower-middle-peasant status.

In addition to searching for contradictions within ourselves, we were supposed to be on the lookout for class enemies outside. Several classmates and I managed to find a class enemy right outside the school's main gate. We came upon a peddler soliciting orders for name seals carved from pear wood. He was charging only three *mao* a seal, so we eagerly placed orders and paid him in advance. He said the seals would be ready that afternoon, but when we came back he had disappeared. We introduced the swindle in politics class as a real-life example of class struggle. For once, Teacher Guo looked a little pleased.

This campaign dominated our political study well into my second year at Yizhong. Then the Four Cleanups moved from the countryside into the towns. We took a few trips to a Four Cleanups exhibition in Yizhen, which displayed photographs from all over the country of land deeds, silver and gold coins, and even weapons that landlords, rich peasants, and other bad elements had been hiding since Liberation.

One morning before breakfast, our class monitor, Caolan, called a meeting of the boys and instructed us to fill out forms listing how much medicine we had received from the school clinic, and at what price. Caolan called a separate meeting of the girls. Yuling told me afterward that Caolan had asked if there were any complaints about medical treatment, and specifically, about Dr. Zhang. It did not take long for the news to spread that Dr. Zhang had been charged with embezzling and indecent behavior. Some of the girls had complained that he always insisted on giving injections in the buttocks, claiming it would hurt too much in the arm. Pretending to have a headache, I went to get a last look at the villain. To my disappointment, Dr. Zhang already had been replaced by a woman, Dr. Yang. She told me that Dr. Zhang was in custody, writing his confession.

The Yizhong faculty had been holding political study sessions practically every evening. Dr. Zhang was the only culprit they were able to ferret out. Although many of our teachers came from less-than-perfect backgrounds, none of them turned out to be a bad element. I felt relieved, because I liked most of them. Teacher Guo was the only one I disliked; and her politics were above reproach.

My favorite teacher was Teacher Li, who taught us Chinese. He had been a Kuomintang army major and was rumored to have worked closely with Chiang Ching-kuo, Chiang Kai-shek's son, in the Kuomintang's central guard regiment. Right before Liberation, Li had gone over to the Communist side and stayed on the mainland when the Kuomintang fled to Taiwan. Teacher Li still had an officer's bearing. He walked with his back straight and his chest thrust out. He was going bald, but his skin was as smooth as a youth's. He always wore an old-fashioned high-collared jacket. At the start of class, he would stride into the room, take off his cloth cap and scarf, carefully fold the scarf and place it on a corner of his desk, and then place the cap on top of the scarf. We would rise—students always stood when a teacher came in— and greet him in unison, and he would respond with a stiff little bow. Then he would square his shoulders, clasp his hands behind his back, and begin the day's lesson.

Li read with great feeling, often acting out scenes from our books and from the lives of their authors. Once when he was reading a piece about a woman Communist going to her execution, his voice suddenly broke and his eyes grew teary. I pondered how a veteran Kuomintang man, a friend of Public Enemy Chiang Kai-shek's son, could be so moved by the story of a Communist heroine.

Li mixed freely with students. Sometimes he played ping-pong with us before class. We would beg for demonstrations of his favorite trick—furiously pedaling a bicycle without moving forward an inch. He also showed off his military prowess by holding a rifle steady with one hand for ten minutes, with a brick suspended from the barrel for extra weight.

Teacher Liu taught geography. He always brought the same props to class: a pointer and a globe. None of us could forget that China was shaped like a chicken, with two eggs representing the province of Taiwan and the island of Hainan. Liu described the mountains, jungles, deserts, and oceans of the world, and the plants, animals, and cultures of different countries. He talked about the different races of mankind. According to him, the Eskimos and American Indians were descended from the Chinese.

I had heard that Teacher Liu had been labeled a rightist during the Anti-rightist movement of the late 1950's, and that his salary had been cut to thirty yuan a month, just enough to buy necessities. Teacher Liu also mixed with us outside class, sometimes joining us for meals instead of going to the teachers' dining hall. He seemed to know all the words of all the revolutionary songs that had ever been written. A meal with Teacher Liu usually ended with a rousing rendition of "See the Five-Star Red Flag Flying High." All the boys in my class would try to imitate his deep baritone.

We had history class with Teacher Yang, who combed his smooth black hair back over the crown of his head like Chairman Mao. Teacher Yang fit my image of a modern scholar. He talked without pause, lacing his lectures with legends and anecdotes. When he came to a crucial point, such as Stalin's declaration of war on Japan in 1945, his voice and his eyebrows would rise at the same time.

Teacher Feng taught us physics. I had heard of the "American" at Yizhong while I was still at Democracy Street Primary School. Feng actually was only half American. His father, a U.S. navy officer, had married a Chinese woman in Tianjin. Feng had been born in Tianjin's American concession in the 1930's. He was more than six feet tall—because of his American blood, we assumed. He performed miraculous feats on the basketball court, which had earned him the nickname Kongzhong Youshi, "aerial superiority." That was the phrase the press used to describe American airpower in the Vietnam War. Feng was adviser to the radio club. When I became head of the club in my second year, he trusted me enough to give me the key to the physics lab in the bell-tower courtyard, where we did our tinkering. We built everything from the simplest single-diode receiver to seven-transistor radios. The best radios picked up signals from Moscow.

Our English teacher was Teacher Shen, who had the short stature, dark complexion and simian face that were said to be typical of southerners. Shen had worked in Hong Kong for a trading company until Liberation, when he returned to serve the new China. He was reputed to be the best teacher of English in the province. He used riddles to make things stick in our minds. Most of us learned not to answer them, since we would only end up looking stupid, but Little Mihu never caught on. When we were learning numbers, Shen asked us: "There were forty birds in a tree. A man shot five. How many were left?" "Thirty-five!" Little Mihu shouted proudly. "Wrong," said Shen. "None. The others all flew away."

One day, we all had to answer the question, "What shall I be when I grow up?" We went around the room. Erchou, who came from the countryside, said he wanted to be a soldier. I knew that he really wanted to be an air-force pilot but had abandoned the idea because he could never meet the strict physical requirements. He was tall and thin, with a disproportionately large head. Little Bawang, whose father was a retired army officer of fairly low rank, said he wanted to be an army commander. Little Mihu, like Little Bawang, a village boy, said perhaps he would be a clerk for a leading cadre. Zongwei, the most artistic member of our class, wanted to be a master of traditional Chinese painting. Yuling wanted to be a doctor. I said I would be a journalist, or perhaps a poet.

The Thirty-Six Stratagems

In the spring of 1966, just before the earthquake, Fangpu and I had entered the school's annual poetry contest. My dream was to become poet laureate for the year. Fangpu had the same desire. My poem told how the workmen had discovered the inscription showing that General Zhao Yun could not have watered his war-horse at the giant stone trough in Dafo Temple because the trough was made long after Zhao Yun's time. Fangpu told me he liked the poem, but he sounded unhappy. I felt a bit guilty, knowing Fangpu was going to graduate and would not have another chance to win the poetry contest, whereas I had four more years to try.

Once the aftershocks were over, my class spent two days building temporary wooden shelters on the basketball court, two for the boys and two for the girls. It was embarrassing to live so close to the girls. At night, if one of them got up to piss, I could hear the ringing of the chamber pot through the thin walls. Some of the other classes were living in even closer quarters. In some cases, one long shack housed everyone, with just a sheet hung in the middle to separate the girls from the boys. In a few senior classes, girls were sleeping in bunk beds right beneath the boys.

Those arrangements did not last more than a few days. Secretary Ding called an assembly and ordered all classes to segregate the sexes, saying it was improper to put boys and girls together. He further admonished us against any romantic notions we might be entertaining. Everyone knew that this was directed at the seniors. "Falling in love at this early age is bourgeois and individualistic," Secretary Ding said. "Keep your minds on your studies."

We had set up our desks and chairs in proper rows near our shelters and propped the blackboard against a tree. We left Chairman Mao's portrait hanging inside. Our classes went on as before. Despite the distractions of the outdoors, we studied harder than ever, for only a couple of months remained until finals.

The pressure was greatest for the graduating seniors. They were preparing for college entrance examinations, which would be held in early summer. Most were confident of passing; Yizhong was a key school, and over 90 percent of its graduates went on to college, compared with only 4 or 5 percent in ordinary middle schools. The main question for the seniors was whether they would score high enough to get into the most prestigious schools. Simply passing the exams might bring admission to a provincial normal college, but top marks were required to enter the famous universities in Beijing or Shanghai. Students who were good in sciences hoped to go to Qinghua University in Beijing, and most of those interested in liberal arts aimed for Beijing University, which we called Beida.

Beida was where I hoped to go. I had made up my mind the very day I entered Yizhong in the fall of 1964, when I had seen the results of the previous summer's college entrance exams, inscribed in gold ink on red paper, posted on the front wall of the Teachers' Building. The names and scores of students who had been admitted to Beida and Qinghua headed the rest.

Red paper, golden characters. The imperial examiners of the Qing dynasty had announced the results of the court examinations on the wall outside the Forbidden City in the same way. Now things were different, of course. High marks were not supposed to mean power and prestige. Those who excelled were expected to serve the revolution, to go wherever the country needed them and do whatever jobs they were assigned. Still, we looked with awe upon the names of alumni who were now students in those famous universities. The list stayed up for two weeks. I looked at the Beida names so many times that I soon knew them by heart.

Now, in the spring of 1966, I knew Fangpu was studying hard in the hope of going to Beida. I discussed his plans with him just once. I told him he should not be too concerned about going to a famous school; after all, we were not imperial scholar-bureaucrats seeking fame and fortune. Sarcastically, he asked me, "Then why do you have a Beida sticker on your desk?" Over the next few days, I tried to scrape the sticker off nonchalantly, hoping Yuling would not notice.

The next time I talked with Fangpu, he called my attention to a debate on art and literature that was going on in the

The Thirty-Six Stratagems

press. Fangpu read the newspapers posted outside the Teachers' Building with care, but I only glanced at them in passing from time to time. "Remember the controversy over the historical play *Hai Rui Dismissed from Office*?" Fangpu reminded me. Six months earlier, the major papers had carried criticism of the play, calling it a veiled attack on the Great Leap Forward and the people's communes. "This debate broadens and deepens the criticism. I think it is the most important development on the cultural front since Chairman Mao's talks at the Yenan forum on art and literature," Fangpu said in an authoritative tone. "Certain people are using art and literature to attack the Party and socialism. Their methods are pernicious. We all have to be on guard."

A few days later, Secretary Ding announced that every class would devote two afternoons a week to discussing the current debate on the literary front. After morning classes, I decided I had better look at the newspapers. Others evidently had the same idea; I had not seen so many students clustered around the display case since China's first atomic-bomb test in the autumn of 1964.

The *People's Daily*, *Guangming Daily*, *Hebei Daily*, and *China Youth News* all carried articles criticizing a series of essays by three authors who called themselves the Three Family Village. One was Wu Han, the author of *Hai Rui Dismissed from Office*. He and his two fellow villagers were accused of using innuendo to oppose the Party. But at the same time the papers referred to the three as comrades, suggesting that their mistakes might not be irredeemable.

At our afternoon political-study sessions, my homeroom teacher, Wen Xiu, merely repeated the words in the newspapers. Even the class Youth League secretary, Congfang, had nothing to add. I began to check the newspapers every day. "Poisonous weeds" were cropping up everywhere, on the stage, in the cinema, in books and magazines. But the main target was still the Three Villagers. The criticism grew harsher. And the three were no longer called comrades.

One day, the *People's Daily* carried an editorial against them entitled "Open Fire at the Anti-Party Black Line!" Secretary Ding called another assembly. He and the Party Committee sat on the stage beneath a streamer that read, "Open Fire at the Anti-Party Black Line!" Ding Yi's speech was almost a verbatim reading of the editorial. He began practically every sentence with, "Holding high the great banner of Mao Zedong Thought . . . " At the end, he announced that we now would devote every afternoon to criticizing the Three Family Village. Each class could pick up poster-making supplies at the school Logistics Office.

In class the next morning, Teacher Shen wrote Three Family Village in English on the blackboard and announced that the English version of Chairman Mao's book of quotations would soon be off the press. Most of us had copies of the Chinese edition. The army's Political Department had designed the book for soldiers who could not read very well. The quotations were arranged in handy categories such as Party, Army, Women, Youth, and Revolutionary Heroism. It made a nice, pocket-sized souvenir.

That afternoon, we set to work making *dazibao*, "big-character posters." The Logistics Office dispensed bundles of brush pens, bottles of ink, and stacks of used newspaper. In the dining hall, a big cauldron had been set up to make glue from sweet-potato starch. My classmates and I spread newspaper over the floor of our empty classroom and began painting big, bold characters, one to a sheet. Little Mihu, who had

The Thirty-Six Stratagems

volunteered to help cook the glue, returned with a bucketful. We used brooms to paste the posters on the outside walls.

Our classroom building soon was covered with a collage of slogans we had seen in the newspapers: "Down with the Three Family Village!" "Smash the black gang!" "Down with the antisocialist cabal!" "Carry the revolution through to the end!" Zongwei, the class artist, had made a few exemplary specimens in his handsome calligraphy. Most of the other writing was crooked and crude, but seemed to suit the messages we were proclaiming. At the end of the afternoon, we stood back to admire our handiwork, our hands and faces smudged with black ink.

I took a tour of the campus. The scene was spectacular. Posters denouncing the Three Family Village covered every wall so that hardly a brick was visible. Some classes had festooned their areas with colorful streamers that waved in the breeze like the willow branches dangling over the paths. Most of the slogans were, like ours, copied from newspaper headlines, but a few were original. A couplet signed by Fangpu caught my eye: "The Three Family Village offended seven hundred million people, setting off a spiritual bomb greater than the A-bomb!"

Many students were strolling around reading posters. So were Secretary Ding and Vice-Principal Lin. Ding Yi, a paunchy man who walked with a limp, the result of a wound he got in the civil war, puffed and laughed delightedly as he read slogans aloud. Lin Sheng, a tall man with the stooped shoulders of someone who seldom left his desk, had a smile of satisfaction on his lips.

The next afternoon, we made more dazibao. The Logistics Office was running out of used newspaper and began to hand out clean newsprint in pastel shades. Inspired by Fangpu's poem, I dashed off a new slogan: "Even the A-bomb cannot rival the masses' anger at the Three Family Village counter-revolutionary cabal!"

After a few days of frenetic poster-writing, I realized that I still did not know very much about this Three Family Village. Curious, I went to the library to review all the papers of the past few weeks. All three Villagers, it turned out, were municipal officials in Beijing. Wu Han was a vice-mayor. Deng Tuo, former editor of the *People's Daily* and now chief editor of the *Beijing Evening News*, was propaganda director for the Beijing Party Committee. Liao Mosha, a writer and scholar, did propaganda for the city government. It seemed the trio had been carrying on anti-Party activities for years. They had started writing their Three Family Village essays for the Beijing Party Committee's monthly journal, *Frontline*, back in 1961.

Deng Tuo was the focus of additional criticism for his column in the *Beijing Evening News*, "Evening Chats at Mount Yan." The national papers had reprinted some of the "Chats" for study and criticism. I found them witty and engrossing, so I needed the newspaper commentary to help me understand what was wrong with them. Two of them, "Great Empty Talk" and "Stories About Bragging," were said to be attacks on the Great Leap Forward. "Special Treatment for Amnesia," which referred to the quack remedies of hitting a patient with a rubber club and pouring dog blood on his head, signified hatred of the Party. "Plain Water Tastes Best," about the belief that drinking plain boiled water is good for one's health, was a smear of the Party's economic policies.

Some of Deng Tuo's columns retold traditional folk tales. "The Family Fortune of a Single Egg" was typical. A cautionary tale, it related how a poor man, finding an egg on the street, took it home and announced to his wife that the egg held the family fortune. But it would take a decade to realize the wealth. He outlined his plan to her. First, he would give the egg to his neighbor to hatch under the neighbor's hen. When the chick grew up, it would lay eggs, which would hatch into another fifteen chickens a month. Within two years, his new hens would have produced 300 chickens, which he would sell for ten taels of silver. With the money, he would buy five cows, which would give birth to more cows. In three years, he would have 25 cows, and in three more, 150. He would sell those for 300 taels of silver. Then he would become a moneylender. Within another three years, he would have 500 taels of silver. Being a rich man, he could now buy a concubine. Hearing that part of the plan, the man's wife became angry and crushed the egg in her hand.

The newspapers said that Deng Tuo had meant that story as an attack on the people's communes.

The "Chat" that intrigued me the most was the last in the series, "The Thirty-Six Stratagems." It listed strategies developed by Chinese military experts over thousands of years, summed up in four-character idioms. Deng Tuo had written that the best was No. 36: "Run away." The newspapers said that was a secret warning to his fellow anti-Party conspirators to disband. These were the stratagems:

Cross the sea under camouflage
Besiege the kingdom of Wei to save the kingdom of Zhao
Murder with a borrowed knife
Wait calmly until the enemy is exhausted
Plunder a burning house
Make a feint to the east and attack in the west
Create something out of nothing
Advance secretly by an unknown path

The Thirty-Six Stratagems

Let the fire burn on the other side of the river
Hide a dagger in a smile
Palm off a substitute for the real thing
Take the opportunity to pilfer a goat
Beat the grass and startle the snake
Revive a dead soul in another's corpse
Lure the tiger out of the mountains
Let the enemy off the hook in order to catch him
Cast a brick to attract jade
Catch the ringleader to nab the bandits
Take the firewood out from under the cauldron
Fish in troubled waters
Leave the molting cicada's shell behind
Close the door to catch the thief
Befriend the distant enemy while attacking the near one
Seek safe passage through the kingdom of Yu to conquer the
    kingdom of Guo, and take Yu on the way back
Steal the beams and pillars and substitute rotten timbers
Point at the mulberry and abuse the locust
Pretend to be foolish while remaining intelligent
Pull down the ladder once the enemy has mounted the house
Deck the tree with false blossoms
Make the host and guest exchange places
Use a woman to ensnare a man
Fling open the gates of the empty city
Sow discord among the enemy
Inflict injury on oneself to win the enemy's trust
Shift the burden to your enemy
And finally, the best policy, run away

Chairman Mao had applied the last strategy in the Long
March, moving the revolution north to escape Chiang Kai-
shek's fifth Encirclement and Annihilation Campaign. I wondered whether I would ever find a use for any of them. Then
I thought up another I could use right away: "Wait and see."

The Thirty-Six Stratagems

Hidden Messages

One afternoon when we were making dazibao, Little Mihu came running into the classroom waving a magazine and shouting, "Big discovery, big discovery!" We clustered around. Little Mihu was holding the May issue of *China Youth*. He jabbed his finger at the back cover, a scene of young people carrying bundles of wheat in baskets slung on shoulder poles. Behind them stretched a golden ocean of wheat.

"Look at the red flag in the background," Little Mihu said excitedly. "It's fluttering toward the right. On the map, right is east and left is west. So the wind must be blowing from the west. Chairman Mao says the east wind should prevail over the west, but here the west is prevailing over the east!"

That was not all. Little Mihu turned the back cover sideways and traced his finger through the wheatfield, pointing out some light-colored streaks. "Here are four characters, do you see?" "Oh my!" somebody gasped. "Long live Kai-shek!" I saw it too, the veiled message in praise of Kuomintang leader Chiang Kai-shek.

The magazine passed from hand to hand. We were shocked that the enemies of socialism would be so bold as to issue a public challenge and amazed that they had figured out such a clever way to do it. Now we understood why the newspapers were warning us that counterrevolutionaries had wormed their way into the very heart of the Party's cultural apparatus. Nothing could be taken for granted anymore.

A few days later, Little Bawang pointed to Chairman Mao's portrait at the front of our classroom and exclaimed, "Look! Chairman Mao has only one ear!" Sure enough, the face was turned slightly to the right, showing only the left ear. A few students laughed. "What are you laughing about?" Little Bawang snarled. "This is a serious political problem. Every normal person has two ears, so why did this painter paint Chairman Mao with only one?" The class divided into two schools of thought. Yuling and I and a few others saw the missing ear as a question of artistic realism. But Little Bawang's view won over a majority. They began discussing whether to report the missing ear to the School Party Committee.

The *China Youth* cover was the talk of Yizhong. Everyone was on the lookout for more incriminating evidence, and every day fresh dazibao reported the latest findings. One group of students claimed to have found a snake on the face of Lenin, whose portrait hung beside the portraits of Mao, Marx, and Stalin in the back of the school auditorium and several other meeting rooms. Others said the snake was no more than a shadow on one side of Lenin's nose. Another group found a sword hanging over Chairman Mao's head in a photograph that showed him standing on the rostrum in Beijing's Tiananmen Square. Others said the sword was a painted beam. There were a few more imaginative discoveries, but none was as convincing as that pernicious message on the back cover of *China Youth*.

The search spread. Nothing was immune from suspicion. Taking their cues from the newspapers, students found problems with short stories, novels, movies, and plays. The critiques that appeared on the walls each day became more and more intricate. The headline-style dazibao were joined by much longer *xiaozibao*, "small-character posters." Many students tried to imitate the prose style of the Shanghai essayist Yao Wenyuan, who had written the first critique of the play *Hai Rui Dismissed from Office*. The method was, first, to declare yourself a defender of Marxism-Leninism and Mao Zedong Thought; second, to pose a series of accusatory questions about your target; and third, to expose it as yet another example of counterrevolutionary infiltration of the Party.

We discovered that this campaign was more than mere academic debate; our writing had effects. One evening, a group of students went into town to see a visiting song-and-dance ensemble from Tianjin. The next day, posters appeared around campus accusing the performers of attacking socialism and spreading bourgeois ideology. The critics were outraged by a dance that depicted peasant girls plucking cucumbers; they said the ugly hip-twisting motions made a mockery of poor and lower-middle peasants. Students sent copies of the posters along with a letter to the ensemble leaders. The troupe canceled its remaining performances and left town.

Then students began to scrutinize textbooks, teaching methods, and even teachers themselves. One poster criticized a literature textbook for spreading decadent bourgeois ideas because it included a poem about young people's minds turning to love in the spring. One chastised our geography teacher, Teacher Liu, for entrancing us with descriptions of the grasslands of Mongolia and the mountains of Xinjiang instead of inspiring us with Mao Zedong's revolutionary thought. Another accused our English teacher, Teacher Shen, of writing a double-entendre poem for a provincial literary magazine. Shen's poem was an ode to the lotus:

Hidden Messages

Though rooted in stinking mud,
Your body is smooth and clean;
Though you drink bitter water all your life,
Your flowers are fresh and fragrant;
In summer, you please us with your beautiful blossoms;
In autumn, you wither and leave us your delicious roots.

The phrase "drink bitter water all your life" was said to be a slur on socialist society.

More posters went up questioning various teachers' backgrounds. Why did Teacher Feng have an American father? What were the circumstances surrounding Teacher Li's defection from the Kuomintang to the Communists? By now, layer upon layer of paper covered the school walls. The debate had expanded far beyond the bounds of the Three Family Village, although the Three Villagers' names still appeared here and there, usually covered with big red X's, the symbol used on court decrees to signify the death sentence.

It was already June. Yizhong's anniversary had come and gone without the annual fish feast. The school leaders had not issued any schedule or instructions for examinations, graduation, or summer vacation. No poet laureate had been chosen for the year. We continued with open-air classes each morning but were given less and less homework.

Secretary Ding called assemblies frequently to recite the latest *People's Daily* editorials. But he also advocated restraint. After the incident involving the Tianjin performers, he cautioned us to keep our criticism within the school walls. When posters about teachers surfaced, he told us to avoid personal attacks. He said we should concentrate on important political and cultural matters instead. Then he announced an outright ban on criticizing teachers.

The movement had acquired a name: the Great Socialist

Cultural Revolution. The newspapers and radio brought us news from the center of the movement, Beijing. In addition, my classmate Yuanchao kept us apprised of important Central Committee developments. His father let him read internal Party communiqués, something my father had never let me do.

Even as Ding Yi was trying to narrow our activities, students in Beijing were broadening theirs. Furthermore, the Central Committee was behind them. One day, the central radio station broadcast the text of a poster that had been put up at Beida, attacking the top authorities of the school and calling on all revolutionary intellectuals to plunge into the Cultural Revolution. The poster said that "monsters" and "demons" and Khrushchev-like counterrevolutionary revisionists were undermining socialism. And Yuanchao brought us rumors of an important Central Committee document that said that representatives of the bourgeoisie had infiltrated the Party, the government, and the army, as well as the cultural arena.

The next news from the capital was even more exciting: the entire Beijing Party Committee and the two top leaders of Beida had been dismissed. The reconstituted Party Committee had sent a work team to Beida to make sure students could carry on the movement unimpeded. The *People's Daily* celebrated these events with editorials headlined "Sweep Away All Monsters and Demons!" and "We Are Critics of the Old World!"

Emboldened by the developments in Beijing, Fangpu struck the first blow against the leadership of Yizhong. He pasted a poster on the auditorium wall accusing Secretary Ding of obstructing revolution with regulations, taboos, and commandments. An attack on Ding Yi was no small matter. He was a longtime Party member with a history of loyal service that was known even to the authorities in Beijing. Aside from his Party work during the civil war, he had proved himself anew by opposing a counterrevolutionary incident in 1962. The government was having a hard time arranging work for college graduates because of the country's economic difficulties, and seniors from the Yizhen Geology Institute had lost patience waiting for assignments. They marched across town brandishing flags and demanding jobs. When they got to the railway station, they lay down on the tracks and halted the trains for six hours, until the head of state himself, Liu Shaoqi, arrived from Beijing to negotiate. Ding Yi had become involved when the demonstrators passed by Yizhong and tried to get students there to join them; he had ordered the school gates barred. Ding Yi had always stood on the side of the Party. He seemed unassailable.

At our next assembly, three strangers sat on the auditorium stage beside Secretary Ding. They were introduced as a work team that would be investigating the progress of the Cultural Revolution at Yizhong. The young woman in charge of the team was exemplarily red and expert. She had graduated from Beida in history and already was a vice-head of Yizhen county. Accompanying her was another college graduate in his early thirties and a dour-looking older man.

The team made rounds of the school over the next couple of days and then issued a report pronouncing Ding Yi's supervision impeccable. Fangpu was required to write a public apology. I went looking for Fangpu after the poster appeared and found him in the library. "I went along as a tactical maneuver," he confided to me. "It doesn't mean that I have changed my mind."

Although the work team had defused Fangpu's assault on

Ding Yi, it lifted the ban on criticizing teachers. The team also suspended classes altogether so we could make Cultural Revolution full time. Once again, posters about teachers proliferated. Their tone grew harsher. "Down with Big Traitor Lu!" said one headline. Lu, who taught senior-level history, had done underground Party work in Shanghai before Liberation. He had once been arrested by the Kuomintang, and the poster charged that he had taken the occasion to betray some of his comrades to the enemy. Another poster was headlined "Ultra-rightist Zhu Is Rubbish!" Zhu taught senior Chinese. The poster said he had not shown repentance since being labeled a rightist in 1957. It referred to him as "Eclectic Zhu" because he wrote essays that blended Confucian, Mohist, Logician, and Legalist thought.

Another read "Leng, Reactionary Student of American Imperialist Leighton Stuart, Must Confess to the People!" The target was an old philosophy teacher, an eccentric bachelor who wore a Western-style suit to class. Leng had graduated from Yenching University, founded by Americans and later absorbed by Beida. The poster alleged he had made underhanded deals with the last U.S. ambassador to China.

More posters appeared about our physics teacher, Feng, accusing his father of representing American aggression in old China. Feng's two little children played happily around the posters. Each time they recognized their father's name, they would point and yell proudly, "There's another one for Papa!" Feng wrote a reply, saying his own mother had been a victim of U.S. imperialism. The American navy officer had raped her, insisted she marry him, and then abandoned the whole family. Next to this account, Feng hung a large framed photograph showing a Caucasian man in uniform, with his pretty Chinese wife and several children. One of the children was Feng himself. This family history and the picture attracted a big crowd. No more posters about Feng appeared after that.

The attack on Teacher Shen resumed with renewed vigor. "Ferret Out Old Fritter Shen!" one poster said. It said Shen had been born into a big landlord family and had gone to Hong Kong after Liberation to escape political retribution and to make lots of money by working for a foreign company. Yuanchao wrote a poster claiming that Shen had insulted his father, the veteran of the Long March. Yuanchao had once written on an English test "My father is a cock," instead of "My father is a cook." Shen had cited the mistake in class as an example of carelessness. Yuanchao charged that Shen had read the sentence aloud in a deliberate attempt to tarnish his father's reputation.

More criticism of Teacher Li went up as well. One poster, which began "Rip off Li's revolutionary insurgent mask!," claimed that our Chinese teacher had not really intended to lead his troops in an uprising against the Kuomintang. Instead, it gave the following version: Li's troops were guarding Chiang Kai-shek's residence in Nanjing, the Kuomintang capital. Just before the People's Liberation Army crossed the Yangtze River to take the city in the spring of 1949, Li went on vacation somewhere north of the river. While he was enjoying himself visiting brothels, his men revolted of their own accord and went over to the Communist side. Li was stranded and had no choice but to surrender. When I remembered how the tale of a Communist heroine had moved Teacher Li almost to tears, I was not sure what to believe.

One morning, the news spread swiftly across campus that Leng, the lackey of the American imperialist Leighton Stuart, had cut his throat. He had bungled the suicide attempt, slicing his windpipe instead of an artery. Other teachers found him on the ground outside his single room and an ambulance rushed him to the Army Hospital. He survived but did not return to school.

Leng's drastic action silenced the criticism aimed at him, but not that against others. Old Fritter Shen now was said to have raped a serving girl at his landlord family's estate while he was a youth, and to have written counterrevolutionary poetry in English as well as Chinese. Teacher Li was accused of corrupting students' minds with his tricks of balancing a rifle and riding a bike without moving. He also was said to have told other teachers dirty stories about visiting brothels in Shanghai. I was feeling more and more disappointed with Teacher Li.

Some teachers began to expose other teachers, producing furious poster battles. Liu and Yang waged one such battle on the wall inside the bell-tower courtyard. Yang said the rightist Liu did not really know much about geography but just threw out bits and pieces of bourgeois trivia to dazzle his students. Liu charged Yang with having an affair with the wife of an army officer while her husband was fighting in Korea. The exchange attracted a lot of attention. Neither won the battle, since their posters provided students with more ammunition to use against both of them.

Other teachers followed Feng's example and wrote explanations, confessions, or self-criticisms in hopes of arousing sympathy. Sometimes students took these as evidence of bad faith, accusing the teachers of making false admissions in order to get by—"crossing the sea under camouflage," as the first of the Thirty-Six Stratagems put it.

The concern with the Three Family Village became buried under layers of posters about teachers. Students first concentrated on those with bad family origins, such as landlord or

Hidden Messages

capitalist, or bad personal histories, such as counterrevolutionary or rightist. Later, these factors did not seem to matter. Anyone who had ever said anything suspect in class was fair game.

I liked almost all my teachers and did not want to attack them, but neither did I want my classmates to think me an unrevolutionary misfit. Finally, I decided to criticize Teacher Wen. Although she always spoke to me in a kind and gentle way, I had grown weary of her lectures about being red and expert, and still felt she was singling me out. I entitled my poster "Denouncing Wen Xiu's Persecution of Me" and posted it in the bell-tower courtyard. It ran for thirteen pages on sheets of paper more than a meter high.

Although some students wrote comments in the margins of my poster praising my literary style and my idea of writing in the first person, few were very interested in my complaints. Teacher Wen was small potatoes. I did get enthusiastic support from one person, though—Shuanggen, our class sports manager. Teacher Wen had once suspected Shuanggen of stealing a pen from the classroom. She had ordered all the boys into our dormitory room to strip naked and search each other. Everyone knew it was directed at Shuanggen. The pen was never found. Shuanggen had borne a grudge ever since.

Shuanggen wrote a poster too, accusing Wen Xiu of maltreating him. His poster got more attention than mine, because he called Wen Xiu "the daughter of a filthy capitalist's whore." Our homeroom teacher's old mother, who lived with her on campus, had a frightening, ravaged face. According to Shuanggen, the old woman's deformity was the result of syphilis she had contracted as a prostitute in Shanghai. "Wen Xiu masquerades as a learned intellectual," Shuanggen wrote, "but her family status is really lumpen."

I tried to avoid Teacher Wen when I saw her on the path, but she stopped me and said, "Jianhua, I am so sorry for what I did to you, but I want you to know that I criticized you for your own good. I didn't mean to hurt your feelings." She looked pale and tired, her eyes were red, and her usually tidy hair was mussed. I suddenly felt remorseful. Teacher Wen asked me to come to her home and to bring Shuanggen. We went, partly out of curiosity, but mostly because we were used to obeying our homeroom teacher. She and her mother lived in a two-room flat off the bell-tower courtyard. Sitting with Shuanggen and me in the dingy bedroom, she poured us tea and related her family history, starting with her mother's birth into a poor peasant family in South China.

Her mother's parents, unable to feed their daughter, had sold her at the age of fourteen to a man who traded in human beings. The man resold her to a brothel near a foreign concession in Shanghai. She had both foreign and Chinese customers. When a foreign warship was in port, she serviced as many as twenty soldiers and sailors a day. She ran away several times, but each time she was caught, sent back to the brothel, and given a whipping. A capitalist bought her as his concubine. Wen Xiu was born. The capitalist discovered that his consort had syphilis and threw both mother and child out on the street, where they turned to begging.

"Mama's syphilis went untreated . . . " Teacher Wen began to sob. When she had recovered her composure, she took a small framed picture out of a box. It showed a beautiful young woman in a tight silk *qipao*, the elegant dress of old China. The woman was smiling, but the smile had a tinge of bitterness. She did not resemble the ugly old woman who was sitting in the next room. I glanced at Teacher Wen and discovered she looked much as her mother once had.

Hidden Messages

49

It was twilight when we left Teacher Wen's home. I looked on the courtyard wall. Fresh posters already were encroaching on my tale of persecution. I knew that my handiwork would be completely covered up in a day or two.

A few days later, I chanced upon Little Mihu writing a poster entitled "Expose Wen Xiu's Indecent Behavior!" In childish calligraphy that resembled tadpoles crawling all over the paper, he complained that Teacher Wen often came into the boys' dormitory rooms and put her hands under the quilts on the pretext of seeing if we were warm enough. I told him that people would laugh at his poster, but that did not dissuade him. Then I told him about Wen Xiu and her mother's bitter past. Little Mihu threw his poster out.

Ox Ghosts and Snake Spirits

The *People's Daily* had called upon us to "sweep away all ox ghosts and snake spirits." Caolan, the monitor of class 85, and Congfang, the class's Youth League secretary, decided to organize a unified action against Teachers Shen and Li. Little Bawang was the most enthusiastic. He suggested we take inspiration from Chairman Mao's report on the peasant movement in Hunan province, written in the 1920's, which described how the peasants had put dunce caps on the heads of local tyrants and evil gentry and paraded them through the streets.

The class split into active and passive contingents. The activists took up ink bottles, brush pens, paper, and paste buckets and trooped off to the Teachers' Building. Little Mihu carried two dunce caps made of white paper, topped with white tassels of the type used for funeral decorations. Little Bawang had two wooden boards. The rest of us followed and watched as Li and Shen were dragged out of their offices and onto the porch. "What's the matter? What's the matter?" Li was saying. "What's the matter?" Little Bawang yelled. "We're here to sweep away you ox ghosts and snake spirits!" The two were capped, and the boards were hung around their necks. Li's board identified him as "Reactionary Kuomintang Colonel and Chiang Ching-kuo's Running Dog." Shen's said, "Vile Progeny of the Landlord Class and Imperialist Spy."

I tried to push my liking for Li out of my mind and concentrate on his crimes. The latest posters had accused him of yearning to "change the heavens," to return to the old days, to restore Kuomintang rule. One poster even said that one night in 1962, when Chiang Kai-shek was raising a hue and cry about counterattacking the mainland, Li had donned his old colonel's uniform.

I had been taught that Chiang Kai-shek's rule was the darkest era in Chinese history. Li himself had read to us from the novel *Red Crag*, which described how the Kuomintang reactionaries and the American imperialists had tortured the Communists. I knew that in Chiang Kai-shek's China inflation was so high that one jin of money could not buy even one jin of plain paper. I had read about the armies of beggars, the lanes of brothels, the frozen corpses found in the streets. My father had fought the Kuomintang all his life. We could not tolerate a return to those days.

As I thought of these things, I began to hate Teacher Li. Yet part of me still liked him. I stayed some distance from the

Ox Ghosts and Snake Spirits

porch and tried to hide from his view among the growing crowd of students. "Students, let's talk things over," Li was saying now. Little Bawang motioned to him to stop talking. A struggle meeting was about to begin. Li and Shen stood on the porch with their heads lowered. Caolan led the crowd in shouting slogans: "Leniency to those who confess, severity to those who refuse!" "Li, make a clean breast of your crimes!" "Shen, confess or be damned!" "Long live the Great Socialist Cultural Revolution!"

"Speak!" Little Bawang yelled at Li. "How many people did you kill before Liberation? What crimes did you carry out for Chiang Ching-kuo? Speak!" Other students echoed his commands.

"I killed no one," Li said. "I was guarding Chiang Kai-shek's residence. Chiang Ching-kuo was my chief. I was a battalion leader under his command."

"Did you kill any Communists?" Little Mihu shouted excitedly.

"No, never. I didn't like Chiang Kai-shek's killing. That's why I ran away with my soldiers and surrendered when the People's Liberation Army came to Nanjing. My brother, who crossed over earlier, had a lot of influence on me. He can testify to that. He works in the provincial government . . . "

"Li is not honest," Little Bawang cut in. "Li is playing tricks with us. Don't be taken in by this cunning fox."

"Down with Li!" Caolan shouted, holding both fists high. "Down with Li!" voices chorused up and down the porch and through the crowd.

Suddenly, with a plopping sound, the paste bucket was upside down on Li's head. The sticky brown mixture of sweet-potato flour and water, still warm, oozed down Li's shoulders and over his back and chest. Little Bawang picked up a broom

Ox Ghosts and Snake Spirits

and began knocking on the bucket. Shen was trembling and bowing his head very low, almost to his knees. I wished he would confess his crimes as soon as possible and get the ordeal over with. But he appeared too frightened to talk at all. The students on the porch then ordered both teachers to start marching. They paraded Li and Shen around the campus, shoving and pushing the two teachers with almost every step. Li, unable to see with the bucket on his head, stumbled and fell several times.

Following class 85's revolutionary action, other classes began to organize struggle meetings and parades. The wooden slogan boards grew larger and heavier, the dunce caps taller and more elaborate. Some students hung bricks on the boards to make it harder for the teachers to stand up. One group of first-graders made a cap of sorghum stalks as high as a two-story building for their homeroom teacher; they had to support it with long poles as they marched him around.

The list of accusations grew longer by the day: hooligans and bad eggs, filthy rich peasants and son-of-a-bitch landlords, bloodsucking capitalists and neobourgeoisie, historical counterrevolutionaries and active counterrevolutionaries, rightists and ultrarightists, alien class elements and degenerate elements, reactionaries and opportunists, counterrevolutionary revisionists, imperialist running dogs, and spies. Students stood in the roles of prosecutor, judge, and police. No defense was allowed. Any teacher who protested was certainly a liar.

The indignities escalated as well. Some students shaved or cut teachers' hair into curious patterns. The most popular style was the yin-yang cut, which featured a full head of hair on one side and a clean-shaven scalp on the other. Some said this style represented Chairman Mao's theory of the "unity of opposites." It made me think of the punishments of ancient China, which included shaving the head, tattooing the face, cutting off the nose or feet, castration, and dismemberment by five horse-drawn carts.

At struggle meetings, students often forced teachers into the "jet-plane" position. Two people would stand on each side of the accused, push him to his knees, pull his head back by the hair, and hold his arms out in back like airplane wings. We tried it on each other and found it caused great strain on the back and neck. Still, some students insisted that it was far more humane than the methods the Kuomintang reactionaries and American imperialists had used to torture the Communists at the infamous Sino-American Cooperation Organization Prison in Happy Valley, near the city of Chongqing. The novel *Red Crag* detailed some of those tortures: bamboo splints under the fingernails, electric shock, the rack. A few students even argued that we should use a bit more force. After all, weren't many of these bad eggs Kuomintang and American agents?

At one meeting, Little Bawang and other activists in my class gave History Teacher Yang a jet-plane ride and a yin-yang haircut. We all knew how proud Yang was of his swept-back Chairman Mao hairstyle. I had heard that he washed his hair with cold water every morning and ate walnuts to make it shine. Teacher Yang displayed a stony expression as the students shaved half his scalp. The next day, he was nowhere to be found. The rumor was that he had run away to stay with relatives. His disappearance alarmed the work team, which issued a new order: from now on, we were to keep watch on the teachers at night.

Virtually none of Yizhong's 200 teachers escaped attention in our big-character posters, and almost anyone who was criticized had to stand before a chanting crowd at least once. After attacking the most obvious bad elements first, students went on to milder cases, even a few from excellent family backgrounds. A young teacher from a worker's family was charged with emphasizing academics over politics, and a young woman of poor-peasant origin was criticized for wearing high heels, proof that she had betrayed her class. Each apologized in a public meeting.

We had just about run out of targets among the teachers when attention suddenly shifted to Lin Sheng, the soft-spoken, scholarly vice-principal of Yizhong. A long critique covering an entire wall reported that Lin Sheng's bourgeois, revisionist view of education had exerted widespread pernicious influence. As proof, it quoted at length from his *Collection of Teaching Experiences*, a pamphlet of essays he had written reviewing his four decades in education. The most offensive essays were excerpted in full. Each essay's title was an idiom, famous saying, or line of poetry, and each began with an anecdote or fable. Each was followed by students' comments. "Red Apricot Blossoms Stretching Over the Wall" was typical. It went like this:

One spring day, long ago, the Southern Song poet Ye Shaotang went to visit his friend's garden. His friend happened to be out. Ye wrote a poem that is still popular today.

> After knocking long and gently at the gate of
> intertwined branches, with no response,
> I turned to go regretfully, the mark of my wooden clogs
> imprinted on the dark green moss;
> When suddenly I spied a sprig of red apricot blossoms
> stretching out over the garden wall,
> The bountiful beauty of spring that could not be
> locked up in answer to nature's call.

Ox Ghosts and Snake Spirits

I learned this poem when I was a small child, but not until recently did I discover in it a philosophical meaning that could apply to our education.

Why did a single branch of red apricot blossoms give Ye Shaotang poetic inspiration? Would he have written such a fine poem if he had seen a whole bunch of apricot branches coming over the wall? I think not. The essence of the poem is in that single branch. It caught his eye against the greenery of everything else. Had there been a bunch of branches, he might have ignored them. The one branch's singularity made it precious.

In education as well, a number of gifted students stand out from the rest. We should pay great attention to them and help them excel in their fields of study. Only in this way can we compete with other key schools and produce talented people for the country.

The commentary that followed said that this essay showed how Lin Sheng took the point of view of the exploiting class. "He advocates the bourgeois theory of the ivory tower," one critic wrote. "He wants education to serve a tiny elite, depriving the vast majority of the children of working people the right to schooling."

In another essay, Lin Sheng recalled how his own father had started him on the road to learning. The comments said that Lin Sheng was bragging about his landlord origins. "In the old society, old people from the exploiting class, like Lin Sheng, could afford to go to school. How many workers or poor and lower-middle peasants went to school? Most of them could not even dream of such a thing!"

Although I rather liked Lin Sheng's writing, I felt no urge to take issue with the commentators. The mere fact that Lin Sheng was the son of a landlord was incriminating enough.

The attack on Lin Sheng caused a stir because he was Yizhong's third-highest authority, next only to the Party secretary, Ding Yi, and our principal, Wu Du. Wu Du was difficult to criticize, since we had not seen him for months. He had gone to Beijing before the earthquake to take a political study course at the Central Committee Party School, and nobody knew when he might return. As for Ding Yi, he still was under the protection of the work team.

Within 24 hours, Lin Sheng's revisionist line in education had become the dominant theme on the school walls. The work team announced an assembly at which the vice-principal would be expected to confess his crimes. It would be our first schoolwide struggle meeting.

The work team had set up a schedule for guarding the teachers. The night before the assembly, our class was on duty. We rummaged through the sports equipment room after dinner and picked out baseball clubs, fencing foils, wooden swords, and metal-tipped javelins to arm ourselves like proper sentries. I felt the same kind of excitement I had felt playing spy games in primary school.

I was assigned to roving patrol in the bell-tower courtyard. Clutching a wooden sword, I roamed the darkness among the teachers' residences. Wherever I saw a lit window, I would try to peer inside. I did not have much luck, since most of the windows were curtained or covered with newspaper on the inside. Only one was uncovered. For a few minutes, I watched Teacher Shen. He was lying in bed, a cigarette dangling from one hand, the other hand stroking a furrow that had been shaved up the middle of his scalp.

I came upon Little Mihu sitting on a stoop and sat down beside him. The night seemed long, the work monotonous. Both of us began to doze. Half asleep, I heard a thump that sounded like a thermos falling. Early in the morning, I opened

Ox Ghosts and Snake Spirits

my eyes to find people already scurrying across the courtyard. "Haven't you heard?" a passing student said. "Vice-Principal Lin hung himself." A throng of onlookers had gathered at the door of Lin Sheng's home. I elbowed my way toward the front. The vice-principal was sprawled on his back on a bed, fully dressed in a blue suit, surrounded by students who had cut down the rope. His glasses lay on the floor. Dr. Yang pushed her way into the room to take his pulse.

Lin Sheng was the second dead man I had seen. When I was still in primary school, I had attended a public rally in town at which a man from a landlord background was sentenced to death for raping a girl from a poor-peasant family. After the sentencing, a horse-drawn cart took the man to the execution ground on a hill behind the town hall. I was eager to see the execution and followed thousands of people to the hill. Then I hesitated. I lingered behind until I heard the gunshot. When I got up the hill, the body was lying by a pit. An old peasant stooped down, scooped the brains out of the skull with his hands, wrapped them in a big leaf, and carried them off.

That lifeless body had been a criminal and a stranger. This one was someone I knew. I thought back to my only personal encounter with Lin Sheng, during my first term at Yizhong. Teacher Wen had criticized me for melting down candles and playing with the wax during class. When I refused to stop, she sent me to see the vice-principal. I arrived at his office expecting a reprimand. Instead, he gave me a cup of hot tea and a lesson on how candles were made. The wax was a by-product of petroleum processing, and workers at the Daqing oilfield worked very hard to get that oil, he said. By the time he was finished, I felt very guilty about having ruined good candles. I went back to the classroom and apologized to Teacher Wen.

As one of the night guards, I could not help feeling partly at fault for Lin Sheng's death. At the very least, I should have investigated the thump I heard as I was nodding off to sleep. On the other hand, the student right outside his door had failed to hear anything. Even with a guard by his bed, Lin Sheng probably would have found a way sooner or later. He was one of those people who subscribe to the notion, "Better to be a shattered jade vessel than an intact clay pot."

Our class had the privilege of sleeping all morning because we had been on guard duty all night. In the afternoon, we attended an assembly in front of the Teachers' Building. Secretary Ding and the other Yizhong Party Committee members stood on the porch. In a monotone, the head of the work team read out a statement: "Anti-Party element Lin Sheng alienated himself from the Party and the people, and committed suicide. On behalf of the County Party Committee, I hereby announce that we have decided to expel anti-Party element Lin Sheng from the Party and dismiss him from his posts both inside and outside the Party. We call on all revolutionary students to rise and criticize Lin Sheng's counterrevolutionary revisionist line in education." Some deafening slogan-shouting ensued.

Lin Sheng was to be buried the next morning. His wife and children refused to come to the funeral, saying they wanted to cut off all relations with this anti-Party element. Some teachers and students volunteered to escort the body to its burial spot.

I took one last look at him in the bell-tower courtyard, where he lay on his own quilt in a flimsy wooden coffin. His eyes were closed, and someone had put his glasses back on his nose. Students covered him with another quilt, nailed on the coffin lid and lifted the coffin onto a cart. The procession set off, with one student at the head holding a signboard and several others pulling the cart. A scattering of students and teachers walked alongside with heads bowed. Others who were neither activist enough to carry a slogan nor soft-hearted enough to grieve—among them myself—trailed at a safe distance.

Lin Sheng was buried outside the north side of the city wall by the grass-covered grave of the student who had drowned in the Hutuo River. The signboard was planted atop the new burial mound. It read: "The Tomb of Anti-Party Element Lin Sheng."

Winds and Waves

By July, the earthquake danger seemed to have passed and the summer rains were beginning. We dismantled our shacks and moved back into the dormitories. It seemed certain now: there would be no finals or college entrance examinations, no poetry contest, no graduation, no summer vacation. The Cultural Revolution took precedence over everything else.

Weihua and I had skipped our monthly visit home two months in a row. Both of us were so busy making revolution with our classmates that we rarely saw each other anymore. When I did run into him, on the path or in the dining hall, I generally asked him the questions I did not want to ask anybody else—such as where the Cultural Revolution was going and how long it would last.

"Nothing is certain in the world," was Weihua's answer to that. "Laozi is not the only philosopher who says that. Marxist dialectical materialism says so too. Or didn't you get that far in politics class?"

"We were just starting dialectics when classes stopped," I said. "Chairman Mao uses dialectics. He says one divides into two, and a bad thing can be turned into a good one."

With Lin Sheng gone, the biggest remaining monsters and demons were teachers like Shen and Li. The activist students interrogated them almost daily and confined them to their offices to write self-criticisms. Little Bawang brought us regular reports on the interrogation sessions. Shen had admitted to deflowering a maidservant while growing up in his landlord family. Li still refused to confess to killing any Communists.

Some students were beginning to talk about linking up with rebel movements elsewhere. By chance, I met two rebels from Beijing who were on a secret mission to Yizhong. Two girls I had never seen before were washing their sandals at a spigot in the bell-tower courtyard. I asked them who they were. Their names sounded familiar. They had graduated from Yizhong two years before and were now university students, one at Beida, the other at Qinghua. Their names had been near the top of the list written in gold on red paper that I had seen my first day at Yizhong.

The two girls told me that their revolutionary rebel headquarters in Beijing had sent them back to their old school to help make revolution. "The movement here lacks vigor," the one from Beida declared. "At Beida, we rebels, under the leadership of Nie Yuanzi, have already kicked out the Party secretary, and the work team is retreating." Nie Yuanzi was the young philosophy instructor who had put up that first poster attacking the authorities at Beida.

The girls asked me if I knew Fangpu. I told them we were good friends, although I had not talked with him since his apology for the ill-fated critique of Ding Yi. "Fangpu is the real revolutionary rebel here," said the one from Qinghua. "He's been suppressed by the work team. He's just like Qinghua's Kuai Dafu, who was persecuted by our work team." I added Kuai Dafu to my ever-growing mental list of Cultural Revolution luminaries. The two visitors urged me to organize my classmates to support Fangpu. "I'll follow the situation," I said.

Chairman Mao had not appeared in public for months, when suddenly in mid-July he made a long-distance swim up the Yangtze River. The work team at Yizhong marked the occasion by organizing a school excursion to the Hutuo River. We lined up by class and walked for an hour, through the town and out the southern gate to the river's north bank. Most of the boys wore gym shorts, and the girls wore shorts and T-shirts, for few of us owned real bathing suits.

The runoff from the Taihang Mountains had filled the channel on its way to the Bohai Sea. Ribbonlike beaches of white sand lined both banks as far as the eye could see. Here and there were patches of hardy "awl grass," whose tentacled roots could tunnel beneath the sand to send up new sprouts. I had acquired a taste for awl grass, as I had for horse greens, during the Three Difficult Years. The sprouts were delicious, and the roots even better. After paddling around in the shallow water, I lay down beside a patch of awl grass to pull up a few sweet roots.

Someone called my name. Fangpu was lying nearby. His chest looked like a washboard and was almost as white as the sand. "Did you see Chairman Mao's poem today?" he asked me. The *People's Daily* had run the poem, entitled "Swimming," on the front page. Beside it was a photograph of the chairman, dressed in a robe, standing aboard a boat and waving his hand. An accompanying editorial called on everyone to temper himself in the great winds and waves of class struggle.

I had learned all 37 of Chairman Mao's published poems by heart, including this latest one. I recited the lines I especially liked:

> Heedless of blowing winds and surging waves,
> I tread the water as if strolling in a quiet
>   courtyard. . . .
> Were the goddess still in good health,
> She would be amazed by all the changes in the world.

Fangpu looked at me approvingly. "Chairman Mao's new poem is very encouraging," he said. "It is a message to us young people. It symbolizes revolutionary heroism." Fangpu's eyes sparkled behind his glasses. He seemed happiest when he was talking about revolution.

"Your father, my father, and all our revolutionary forefathers fought all their lives for the revolution," he went on. "We revolutionary descendants are obliged to carry on the great cause. Although our country is besieged by the U.S. imperialists and the Soviet revisionists, reactionaries of other countries, and the Kuomintang on Taiwan, we do not fear them. The greatest danger comes from the enemies hidden right among us. We must ferret them out!"

Fangpu glanced meaningfully at a group of people standing

Winds and Waves

on the beach. They were Secretary Ding, the two men on the work team, and Teacher Guo, who wore an eye-catching scarlet swimsuit. Most of the teachers had remained behind on campus; she was one of the few untainted ones who had come along. "Ding Yi is trying to stop us from exposing these hidden enemies," Fangpu said. "He and the work team diverted the students' attention to Lin Sheng, who was a much lesser threat. We will expose their tricks."

I asked Fangpu where he had been since he wrote his self-criticism. "I've been in my dormitory room, reading Marx, Lenin, and Chairman Mao," he said. "Soon I'll be coming out of seclusion. Two revolutionary rebels from Beida and Qinghua are helping me prepare." I did not tell him about my meeting at the well.

"The confrontation between the students and the work teams in the schools in Beijing is intensifying," Fangpu said. "The real revolutionary rebels want to follow Chairman Mao's instructions and expose the hidden enemies in the Party, while the work teams want to protect them. The contradiction is the same at Yizhong. Don't forget, we're one of the four key schools in the province. Imperialists and revisionists can always find a way to plant their agents in the most influential institutions." As Fangpu talked, I realized that he was a perfect example of the unity of opposites, which Chairman Mao explained in his article "On Contradiction." Pale, spindly, and bookish on the surface, he was zealously revolutionary at heart.

Fangpu left me to rejoin the seniors for the walk back to school. I got into formation with class 85. By the time we reached the city's southern gate, my shorts were dry. Secretary Ding, Teacher Guo, and the three work team members passed us on bicycles. Teacher Guo's swimsuit had made a damp print on her blouse and pants. She looked happier and more relaxed than the fragile, pinched woman I knew from politics class.

At the end of July, Yizhong took part in a nationwide display of support for the valiant struggle of the Vietnamese people against U.S. imperialism. We assembled outside the Teachers' Building to listen to a live broadcast from Beijing, where a million people were rallying in Tiananmen Square. Head of State Liu Shaoqi made a speech, declaring, "China's seven hundred million people are the Vietnamese people's powerful backup force, and China's vast territory is the Vietnamese people's trusted rear area." We also held our own outdoor rally. To my surprise, the work team had picked Fangpu to speak on behalf of the students.

Fangpu's oratory seemed more fiery than ever after his month in ignominy. "The United States is the source of war in the world!" he shouted. "We have dealt the U.S. imperialists one blow after another, but they persist in their vicious ambitions to swallow China up. We drove them back in the Korean War. We have knocked down two U-2 reconnaissance planes. We have wiped out many Kuomintang troops that landed on our southern coast with the help of the U.S. marines. But the U.S. imperialists still occupy our treasured island of Taiwan. Under U.S. occupation, our compatriots on Taiwan live in abject misery. Our Taiwanese sisters are often kidnaped by U.S. soldiers and raped in speeding jeeps. Our Taiwanese brothers are often used by U.S. soldiers for target practice."

As Fangpu ended, his audience took up his final words: "Down with the U.S. imperialists! Resist the United States and aid Vietnam! We must liberate Taiwan!" We kept on shouting as we marched into town to join the rest of Yizhen

Winds and Waves

in a demonstration. It happened to be market day, which fell on every fifth day in Yizhen. Throngs of peasants from the surrounding countryside were in town to sell their produce, go shopping, see local opera, or just sightsee. They mingled with the townsfolk, who had poured into the streets with banners and signs.

The demonstration converged at the intersection of the city's two main streets, Four Harmonies Street, which ran north and south, and Perpetual Victory Street, which ran east and west. We formed a big circle, creating an open-air stage, where our school gave a show on the theme, "Resist the United States and aid Vietnam." Every class had prepared a song, dance, or skit. Our act starred Little Mihu, Little Bawang, and Erchou. Little Bawang played the role of an American soldier, Erchou was an American pilot, and Little Mihu, who had an older brother fighting with an antiaircraft artillery unit in North Vietnam, was an American sailor. They wore paper caps and large red paper noses. Each confessed his crimes and stupidities in Vietnam. At the end, they flung off their props, turned into Vietnamese villagers, and yelled anti-American slogans.

The peasant spectators were delighted at the unexpected entertainment. The bartering on the sidewalks came to a virtual halt. The intersection became totally clogged when Leiting, one of Yizhong's best performers, appeared dressed as Uncle Sam to recite a clapper ballad. In a thick, rustic accent, he ridiculed the American capitalists for their greed and cruelty, his copper clappers clicking and clacking away. "The American capitalists take baths in milk or dump it into the sea while others are starving!" he said. The peasants laughed and talked among themselves excitedly. By the end of the show, they were shouting slogans along with us.

That night, messengers came around to all the dormitory rooms to tell us to report for emergency muster. We got dressed in the dark, since lights were not allowed, and went to the South Gate. The secretary-general of Yizhong's Youth League branch, Tang Hong, announced that she had received an urgent order to collect supplies to send to the Vietnamese front. I donated my quilt, plus two mao that I found in my pocket. Other students gave everything from clothing to mosquito nets and canteens. The collection continued for nearly an hour. When it was over, Tang Hong told us it was nothing but an exercise to see whether we were prepared. She looked pleased as she instructed us to retrieve our things and go back to sleep.

The Degenerate and the Worn Shoe

Ferret Out Alien Class Element Guo Pei!" I was astonished to see this slogan appear one morning on the wall of the Teachers' Building. Guo Pei in trouble? Teacher Guo was our authority for political questions. I had never heard her say anything that could be faulted. And she was the greatest Cultural Revolution enthusiast among all the teachers. She had worked closely with the Yizhong Party Committee and the work team in arranging our political activities during the past several months.

The poster revealed that Guo Pei had been hiding something. It said she was the daughter of a general in the service of one of Chiang Kai-shek's most notorious strongmen, Yan Xishan. Yan had been warlord of Shanxi province before submitting to Kuomintang authority. He had slaughtered countless Communists. Among his victims was the child heroine Liu Hulan, whom his troops had chopped up with a hay cutter.

According to the account, Guo Pei had taken a plane to Tianjin with her father on the eve of Liberation. He had fled to Taiwan with Chiang Kai-shek, but she had stayed behind. "Guo Pei was left behind to sabotage our socialist construction," the poster charged. "For years, she has been opposing the red flag under cover of the red flag. She is a counterrevolutionary who wormed her way into the heart of the Party and assumed the most important of positions, teaching politics to the younger generation."

My eyes moved to an adjacent poster. "Guo Pei is a venomous snake who disguised herself as a beautiful woman," it began. It went on to say she had used one of the Thirty-Six Stratagems, "Use a woman to ensnare a man," to corrupt her husband, a physics teacher who came from a working-class background. "We must break the venomous snake's spine!" the poster exhorted. I had always thought Guo Pei and her husband ill matched, but not for political reasons. He was tall and well built, and Sanxi often joked that he could easily crush his slender wife into minced meat in bed.

The criticisms of Guo Pei were signed "All Revolutionary Students of Class 35." That was Fangpu's class. Furthermore, Fangpu was leading a new assault on Ding Yi. Fresh posters charged the Party secretary with suppressing the Cultural Revolution, and called on students to revolt against him.

Fangpu was now on firmer ground because of recent developments in Beijing. Chen Boda, Chairman Mao's personal secretary for decades, had become head of the Central Cultural Revolution Group that was directing the movement. Official documents now referred to the movement as the Great Proletarian Cultural Revolution, a name that had been appearing more and more frequently in the press, replacing Great Socialist Cultural Revolution. Most important for Fangpu's purposes, the central authorities had called on schools throughout the country to elect Cultural Revolution preparatory committees of their own to replace the work teams. That meant that Ding Yi's protectors would soon be leaving.

Secretary Ding put up his own poster, headlined "Sincerely Welcoming Criticism from Revolutionary Students and Teachers." Immediately, students began filling up the margins, warning that Ding Yi was playing tricks. Other students defended him with posters urging us to have faith in the Party's leadership. The rebellious students responded by calling the defenders "royalist clowns."

The political atmosphere was heating up to match the midsummer weather. A heat wave had set in, and before going to bed, we would strip naked in the dark outside the dormitories and pour basins of cold water over our heads. The boys in class 85 often stayed awake past midnight now, listening to Little Bawang. He would stretch out in bed without a stitch of clothing on, displaying his pubic hair and bulging thigh muscles, as he reviewed the day's events. An activist in the campaign to criticize teachers, he was in a position to bring us the latest allegations against Ding Yi and Guo Pei.

"We made a great breakthrough today in interrogating Guo Pei," he announced one evening. "Fangpu, the martyr's son, led us in storming her office. We took her to an empty room in the bell-tower courtyard. At first, she refused to come

The Degenerate and the Worn Shoe

69

with us, so we had to drag her. We ordered her to lower her head and confess her crimes. She said she hadn't committed any crimes and refused to lower her head. So I pushed her head down. She resisted as desperately as a pig about to be slaughtered. I got so angry that I slapped her face. I didn't slap her very hard, but she's such a weakling that she fell down. I ordered her to get up again.

"We took turns eating dinner while we interrogated her. We brought her some food, but she wouldn't eat. She was such a diehard devil that we almost gave up. Then Fangpu got an idea. He made up the story that Ding Yi had confessed to having sexual relations with her. You know what? She believed it! She almost fainted. Seeing this, we all knew they must have done something. We pressed her to confess. Finally she admitted that she's been Ding Yi's mistress for more than a year!"

Little Bawang's triumphant announcement took us by surprise. Sanxi broke the shocked silence. "How incredible! Every day, Teacher Guo taught us to observe socialist morality, but she herself is a worn shoe!"

"Guo Pei's hair was loose and all over her face, making her look like a spirit," Little Bawang continued. "I urged her to spill out her secrets if she wanted lenient treatment. She told us how the whole thing started. In the winter of 1964, Ding Yi came to her home to discuss the Four Cleanups. Somehow, he began to tell her about his personal life. He complained that he was lonely because his wife was working for the Women's Federation in another county. Guo Pei said she wanted to comfort Ding Yi—though our analysis is that she wanted to use her flesh to curry political favor. They made an arrangement. One snowy night when Guo Pei's husband was away at a meeting, Ding Yi limped all the way from the lead-

The Degenerate and the Worn Shoe

ers' courtyard to the bell-tower courtyard and tumbled into bed with Guo Pei, just like the King of Chu meeting the Goddess of Mount Wu in the clouds and rain."

"I'll bet Secretary Ding really crushed Teacher Guo into minced meat!" Sanxi exclaimed.

Little Bawang was enjoying our attention. He went on: "Guo Pei's confession was so fascinating that we kept asking her for more details. We asked her what they talked about in bed. She turned red and said, 'Just pillow talk.' We urged her to be more specific. She finally said, 'I asked him what the difference was between me and his wife. He said his wife's place was too loose while mine was tight and sensual.' We really hadn't expected her to be so frank. We felt a little embarrassed and ended the interrogation."

"How often did they do clouds and rain?" Sanxi asked.

"Whenever there was a chance," Little Bawang said. "Guo Pei's husband may be tall and strong, but he's henpecked. He probably knows he's a cuckold but is afraid to speak out. Guo Pei usually went to Ding Yi's house because it's more isolated. She confessed that one night she ran over there barefoot in the snow."

"This wild pheasant is not afraid of cold when in heat," Sanxi declared.

Little Bawang said the activists planned to drag out the Party secretary the next day and parade the adulterers downtown. When I fell asleep, he was still talking, with Sanxi interjecting from time to time.

The next morning, the whole school was plastered with new posters about Ding Yi and Guo Pei. Fangpu and his fellow rebels must have worked all night. The Party secretary was described as morally rotten as well as reactionary, a degenerate as well as a revisionist. Our politics teacher was a

The Degenerate and the Worn Shoe

71

worn shoe, a wild pheasant, and a whore, as well as an alien element and a venomous snake. One poster said that revolutionary rebel students had seized and interrogated Ding Yi during the night, and that he had confessed his crimes. The poster announced that "degenerate counterrevolutionary revisionist Ding Yi and his alien-element mistress Guo Pei" would be on parade that afternoon.

In the leaders' courtyard in the southwest corner of campus, students were searching Ding Yi's office and tossing his books out the door. A couplet had been posted around the door frame. The first set of characters on the right side read, "Eat, drink, shit, pee, sleep," and the second set on the left side listed five inert elements, "Helium, neon, argon, krypton, xenon." Four characters above the door read, "Inertness is your nature." All this was a clever way of calling the Party secretary a lazy good-for-nothing. The handwriting looked like Weihua's, but he was nowhere around. I found him in front of the Principal's Building, pasting up a poster entitled "Kick Out the Party Committee and Make Revolution Ourselves!"

I asked my brother if he had written that couplet, and he said that he had. I reminded him that Mama and Papa had always told us not to get involved in ambiguous matters. "I've been very cautious," Weihua insisted. "I wrote that for our homeroom teacher's door, but my classmates said it would go to waste there and took it over to Secretary Ding's place. Anyway, the matter no longer seems ambiguous. The work team came out in support of the rebel students and is helping them prepare an exhibition on Ding Yi's corrupt life."

"Does that mean anything?" I asked. "The work team members are but grasshoppers in late autumn; they will soon be replaced by an elected committee."

The Degenerate and the Worn Shoe

"Of course they're not so stupid as to defend a pair of adulterers," Weihua said. "In this part of the country, people think extramarital affairs are worse than burglary, or even murder. But the team members could have just stayed silent. The fact that they are backing the rebellion against Ding Yi gives it some legitimacy. It also makes logistics easier, since the work team still is in charge of supplies."

The exhibition was up by the time breakfast was over. A banner strung between two willow trees in front of the Teachers' Building heralded "The Startling Realities of Class Struggle." Property seized from Ding Yi and Guo Pei was arrayed over a row of desks—big piles of grain coupons, wads of money, cigarettes, good wine, a desk lamp, a potted orchid. Ding Yi had owned an eight-transistor Panda-brand radio, testimony to his decadence. Guo Pei somehow had obtained some American-made razor blades for her husband, evidence that the Kuomintang had planted her as a spy.

I was most impressed by the heaps of grain coupons. Where had the Party secretary gotten so many? Did he have so much meat and fruit to eat that he could not use up his grain rations? Or maybe the cook in charge of the teachers' dining hall had given him extra coupons as a bribe.

I thought of the small dining hall where the teachers and administrators ate. Once during the winter, after months of eating tasteless cabbage, I had peered into a window there and seen big chunks of meat in the teachers' bowls. The teachers still ate there, even though most of them were monsters and demons. Now that the top leader of the school had become a demon too, why should they eat so well?

The more I thought about the small dining hall, the more indignant I felt. I rounded up Little Mihu, Shuanggen, Zongwei, and a few more classmates and suggested we shut it

The Degenerate and the Worn Shoe

down. They were enthusiastic. We took up the usual weapons—paper, brush pens, ink, and a pail of glue—and marched into the small kitchen. We found the cook, Wuxiang, meaning "five spices," preparing the teachers' lunch. Wuxiang had a special affection for boys. One night when I had run into him on campus he had put his arms around me and squeezed me. I had broken loose and run away. Seeing the group of us, he smiled awkwardly and asked what we wanted.

"We want to shut down your dining hall!" I said boldly.

"You must be joking," he said. "Where on earth did you get such a strange idea?"

"We're not joking. This is serious. Don't you know that all but three of your diners have become monsters and demons? Do you want to keep serving to ox demons and snake spirits?"

"No, I don't. But you can't close down my kitchen without a formal order from Secretary Ding."

"Secretary Ding is now a demon too!" screeched Little Mihu.

Wuxiang looked puzzled. "That can't be."

"Just go out and see for yourself," I said.

Now Wuxiang looked worried. "What shall I do if you shut down this dining hall? Let's discuss it." He picked up some steamed pork knuckles. "How about this? I give you a few of these and you go away."

"Wuxiang," I said, trying to sound severe, "Ding Yi had a whole lot of grain coupons. They're being exhibited outside as proof of his crimes. Did you bribe him?"

"No, I didn't. I'm a clean person. It has nothing to do with me."

"Then why did you try to bribe us just now?"

The Degenerate and the Worn Shoe

"I was wrong. I apologize." Wuxiang nodded his head like a chicken pecking rice.

"You had better talk with the cook in charge of the main dining hall to see if you can go to work there," I said. "From now on, this dining hall is closed forever!"

We swept by Wuxiang and set to work. First we carried all the tables and stools to our dining hall. Then we pasted up some posters denouncing the teachers' bourgeois lifestyle. Finally, we shut the doors and sealed them with an X made of two strips of paper, on which we wrote "Closed by revolutionary teachers and students." Looking at the sealed door, I felt pleased. It was so easy to accomplish things nowadays.

The procession with Ding Yi and Guo Pei passed out the South Gate in the afternoon. New information about the Party secretary's decadence had continued to surface all morning, and now we had a third culprit—Tang Hong, the Youth League secretary-general who just a few days earlier had summoned us for emergency muster to aid Vietnam. Ding Yi had admitted to sleeping with her too. One poster, headlined "One Cavalier Riding Two Horses," charged that he had rolled into bed with both women at once.

Ding Yi headed the parade, wearing a five-meter-high dunce cap decorated with paper cutouts of skeletons, monsters, turtles, and ox heads. A drum hung from his neck. He held a drumstick in one hand while trying to support the swaying cap with the other. Guo Pei, beside him, wore a long pink silk qipao that students had found in her wardrobe. A pair of frayed red satin shoes hung around her neck. Her shoulder-length hair had been cut into a tangled haystack, with patches shaved to the scalp. She held a gong and a stick. Tang Hong wore a long black gown and had a pair of old leather shoes dangling around her neck. All that was left of

The Degenerate and the Worn Shoe

75

her hair was a long strip down the middle. She held a pair of cymbals. The trio sounded their instruments as they walked. The students of Yizhong followed along.

It was market day again, so a big audience was in town. The crowds gawked as we escorted the three new demons through the streets. On orders from rebel leaders, the three had to chant in turn as they walked: "I am Ding Yi, ox demon and snake spirit." "I am Guo Pei, and I am a worn shoe." "I am Tang Hong, and I am a worn shoe too."

At the main intersection, we ran into another parade. Students from the normal school were taking a group of school leaders through the town as well. Our two processions cheered each other.

The sun beat down like a ball of fire over the ancient city. Our three demons were drenched in sweat. Guo Pei's tight dress clung to her so that her underwear could be seen. Ding Yi's paper dunce cap was soggy and coming apart. Rivulets of perspiration ran down his red, puffy face.

The Red, the Black, and
the In-Between

During the movement to criticize teachers, Yuling had grown more and more withdrawn, until I almost forgot she was around. One day, she came up to me on the verge of tears. She had never before asked me for help with anything except math problems, but now she said that she needed my advice. We went for a walk by Rear Lake. Yuling told me that some of her father's medical students had come from Shimen to search her family's house that morning. Only her grandmother had been home. A sympathetic neighbor had summoned Yuling from school, and she had run home to find the intruders looking through her father's diaries. The diaries were the only thing they had taken away.

"Those diaries recorded my father's whole life, including the period he spent abroad," Yuling said, her voice trembling. "Those students said my father is a spy working for the CIA. I know he is not a spy. He works very hard, and cares very little about comfort. He never does any of the things a spy would do."

I told her not to panic. "They can't just claim he's a spy; they have to have solid evidence," I said, trying to convince myself as well as her. "The current situation is very confused. All the teachers everywhere are getting criticized. They can't possibly all be bad. After some time, things will calm down."

Yuling's mother was in trouble also; her students at the normal school had charged her with teaching bourgeois music. "I'm really worried," Yuling said, and began to cry. I searched my mind for a way to comfort her. "Good people who are wrongly accused will be cleared in the end," I said. "Take the case of my father. He once was labeled the leader of an anti-Party clique, but later he was rehabilitated."

The charges against Yuling's mother sounded mild, so I assured her not to worry. As for her father, I advised her not to tell anyone that he was suspected of being a CIA spy. If anybody should find out, she should say that she had severed all ties with him. Many children of teachers under criticism at Yizhong had publicly disowned their parents, and a few

The Red, the Black, and the In-Between

were even helping to expose their parents' crimes. It was only practical.

Our classmates soon found out about Yuling's mother from students who had visited the normal school to read dazibao. I had to agree with Yuling that it was only a matter of time before rumors about her father would reach our school. She was growing increasingly nervous about her family background. When the name Great Proletarian Cultural Revolution replaced the name Great Socialist Cultural Revolution, she asked me if "proletarian" excluded intellectuals. Finally, she decided to forestall any trouble. She put up a poster, the first she had written since the Three Family Village days, announcing that she was severing relations with her parents, politically and economically. That act seemed to lift a burden from her mind. Once again, she began taking part in the rallies, marches, and slogan-shouting that occupied the better part of our days.

After several mass meetings to struggle against Ding Yi and Guo Pei, we turned our attention to the business of forming a Cultural Revolution Preparatory Committee. The work team, which would still be in charge in the meantime, announced the procedures. Each class was to elect its own Cultural Revolution group of five members, who would serve as delegates to a meeting to elect the committee.

Our class convened in the classroom for a nominating session. A crack from the earthquake stretched across the plaster ceiling. The back wall was covered with essays criticizing the crimes of Guo Pei and Ding Yi. There were eight nominations. They included several class officers—monitor Caolan, Youth League Secretary Congfang, and Daily-Life Manager Erchou—as well as Little Bawang, Yuling, and me.

Just as Caolan was about to pass out the ballot paper, Little Bawang stood up, a grim expression on his face. "Comrade Monitor," he said, "I oppose Yuling's nomination. She herself admitted in her poster that her father is suspected of being a CIA spy, and we all know her mother is under attack for teaching bourgeois music. I suggest her nomination be canceled."

I rose angrily. "Yuling's classmates nominated her fairly. You have no business interfering."

Little Bawang became furious. "We are electing a committee to lead us in the Great Proletarian Cultural Revolution! As Chairman Mao says, revolution is not a dinner party. This is a serious matter. If someone whose parents have problems gets into our leading body, who will be responsible if something goes wrong?"

"Yuling has been an active participant in the Great Proletarian Cultural Revolution," I retorted. "She's just as qualified as anybody else."

"Our class has many students with pure family backgrounds; why should we accept a nominee from a questionable one?" Little Bawang said. "We must take a firm proletarian stand in handling this matter. What we need is a Paris Commune–style group, not a bourgeois parliament. If you insist on allowing her nomination, we'll have to postpone the vote to study the matter."

Yuling buried her head in her arms on top of our desk. Her shoulders began to heave. After a few minutes, she lifted her tearstained face and said, "So that the voting may go on, I surrender my right to be a nominee." I was both disappointed and relieved at this quick resolution. Monitor Caolan accepted Yuling's withdrawal. Sports Manager Shuanggen was nominated instead. The voting could proceed.

We filled in our ballots and dropped them into a box. Little

Mihu, under the watchful eyes of Caolan, read out the names on each ballot while another student tallied them on the blackboard. The top five were Caolan, Congfang, Erchou, Shuanggen, and I. Little Bawang could only scowl fiercely.

The next day, 120 delegates representing all 24 classes sat down with administration and faculty delegates to make nominations for thirteen committee positions—ten students, two teachers, and one administrator.

Nowadays, the administration meant the work team, for Yizhong's entire Party Committee had dissolved in the wake of Ding Yi's downfall. As for the teachers, only a dozen were not monsters and demons, and only three were entirely above suspicion. So the dozen sent the three as their representatives. One was Guo Pei's cuckolded husband. As soon as his wife's unfaithfulness became known, he had put up a poster saying that he would have nothing more to do with her. The next day he filed for divorce. He was praised for taking a firm proletarian stand.

We did not have much difficulty choosing students for the committee; there were plenty of three-good students, Youth League leaders, and Cultural Revolution activists among us. Most of the student nominees were seniors. One was Fangpu, now very popular among student revolutionaries for his leading role in bringing down Ding Yi.

It was harder to choose among the teachers. Guo Pei's husband had come to public attention only because of his wife. The other two had never done anything to distinguish themselves. When we finally cast our ballots, a teacher I had never heard of before emerged as chairman of the committee. His name was Deng Zeng. He was a graduate of People's University in Beijing and taught senior-level political economy. Short, stocky, a man of few words spoken with a nasal twang, he was the purest teacher left at our school. He had a clean personal history and a good proletarian class background, and was a Party member besides. The other teacher chosen was a physics instructor.

Although the work team was about to depart, we chose the head of the team to fill the one administration position for lack of other suitable candidates. She congratulated us on our success in selecting a Cultural Revolution Preparatory Committee and then promptly resigned. The team members left that very afternoon for the county government headquarters in town. The students saw them off at the South Gate.

The Preparatory Committee's first significant action was to buy a new microphone. Then it called a schoolwide struggle meeting against Ding Yi. The Party secretary had to stand on the stage of the auditorium with his head lowered for nearly three hours as each class sent up a speaker to denounce him. His lame leg was shaking uncontrollably. Finally, Deng Zeng let him sit down.

One senior student pounded the podium so hard that the shiny new microphone fell off its stand. Deng Zeng darted over to pick it up and examined it with concern. We soon learned that he was rather tightfisted. When the committee had to have an official stamp made, he spent three days looking for the cheapest place in town. Some students began to complain that he was too stingy and cared too much about trivial things to make a good revolutionary leader.

In mid-August, more important news arrived from Beijing. The Eleventh Plenum of the Central Committee had just concluded. Defense Minister Lin Biao had been named vice-chairman of the Party. Moreover, he was the only vice-chairman. There had once been six: Liu Shaoqi, Zhou Enlai, Zhu De, Chen Yun, Lin Biao, and Deng Xiaoping. The plenum

The Red, the Black, and the In-Between

also had issued a sixteen-point resolution about the Cultural Revolution, which provided the first clear guidelines for what we should be doing. It said that our target should be people within the Party who were taking the capitalist road, as well as certain academic and cultural authorities who continued to propagate bourgeois ideology. It called for a struggle against the Four Olds—the old ideas, culture, customs, and habits of the exploiting classes. It said persons in charge should not take measures against students involved in the movement. It said we should use reason, not violence. And it said the vast majority of cadres were good or "comparatively good," but a small number were anti-Party, antisocialist rightists.

To celebrate the plenum's decisions, our Preparatory Committee organized a spectacular parade through town, headed by students holding a giant portrait of Chairman Mao. Each class had formed its own cacophonous marching band with drums, cymbals, and gongs. We marched amid masses of red flags, waving our small red books of Chairman Mao's quotations and singing:

> The mountains are cheering and the seas smiling;
> The Central Committee has issued its communiqué;
> Like a lighthouse it illuminates our advancing path;
> We'll carry the Cultural Revolution to a new high tide!

Then we shouted two chants until we were hoarse: "Resolutely support the Sixteen Points! Warmly propagate the Sixteen Points! Firmly carry out the Sixteen Points! Bravely defend the Sixteen Points!" and "Smash the Four Olds! Smash old ideas, old culture, old customs, and old habits!"

Even more exciting than the announcements from Beijing were the rumors that followed. Chairman Mao, it was said, had put up his first dazibao. Entitled "Bombard the Head-quarters!," it criticized the work teams that had come to Bei-jing's university campuses in June and July for terrorizing and suppressing student rebels.

Chairman Mao's meeting with a group of Beijing students in Tiananmen Square was an even more dramatic declaration of his confidence in youth. We had always seen him high up on the rostrum, but this time he was down among the people, walking right across the Golden Water Bridge to talk with the students. He told them to get involved in state affairs and to carry the Great Proletarian Cultural Revolution through to the end. Students from the middle school attached to Qing-hua University gave him a red armband with three yellow characters written on it in elegant calligraphy—*Hong Wei Bing*, or Red Guard. The newspapers printed a picture of Chairman Mao wearing his armband and waving. He looked healthy and energetic.

Chairman Deng called a meeting of the class Cultural Rev-olution groups to discuss forming a Red Guard organization of our own. We decided that each class would set up its own Red Guards under the leadership of the Preparatory Com-mittee. The committee set only two conditions for eligibility: good ideology and activism in the movement.

When our class met to discuss the plan, Little Bawang ar-gued that only members of the Five Red Categories—worker, poor and lower-middle peasant, revolutionary soldier, revo-lutionary cadre, and revolutionary martyr—should be al-lowed to join the Red Guards. He opposed accepting any of the Seven Black Categories—landlord, rich peasant, reaction-ary, bad element, rightist, traitor, and spy. Once again, I found myself opposing Little Bawang. "We don't have a single Black Category person in our class," I pointed out. "All of us

The Red, the Black, and the In-Between

have taken part in the movement since the very beginning, fighting shoulder to shoulder. I think we should allow everybody to become a Red Guard."

Youth League Secretary Congfang said, "Even though we have no Black Category people, we do have some people who fall between the Black Categories and the Red Categories. Those are the questionable ones here."

"We shouldn't admit them!" Little Bawang said.

"Why not? They didn't do anything wrong," I said.

"They might not have done anything wrong themselves, but their parents didn't support the revolution. When our fathers were fighting the Japanese and Kuomintang, theirs were hiding and trembling like timid mice!"

"That has nothing to do with their children," I said. "All our classmates were born and brought up under the five-star red flag. We all have a socialist education."

Little Bawang was livid. "Chairman Mao says everybody living in a class society is stamped with the brand of his class. 'A dragon begets dragons, a phoenix begets phoenixes, and a mouse's children can only dig holes.' They will waver in the course of the Cultural Revolution. We cannot admit them!"

"That's not necessarily so," I said. "Don't you know the story about Zhou Enlai? Once when Premier Zhou was in Moscow, Khrushchev told him proudly, 'My class origin is peasant; what's yours? Premier Zhou looked at Khrushchev and said, 'My family background is feudal bureaucrat. So we have something in common, Mr. Premier. We both betrayed our class.'"

Little Bawang snickered. "That is a good story. But Premier Zhou is an exception."

Other Red Category students joined in the discussion. The

The Red, the Black, and the In-Between

in-between students stayed silent, listening to our debate. At last, we took a vote. Little Bawang's view won out. So 35 of us became Red Guards by virtue of our heritage, and the other fifteen remained what they were.

Afterward, I tried to comfort Yuling. "Don't worry," I said. "You can still make revolution without being a Red Guard."

"It's useless," she replied in a flat voice. "You can't make revolution unless you're a Red Guard. All you can do is look on. I'm going home to see Grandma." She walked off, her head bowed.

Chairman Deng had put a group of students to work making red armbands. The torn strips of red cloth stenciled with yellow paint were not nearly as elegant as Chairman Mao's. As I put mine on, with Yuling's misfortune still fresh in my mind, I felt a twinge of guilt. But as I walked around the campus displaying my new status, my uneasiness gave way to a sense of importance.

Smashing the Four Olds

News accounts from Beijing described how Red Guards had smashed the old signboards of stores and restaurants and given old feudal streets new revolutionary names. Perpetual Peace Boulevard, which ran through Tiananmen Square, had been renamed East-Is-Red Boulevard; the street once occupied by the missions of the Western powers was now Anti-imperialism Road; and the one where the Soviet embassy was located was Anti-revisionism Road. These reports pointed the way for the Red Guards of Yizhong. Our first task would be to eradicate the Four Olds in Yizhen.

We gathered at the South Gate. Chairman Deng led us in chanting a paragraph from the Sixteen-Point Resolution, which we had mastered so well we could recite it like poetry:

Although the bourgeoisie has been overthrown, it is still trying to use the old ideas, culture, customs, and habits of the exploiting classes to corrupt the masses, capture their minds, and endeavor to stage a comeback. The proletariat must do the exact opposite: it must meet head-on every challenge of the bourgeoisie in the ideological field and use the new ideas, culture, customs, and habits of the proletariat to change the mental outlook of the whole society.

With a red flag reading "Red Guard" fluttering at the head of our column, we set out for downtown. Most of us carried the little red book, as we had seen the Beijing Red Guards doing in pictures in the newspapers. Some students had drums, gongs, ink bottles, and brush pens. As we marched, we bellowed the new "Song of the Red Guards" composed by our comrades in Beijing:

> We are Chairman Mao's Red Guards,
> Tempering ourselves in great waves and winds;
> Armed with Mao Zedong thought,
> We'll wipe out all pests and vermin.

Our first target in town was street names. Yizhen had 72 streets, big and small. Many were named for their location, like Southwest Street and Inner North Gate Street, and others for landmarks, like Flowery Pagoda Street. Perpetual Victory Street was named after the deeds of the invincible general Zhao Yun. Democracy Street had been named after Liberation. We reviewed all the names and decided that only one was inappropriate: Four Harmonies Street. We renamed it the Street of the Four News to commemorate the attack on the Four Olds.

The Empress Guo Wineshop was our next stop. A poster reading "Worker-Peasant-Soldier Wineshop" went up over the gilt lettering of the lacquered signboard.

At the town's main intersection, we encountered a few peasants selling vegetables out of wooden barrows. "Aren't they making capitalism?" one Red Guard asked. "Sure they are. Confiscate their wheelbarrows!" said another.

A group of Red Guards approached the peddlers. "Who allowed you to make capitalism?" one demanded of an eggplant seller.

"I grew these in my yard," he said.

"I grew these cucumbers in my private plot," another vendor chimed in.

"No matter where you grow things, if you're not working for the collective, it's making capitalism."

"I work in my yard after finishing work in the production team's fields," argued the man with the eggplants. "It's permitted by government policy."

"Where do you work harder? Where do you put your nightsoil? If you care about these private matters, how can you concentrate on collective work? You're a capitalist-roader, and we'll have to confiscate your things."

"You can't do that. I saved for a long time to buy this barrow and scale." The peddler held tight to his possessions as his critics tried to wrest them from him.

Another Red Guard stepped in to moderate. "Comrades," he said, "we've barely begun our work. If we take this barrow, it will only be a burden to pull along. Better to just make this fellow promise not to peddle here again and let him go home." After a bit of discussion, the others pasted a dazibao against capitalism on the peddler's barrow and let him go.

Similar scenes were unfolding up and down the street. Several Red Guards surrounded an old woman who was wearing heavy dangling earrings and bangles and ordered her to take off her jewelry. She obeyed without saying a word. She handed the jewelry to the loudest student in the group, who looked at it, dumbfounded, then handed it back and told her to take it home and bury it.

Little Mihu and a few others encircled a white-haired old lady with bound feet. She was a familiar figure in town. She sold popsicles, but rumor had it that her popsicle business was only a cover, and that she was really a prostitute who charged five yuan a visit. Her husband was said to keep watch while she entertained in their house.

"Auntie," Little Mihu said to her in his sternest voice, "take off your old feudal foot-binding rags." This woman was not so compliant. "I've worn my foot-binding cloths all my life!" she shrieked. "The Communist Party has never told me to take them off. How dare you tell me to? Doesn't your grandma wear them? Go home and tell her to take hers off!" The students argued with her for some time, but she held her ground. So they hung a sign around her neck reading "Wild Pheasant," drew a circle in the dust around her, and ordered her to stand there in the sun for four hours. As soon as they had gone around the corner, she disappeared into her house.

We resumed our procession along the Street of the Four News until we reached three elaborately carved marble arches that straddled the street. The triple archway had stood here for two hundred years. The arches had been erected under the reign of Emperor Qianlong of the Qing dynasty to honor the court's minister of personnel, Liang Menglong, a native of Yizhen.

Many of Liang's descendants still lived in this neighborhood. Our family had lived near here also, and I had played street games with the children of the Liang clan. Our favorite was "playing officials." We would set up formations of bricks and throw broken pieces of brick at them. If you knocked down the brick that was largest and farthest away, you became the big official. If you knocked down smaller bricks, you were a petty official. If you missed entirely, you became the criminal and had to run away. The big official would order the petty officials to catch the criminal. If they failed, everyone else would spank them.

Yizhong's Preparatory Committee had decided that the triple archway symbolized feudal oppression of the people of Yizhen and therefore must come down. Although I had happy memories of playing under the shadow of the arches, I did not feel too bad about destroying them. Of all 24 Chinese feudal dynasties, I disliked the Qing most. For one thing, it was a dynasty of invaders, the Manchus. For another, it was under the Qing that the Western powers had begun to subjugate China with opium and gunboats. The Qing was the most corrupt and impotent dynasty in Chinese history.

A nimble boy scaled the first arch and fastened a thick tug-of-war rope around the top. Others began to pry the stone foundation loose with crowbars and pickaxes. Curious neighbors came out to watch. I recognized some of the Liangs. Nobody stepped out to protest, and some of the people even brought tools to help us out. To the clamor of "Smash the

Four Olds!" the resplendent structure came down and smashed into a pile of broken stone. Within two hours, all three arches were gone and piles of stone blocked the street.

Fangpu climbed atop the rubble, his usually white face flushed almost as red as his armband. Waving a fist in the air, he yelled, "Revolutionary comrades-in-arms, we have successfully knocked down this feudal relic! This is our first great victory! Let us advance on the crest of victory to the next target!"

We wiped our dusty faces and marched on amid the sound of drums and gongs, shouts, and revolutionary songs. We were heading for the south side of town. People of the Hui nationality, many of them practicing Moslems, lived there. So did some descendants of Jews who had come along the Silk Road from the Middle East during the Song dynasty. Their synagogue was long gone, and they had religious services along with the Hui in the mosque. If you went walking through this neighborhood, someone might point out a person with curly hair and tell you that he was a Jew, but if you asked the Jew his religion, he would tell you that he was a Moslem.

With the exception of these non-Jewish Jews, the Moslems looked just like the rest of us Han Chinese. But when a Hui person died, he would be wrapped in a long white cloth and buried in a brick tomb, whereas a Han would be put in a wooden coffin and laid to laid to rest in the earth. The other thing that distinguished the Moslems was their refusal to eat pork. There were quite a few Moslem restaurants in town, and our school dining hall had a special section for Hui students, who got mutton or beef whenever the rest of us had pork.

I had been brought up to consider religion backward and

superstitious—a spiritual opiate, as Marx had said. I had tried some religion only once, just before taking the middle-school entrance exams in the summer of 1964. A group of us from Democracy Street Primary School had gone to see the Goddess of Mercy at Dafo Temple. When nobody else was in the hall, we hastily fell to our knees, put our palms together, bobbed our heads, and chanted for the giant 42-armed goddess to ensure our admission to Yizhong. Only two of us got into the key school. The others went to undistinguished schools. I concluded that the goddess was not very reliable.

The onion-domed mosque stood near the town's southern gate. An old man with a wispy goatee came out and surveyed the crowd of students at the entrance. "What are you here for?" he asked. He was answered with shouts: "We've come to eradicate the Four Olds!"

"Four Olds? There's nobody by that name here."

Fangpu stepped to the front of the group. "Don't play games with us," he said. "We've come to extirpate your superstition."

"What superstition? We don't have any superstition."

"No superstition? What about those people who crouch on the floor with their buttocks to the sky and murmur, 'Allah, Allah'? What is that if not superstition?"

"That is religion, the Moslem faith, permitted by the government. It is not superstition."

"Enough of your nonsense!" Fangpu said. "Your activities belong to the Four Olds and must be wiped out!" He pushed his way past the old man, and the rest of the Red Guards swarmed after him. "Forward, revolutionary comrades-in-arms!" Fangpu shouted. "Chairman Mao teaches us that revolution is not like going to a dinner party, or writing an article, or painting a picture, or doing embroidery. We can't be

Smashing the Four Olds

so tasteful and refined. Revolution is when one class over-throws another. Let's overthrow this reactionary supersti-tion!"

We looked around for something tangible to overthrow. The few worshippers who had been in the mosque when we entered had scurried away, leaving only an empty expanse of cold tile floor. We decided to pull down the onion. It was so high that we had to tie several ropes together. The daredevil who had scaled the arches found his way to the roof, shim-mied up the bronze-plated dome, and attached the first rope to its needlelike point. With hundreds of Red Guards pulling, we easily toppled the onion on the count of three. Great cheers went up.

The old man watched in horror. Somebody had obtained a pig's tail from a butcher shop and hung it around his neck. Others were drawing caricatures of fat pig heads and posting them around the building and courtyard.

We had been smashing the Four Olds since early morning, and it was already midafternoon. So gripped were we by rev-olutionary ardor that nobody had even mentioned lunch. Chairman Deng was waiting with a smile on his face when we came out of the mosque. He recommended that we go back to school for some food and rest. "You little revolution-ary generals have worked all day," he said. "This is just the beginning. We have a long way to go."

The next morning, we set out for Dafo Temple like an army of Monkey Kings eager to make havoc under heaven. We found that a company of People's Liberation Army men had moved in during the night to protect the temple. As the Red Guards in my class approached the front hall, which housed a smiling, big-bellied Buddha and four Celestial Kings, one of the soldiers came up as if to greet us. The four pockets on his jacket indicated he was an officer. He held a little red book in one hand. "Little revolutionary generals," he said, "this temple is on the national register of cultural relics. It does not belong to the category of the Four Olds. Please leave and find your Four Olds elsewhere."

Monitor Caolan, who also clutched a little red book, answered him, "Comrade Soldier, how can you say this place doesn't belong to the Four Olds? Don't you see those superstitious monsters?" She gestured toward the Celestial Kings, who indeed looked monstrous, especially the one with a green face and protruding teeth.

"These statues are the work of ancient artisans," said the officer. "They are the wealth of the people. We should not destroy them."

"Can't you see that they oppress the ordinary working people?" Little Mihu said, pointing to a small figure writhing in agony under the foot of one of the fiendish kings.

"These are figures of legend and have nothing to do with reality," the officer said. Students from other classes had drifted over to hear the debate. The officer seized the initiative. "Come with me," he told the growing audience. "I'll tell you a true story."

Intrigued, we followed him across the temple compound to the hall of the Goddess of Mercy. He led us inside. "You all know that the great Goddess of Mercy has forty-two arms," he said. "But do you know that only the two big arms in front are real bronze? The Japanese aggressors sawed off the other forty arms and melted them down to make bullets to kill the Chinese people. Japan has a long Buddhist tradition, but they didn't care about that when they needed ammunition. They wanted to destroy the whole statue, but they couldn't uproot it. They finally gave up when the temple elders told them that

Smashing the Four Olds

black water would run out and flood the whole city if the goddess was removed."

"Damn those Japanese devils! Death to the Japanese devils!" several Red Guards cursed.

The army officer continued in a gentle voice that resonated through the hall. "This statue was not easy to make. Craftsmen of the Liao dynasty built a small earthen hill and carved out the mold for the lotus seat. Scores of smelting stoves worked at the same time to make enough bronze to fill the mold. After the seat was cast, the craftsmen heaped more earth on the hill to make the second section. They repeated this seven times in all, casting the head last. At the end, they took away the hill, and here the statue has stood ever since." We looked at the Goddess of Mercy with new admiration. "Do you still think we should smash these cultural relics?" the officer asked.

Just then, we heard a series of crashing sounds. The officer's face fell. He rushed outside, and we ran after him. While he had been holding some of us spellbound before the Goddess of Mercy, other students had regrouped by the four Celestial Kings, tied ropes to them, and pulled them down all at once. The painted clay figures had smashed into pieces.

The officer looked at the wreckage with tears in his eyes. "You—You—What kind of Red Guards are you?" he stammered. He barked a command and a platoon of soldiers ran over. They linked arms to blockade the hall entrance. The demolitionists retreated. Nobody wanted to clash with the People's Liberation Army. We marched off, waving our red flags, singing the Red Guard song, and exulting in our latest victory over the Four Olds.

Smashing the Four Olds

Cleaning Our Own Nest

Much more work lay ahead. For one thing, we could not be true revolutionaries unless we purged the Four Olds from our own ranks. Some Red Guards of Hui nationality bravely began to eat pork. One boy gave a public demonstration in front of the dining hall. "Comrades," he declared, "tradition says we Hui can't eat pork. That's nonsense! We must thoroughly wipe out such old customs! Now, watch me eat this chunk of pork. It's delicious, much better than mutton or beef!"

Long hair was another old thing. The girl Red Guards snipped off their braids, emulating the women in the Communist base areas in the 1930's, who had bobbed their hair. Caolan and Congfang prevailed on class 85's best barber, Erchou, to crop their hair as short as the boys'. "Our revolutionary forefathers sacrificed their lives for the revolution, so why shouldn't we sacrifice our hair?" Caolan said.

The girls did not stop with their own heads. They set up a checkpoint at the Small North Gate, an opening in the city wall where people passed on their way from town to the railroad station, and made any woman with long hair get it cut before she could go through. They also checked for tight pants. If there was not enough room for a soda bottle to drop down to the cuff, they would slit the legs up to the thigh. For anyone so ignorant as to protest, the girls explained their actions by quoting the first line of the Sixteen-Point Resolution:

"The Great Proletarian Cultural Revolution now unfolding is a great revolution that touches people to their very souls."

Another thing that concerned us was our own names. We all knew the story of the Qinghua middle school girl who had been among the students received by Chairman Mao. Learning that her given name was Binbin, which meant "gentle and refined," Chairman Mao had told her, "You should be militant!" Afterward, the girl had changed her name to Yaowu, "militant."

Some of my classmates proposed that everyone in class 85 adopt the surname Mao, because Chairman Mao was our great commander and we were all his children. Others suggested the surname Wu, to signify "proletariat," but we dropped that idea after someone pointed out that the same character could also mean "none." Still others suggested the surname Dang, meaning "party," for the Communist Party. Some thought we should use numbers for given names—Party One, Party Two, and so on. Others said that would be too confusing and advocated using a variety of given names—Party Toward the Sun, Party Red Heart, Party Forever Loyal, and the like.

Unable to reach agreement, we decided that everyone could choose whatever name he or she wanted, or keep the old name if it was not objectionable. Almost all of us chose new revolutionary names. They included Bao Dongbiao, for "safeguard Mao Zedong and Lin Biao"; Chongmao, "revere Mao"; Xiangdong, "toward the east"; Jihong, "inherit red"; Yongge, "forever revolutionary"; Fanxiu, "antirevisionism"; and Miezi, "liquidate the bourgeoisie."

Sanxi wanted to add a fourth happiness to his name. "My parents were happy because of Liberation, Land Reform, and my birth," he said. "Now I'm happy because the Cultural

Revolution will consolidate the dictatorship of the proletariat." So he became Sixi, "quadruple happiness." I took my new name from Chairman Mao's poem "Swimming," and called myself Shijie Shu, meaning "changes in the world." But the lengthy discussions were all for naught: we found it impossible to remember all these new names, and our new identities lasted only a few days.

We thought we had recognized just about all the Four Olds in our midst when a poster appeared at Yizhong's main entrance calling our attention to something we had missed. The poster was addressed to "Red Guard Comrades-in-Arms of Yizhong" and said:

You have done a very good job of smashing the Four Olds outside your school, and we congratulate you. However, you have neglected the Four Olds under your own noses. This Western-style marble gate, which represents the cultural aggression of the imperialist powers, obviously belongs to the category of the Four Olds. We trust you will take immediate action to clean up your own nest. If you fail to smash the gate within three days, we Red Guards of Yizhen Normal School will come smash it for you. Salutations in the name of the Great Proletarian Cultural Revolution!

Chairman Deng immediately called a meeting of the Preparatory Committee, which unanimously passed a resolution to pull down the South Gate. Everybody on campus, even demons and monsters who had been sequestered in their rooms writing self-criticisms, came out to witness the historic event. Eclectic Zhu, the ultrarightist teacher of Chinese, showed up with a pickaxe, climbed all the way to the top of the gate from an adjacent wall, and began chopping at the central arch.

"Come down here, Eclectic Zhu!" Fangpu yelled. "Who gave you permission to go up there?"

Cleaning Our Own Nest

Eclectic Zhu looked down sheepishly. "Nobody. I just want to contribute something to the campaign to wipe out the Four Olds."

"Only revolutionaries can take part in this!" Fangpu said. "How dare you pretend you're a revolutionary? You're a die-hard ultrarightist! You'd better go back to writing your self-criticism."

Zhu came down, dropped his pickaxe, and left. But the incident played into the hands of a group of students who wanted to save the gate. Quoting Chairman Mao's saying "Whatever our enemies support, we must oppose, and whatever they oppose, we must support," they argued that if smashing the gate pleased the ultrarightist Eclectic Zhu, the gate should not be smashed. Chairman Deng called a hurried meeting of the Preparatory Committee on the spot. The committee came up with a compromise: we would knock down the arches on top but not the pillars on the bottom. Within a few hours, the arches had fallen. The six pillars remained, and so did the metal grates topped with spikes and red stars that were swung shut each night.

The Preparatory Committee met again to determine what other Four Olds we had overlooked. It assigned tasks to each class. Class 85 got the job of dismantling the school bell tower. Of course, only Red Guards were allowed to participate.

Nobody could deny that the bell tower was old. It had stood in the courtyard at the center of the campus since the Song dynasty, a good thousand years. It was a complicated structure, with a solid square brick terrace for a base, topped by a round silo of brick and wood. This construction fit the traditional mythological view that the earth was square and the sky round. The big bronze bell hung from a thick beam inside.

We started from the top, climbing a ladder to the roof, prying the gray tiles off one by one, and throwing them down until clay shards littered the courtyard. Yuling, who had returned to school after spending a few days with her grandmother, stood below with the other non-Red Guard students. As the others cheered us on, Yuling merely watched, a sad expression on her face. She had become as quiet as a statue.

With the rafters of the bell tower exposed, we noticed several sparrows' nests tucked away beneath the eaves. We suspended our work to raid the nests of their eggs and fledglings. Then we tore down the rafters, uncovering the big bell. As we struggled to lower the bell on ropes, the beam creaked and gave way. The bell hit the brick terrace and broke into several pieces.

Our revolutionary task took almost an entire day. In the evening, feeling tired but triumphant, we wrapped the baby sparrows in mud and roasted them over a campfire. When they were done, the feathers came off easily with the mud cocoons. We popped the naked, steaming little birds into our mouths. It was a good reward for a job well done.

Picking Up the Pieces

Yuling once again sought my help. Her neighbor had brought word that Red Guards from the normal school had come to her home to smash the Four Olds. I readily agreed to go with her to help her grandmother clean up the mess. I had been to her house several times, and her grand-mother had always offered me something good to eat.

We took a shortcut to town along a path through the reed ponds. On the way, I took off my armband. I did not want to alarm the old woman. I also wanted Yuling to know that we were still equals. I told her that I was still angry with my classmates for excluding her from the Red Guards. Yuling gave me a sorrowful look. "It's fate," she said. "Grandma used to talk about fate, and I always told her she was being superstitious. But now I'm beginning to believe that you can't change your fate."

Her pent-up feelings poured out. "Sometimes I hate my parents for not being pure. I hate them for being educated in the old society. I hate them for making so many problems for me that I can't even join the Red Guards. Other times, I don't blame them for anything. They are kind people and good par-ents, and they have always worked hard for the country. From first grade in primary school, I was always a Young Pioneer leader. My teachers and classmates liked me. Now everybody treats me like some sort of criminal. Even you—you've been ignoring me totally for the past week. You're only interested in smashing things. Maybe you think talking with me will harm your political future."

It was true that I had not said a word to Yuling as she followed the Red Guards around. Once again, I felt guilty that I was a Red Guard while she was not. I looked at the ground as we trudged along the path. We finished the walk to her house in silence.

Yuling's home was on Democracy Street. A pair of small stone lions squatted on either side of the carved wooden door to the courtyard. As Yuling opened the door, we could see that the lions had proved impotent guards. It looked as if a hurricane had swept through the courtyard. Books, sheet music, and anatomy and acupuncture charts were scattered all over. A pair of large porcelain vases lay broken beneath a grape trellis.

We entered the house, a traditional one with a tiled roof and latticework on the windows and doors. Yuling's grandmother sat on a couch, a blank expression on her face. Her white hair, which she always put up in a bun, had been cut.

"Grandma, Jianhua's come to help us clean up," Yuling said, her voice suddenly cheery.

The old woman stirred from her trancelike state. "Child, you're home," she said. "I've been wondering how to clean up, or whether it's necessary."

"Of course it's necessary," Yuling said. "Our home is not the only one in this condition. Many others have been ransacked too. This is life. We should pick up the pieces and start over again." Now she sounded like the old Yuling; but I knew she was covering up her pessimism for her grandmother's sake.

I took a good look around. An upright piano stood in the living room, its keyboard and cover smashed, its strings sprung out in all directions. A gramophone lay on its side on the floor, bits and pieces of smashed records all around it. Potted flowers, incense burners, vases, and pictures in glass frames lay broken among more piles of books.

Yuling's grandmother related how a dozen Red Guards had burst into the courtyard and turned everything upside down. "They said your father is a spy and your mother worships foreign things," she said. "They called me a capitalist." A wry smile came over her face. She had been a shopkeeper in the old society, so she had always been classified as petty proprietor.

Picking Up the Pieces

It turned out that the Red Guards had taken all the old woman's wealth without even knowing it. A few days earlier, she had hidden a gold brick and some jewelry inside the frame of Yuling's old Pigeon-brand bicycle. The Red Guards had wheeled the bike away, saying that the emblem—a white pigeon with a blue sky on a red background—was a camouflaged Kuomintang flag.

Yuling and I spent several hours sorting through the rubble, righting furniture, and returning books to shelves. I looked up and down the street as I left, just to make sure that nobody who knew me was around to see.

Rebels and Royalists

In calmer times, Weihua and I had gone home once a month to see Grandpa and our brothers and sisters. Sometimes we took the bus to Lingzhi, and sometimes we walked half a day to save the fare. If we were lucky, we could hitch a ride on a cart and get home before dark.

Our last visit had been early in the poster-writing campaign, when classes were still in session. We had set out on foot on a Saturday afternoon, buying a few sesame buns at the railway station near school before turning onto the road from Yizhen to Lingzhi. Fields dotted with shocks of newly harvested winter wheat stretched endlessly around us. Wheat also covered some stretches of the road that the peasants had taken over for threshing grounds.

We passed one small village after another, each a cluster of mud and brick houses partially hidden by courtyard walls. Some of the walls closest to the road were whitewashed and bore slogans in huge red characters: "Never forget class struggle!" "Carry the Four Cleanups through to the end!" It looked as if the Cultural Revolution had not even touched the countryside.

We had made this trip dozens of times, but I always found it exhilarating. The terrain changed gradually, flat plains giving way to gently rolling hills. Even the slopes had been planted with wheat. Peasants in the plains pulled the wheat up by the roots, but here they harvested by sickle, leaving a golden-brown stubble. With dusk approaching, the Taihang Mountains shimmered light blue in the distance.

Papa had fought the Japanese in the Taihang Mountains, and then led militia reinforcements to help the People's Liberation Army fight the Kuomintang. He had given Weihua two mementoes of those days: a Japanese soldier's green wool blanket and an American-made Parker fountain pen. Papa had received two blankets after a victorious battle with the Japanese in 1941, but had sold the second after marrying Mama. His unit had captured the pen from a Kuomintang army officer in 1948. My brother kept his two treasures at school. I could not help feeling envious whenever I saw him unfold and refold the blanket or cradle the Parker pen in his hand.

After we crossed the Yizhen-Lingzhi county line, the road ran along a river. Bluish-gray cooking smoke curled from the stovepipes of the houses on the riverbank. An ox-drawn cart laden with wheat lumbered ahead. We ran to catch up with it. The driver, an angular old peasant with a straw hat pulled over his forehead, was leaning against the load of wheat humming a high-pitched opera tune. A long-stemmed pipe with a brass bowl, the kind Papa smoked, dangled from his lips. We gladly accepted his offer of a lift.

When Weihua mentioned that the winter wheat harvest looked good, the old peasant said that it was, thanks to County Head Gao. "Is that County Head Gao Shangui?" Weihua asked. "None other than Gao Shangui," he said.

"Thanks to County Head Gao, we dug extra pump wells last year," the peasant said. "Otherwise, the dry winter would have ruined a big part of the crop. County Head Gao came to our village in person and told us to dig more wells. He even tied on a rope and went down a hole himself to help dig. The water was miserably cold, and he looked as weak as a scholar, but he insisted on going down. I'm sixty-five, and I've never seen an official who's nicer to us peasants. He knows something about farming, unlike most of those city bureaucrats."

I asked the old man if it was true that County Head Gao dressed like a peasant. "That doesn't impress us," he said. "Many officials do that for show. We watch how he acts. When he goes on inspections, he carries a manure basket on his shoulder and picks up stray dung. Then he dumps it in our fields."

The man told us that lately Gao Shangui had been going around incognito. "A lot of people wrote him letters complaining that workers at the county coal station were slipping coal to friends and relatives through the back door. So he showed up in his shabby peasant clothes to buy coal, and the manager said it was all sold out. He insisted, and the manager got impatient and gave him a shove. Then his aide spoke up and told the manager not to be so rude to the county head. The manager was terrified and begged for forgiveness. County Head Gao criticized him and told him to treat the peasants with respect and to shut his back door. How about that?"

Rebels and Royalists

When the old man let us off and turned down a dirt path to his village, I pondered why Papa would want to stay on in this backward mountain area. "Weihua, does it sometimes seem to you that Papa loves the peasants more than he loves us?" I asked my brother. "Don't be silly. Papa's just that way. He's busy," Weihua said.

The county seat appeared before us, set in a basin surrounded by low hills on three sides and bordered by the river on the fourth. The haze of cooking smoke mingling with the twilight made the scene look like a mirage. We began to run down the hill, as we always did when we got to this point. We knew just what waited below. Grandpa would make us a good dinner. Since Grandma's death, when Weihua and I were infants, he had learned to do all the things that women were supposed to do around the home. Zhihua and Xinghua would bring us a basin of warm water and clean towels. Meiyuan would help Grandpa pump the bellows at the stove. Yiyuan, with her big eyes and thick hair, would sit on our knees and, after a bit of coaxing, perform the newest song and dance she had learned in primary school. Papa probably would be out in the countryside on inspection, but Mama might drop in to say hello.

We found things as we expected, except Grandpa's chronic bronchitis was a little worse than before. After eating, all of us sat together in the front room of the small house and talked late into the evening. Feeling important, Weihua and I described the activities going on at Yizhong. The Cultural Revolution had hardly made a ripple in Lingzhi.

The younger children went to bed on the *kang*, the heated bed in the back room. After converting the dining-room table into a bedboard and fluffing up some quilts, Weihua and I joined them. My last sight before I dropped off to sleep was

Grandpa sitting by the lamp in the corner, leafing through one of his thick books on herbal medicine. During the Three Difficult Years, he had sewn patches on our pants in the same posture by the same dim light.

That had turned out to be our last visit home for quite a few months. In late August, I decided to take a few days off from the campaign to smash the Four Olds. I wanted to check on Grandpa's health and to ask Mama for some extra money for a train ticket to Beijing. Rumor had it that Chairman Mao was going to receive a second batch of Red Guards in Tiananmen Square, so Yizhong's Preparatory Committee was organizing a school trip to Beijing.

To save time, I took the bus home. Lingzhi seemed tranquil as the bus pulled into the terminal. The buildings and walls and streets looked naked compared with Yizhen's; there were few posters. I supposed that the difference had something to do with Lingzhi's quiet political history. The Western imperialist armies had marched into Yizhen in pursuit of Boxers; the Catholic Church had won converts there; the Japanese had occupied the town for eight years and the Kuomintang for two more. It was logical to find spies, reactionaries, collaborators, and traitors there. Lingzhi, on the other hand, had never been of interest to the Western powers and had been under the Japanese only briefly. When the People's Liberation Army took over there, no struggle with the Kuomintang for control had ensued.

I walked through the town with big strides, conscious of my eye-catching Red Guard armband. I had not seen a single person in the streets here wearing one. I swung my arms back and forth grandly so that everyone might notice the first Red Guard ever in Lingzhi. Turning a corner, I approached the county theater. A collage of slogans, written in sloppy calligraphy on strips of coarse brown paper and pasted haphazardly on the theater's front wall, brought my proud march to a halt. "Down with Gao Shangui!" I read. I could not believe my eyes. I looked again, carefully. The slogan did not change. I moved on, my heart beating wildly. "Strongly protest Gao Shangui's suppression of revolutionary students!" "Gao Shangui, lower your head and confess your crimes to the people of Lingzhi!" "Denounce executioner Gao Shangui for suppressing the Cultural Revolution at Lingzhi Middle School!"

I broke into a run. Breathlessly, I burst into the house. Grandpa was making dinner. He listened serenely as I blurted out the news about the slogans on the theater wall. My younger brothers had already told him, and he had gone out to see them himself. "Don't worry," he reassured me. "Storms come and go. I've witnessed many political movements and they're all the same. Now, wash you face and hands and have some watermelon."

Grandpa said that the middle-school students were causing trouble over the work team sent there by the County Party Committee. The Party secretary was on leave to lead the Four Cleanups in another county, so Papa was acting secretary as well as county head, and the students blamed him for the work team's presence. Grandpa told me several more times not to worry. He said that Papa had acted in line with instructions from above and was not to blame for any problems with the work team. Furthermore, even if the students opposed him, the local peasants would always support him.

Mama came over the next morning looking troubled. Papa had just returned from the countryside, and the students were looking for him in order to hold a struggle meeting. Lingzhi did not yet have a Red Guard organization, Mama said.

Rebels and Royalists

"Why don't you go talk to the students?" she urged me. "Since you have that Red Guard armband, they might listen to you." The idea made me uncomfortable. What would the students think of a rebel talking like a royalist? Would they even listen to me? Nonetheless, I agreed to try.

I went first to the county government headquarters, but found no students, only a man painting the Sixteen Points onto a billboard by the gate. I headed for the County Party Committee headquarters. On the way, I noticed that the marble archway at the town's western entrance was still standing. During the Warring States period, the king of the state of Zhao had ordered the arch built to commemorate his sixtieth birthday. The movement against the Four Olds had not made much headway here.

The students milling about the Party Committee courtyard eyed my armband as I approached. I went directly to the dormitory room where my father sometimes stayed. The door was shut and sealed with two crossed strips of paper that read "Closed by revolutionary students of Lingzhi Middle School."

Returning to the courtyard, I asked one boy what the students were waiting for. "We're waiting for Gao Shangui to come back," he said, looking longingly at my armband. "We haven't set up our Red Guards yet, but we're discussing it."

"Why are you waiting for County Head Gao?"

"He's to blame for the work team's mistakes at our school. He also supported our principal, who is a capitalist-roader. We want him to make a self-criticism."

"Comrade," I said, "we Red Guards in Yizhen drove out our work team without resorting to extreme means. We even saw them off at the gate. We didn't go in hot pursuit and blame the County Party Committee for their mistakes."

"Maybe your work team wasn't too bad. The work team at our school put a student under house arrest for a month. Now he's our leader."

"Everybody I've met here says Gao Shangui is a good county head. He spends most of his time living in the villages and working in the fields with the peasants. Why pursue a good man?" I felt uneasy praising my father, but it was the only tactic I could think of.

"We hear a lot about his good deeds too. But we're making revolution. We can't be blinded by his good side. County Head Gao cares only about *liang, mian, you*—grain, cotton, and oil—and doesn't distinguish between *di, wo, you*—the enemy, ourselves, and our friends. He doesn't hold high the banner of Mao Zedong Thought. He neglects class struggle. Two rebels from Nankai University in Tianjin made an investigation and discovered these things."

The middle-school students were not likely to give up if they had university students egging them on. I tried one more thing. "Why don't you give him a chance to correct his mistakes, instead of struggling against him?"

"That's what the royalists at our school recommend. We can't wait anymore. We're far behind the rest of the country."

It was hopeless. They were not going to change their minds. I slowly walked toward home, thinking how unrealistic and naïve Mama was to imagine that rebels would give up their rebellion just because of my armband. I began to feel embarrassed. How ridiculous I must have seemed!

I wandered about Lingzhi's narrow streets kicking pebbles, in no hurry to report my failure to the family. I found myself at the county theater again. A noisy crowd appeared on the town's main street, coming toward me. The people in front were pushing a slender man in a peasant's white cotton jacket. As they came closer, I saw Papa's face, wincing slightly with each shove as he tried to stay upright. The wave of people carried him up the theater steps and into the door.

The door closed behind them. The street was empty again, except for a few students left to stand guard outside the theater. I could hear cries of "Down with Gao Shangui!" coming from inside. Faintly, I heard Papa respond, "Long live the Communist Party!" Then the shouting again, "Down with Gao Shangui!" Again, Papa's voice, "Long live Chairman Mao!" How stubborn Papa was. Like a sword of tempered steel, he would rather break than bend. I waited and waited outside the theater for the struggle meeting to end. The shouting seemed to go on forever. When students finally opened the front door and spilled out, Papa was not among them. They had slipped him out the back.

I trudged home. It was dusk. I had planned to go back to Yizhong that afternoon, but the idea of making revolution with my classmates no longer fired me with enthusiasm. If my classmates found out about Papa, they would not want me making revolution with them anyway. For the first time in my life, I faced the specter of joining the Black Categories. My family had always been a revolutionary family, and I had never been anything but the son of a revolutionary. How could this happen to me?

When I got home, Weihua was there. He had investigated the situation at Lingzhi Middle School and had heartening news: some of the students had decided to defend Papa. They had formed a Red Guard organization called the Mao-Zedongism Red Guards. In addition, militiamen from nearby villages were preparing to rescue Papa from the rebel students.

Rebels and Royalists

Papa had been brave enough to go to the school in person that morning. He had put up a poster on behalf of the Party Committee, welcoming suggestions and criticisms. The rebel students denounced the poster as a trick. They demanded that Papa immediately dismiss their principal. Papa argued that he could not do that himself; the whole Party Committee would have to meet and discuss it. That was when the rebels had decided to seize Papa.

The next day, Mama came over to tell us that other county officials were negotiating with the students for Papa's release. She gave Weihua and me money for train fare to Beijing, and a bit of pocket money besides, and told us to go back to school since there was not much we could do at home. Walking to the bus station, we encountered new slogans along the street that made us feel even better: "We are ready to die in defense of the County Party Committee!" "We are ready to die in defense of Gao Shangui!"

Within a few days, Mama wrote us that Papa had been freed. The negotiations between the county officials and the students had broken down. Peasants and militiamen armed with spades and hoes had stormed the middle school, scattered the rebels, and found Papa in a locked room. The Mao-Zedongism Red Guards had cheered on the rescuers. Meanwhile, the rebels had set up their own organization, called the Mao Zedong Thought Red Guards. Papa feared that the confrontation between the Ism Guards and the Thought Guards had only begun.

Rebels and Royalists

Going to See
the Great Helmsman

I could hardly contain my excitement at the prospect of visiting our country's great capital. From Yizhen to Beijing took only four hours by express train, but few of us at Yizhong had ever made the trip. The closest I had come was during my last year at Democracy Street Primary School. I had been visiting relatives in my hometown of Shuiyuan when flooding cut both the road and the railroad to Yizhen. To get back to school, I made a roundabout detour through Beijing. I had spent two hours in the Beijing railway station. Now I would see not only the Forbidden City and Tiananmen Square, but also the Great Helmsman, Chairman Mao!

Yizhong's Preparatory Committee, at the urging of Chairman Deng, had recommended that every student, Red Guard or not, make the pilgrimage to see Chairman Mao. Yuling's spirits soared. She showed me the bedroll she had prepared for the trip: a green canvas shoulder bag, an aluminum canteen, a cup, toothbrush, and towel, and a copy of Chairman Mao's quotations rolled into a quilt. Unfortunately for her, however, the committee left the final decision up to each class. Little Bawang again raised objections against those from questionable family backgrounds. "Only Red Guards have the right to see Chairman Mao!" he declared. "Chairman Mao is the great commander of the Red Guards, and the Red Guards alone!"

This time, Little Bawang had support from Yuanchao, whose combined revolutionary soldier/poor-peasant lineage made him the reddest Red Guard in our class. "Our parents followed Chairman Mao in making the revolution and liberating China. Only we can go!" he said, standing extra straight so that we could get a good look at his new outfit—his father's baggy old Red Army uniform, cinched with a leather belt. He also had pinned on his chest an enameled badge the size of a one-fen coin that showed Chairman Mao's profile, golden against a red background.

I argued that everyone wanted to follow Chairman Mao to make revolution, and everyone deserved to see him. The students with family problems had not chosen to be born into those families, and they had put up posters making a clean break. Yuling and the other non–Red Guard students watched me intently. None of them dared speak for themselves, for fear of being accused of "class retaliation."

My view found even less support than before among the Red Categories. When we voted, my side lost again. Little Bawang and Yuanchao led some of the Red Guards in taunting the others:

> A dragon begets only dragons,
> A phoenix begets only phoenixes,
> A rat's descendants know only how to dig holes.
> A hero's child is a brave man,
> A reactionary's child is a bastard.

Yuling picked up her bedroll and left for home in tears.

Yizhong's delegation to see Chairman Mao, a thousand-strong, boarded the night train for Beijing. Many students were wearing new khaki clothes tailored to resemble army uniforms, which their mothers had bought or made. Each of us carried a bedroll and a lunch bag containing steamed bread, pickled turnip, and two hard-boiled eggs.

We nodded off to sleep on the hard seats, waking periodically to the sound of the train screeching into yet another small station. Peasants pushed onto the cars all through the night, heaving string bags, baskets, and shoulder poles laden with everything from vegetables to live chickens, rabbits, and piglets. The train was packed by the time the darkness began to lift. As day broke, stirring music and the morning news came over the train loudspeakers. Chairman Mao had received a second group of Red Guards in Tiananmen Square. That meant we would be among the third group.

Arriving at the station at the southwest edge of Beijing where most of the local trains stopped, we got off to wait for transportation into the city. Some students began munching on their lunches. Others raised a red flag bearing the characters for "Yizhong Red Guards." In midmorning, twenty army trucks pulled up. We piled into the backs, standing so squeezed together that nobody could possibly fall down, and rode through the unfamiliar streets. I looked in vain for a glimpse of Tiananmen Gate. We were unloaded in front of the entrance to Beijing Middle School No. 101. The main gate was closed but a small door in the middle of it was ajar. An old man sat in a gatehouse to one side.

A few youths wearing Red Guard armbands appeared to be standing guard outside the entrance. From time to time, other Red Guards would go in or out the little door. I could not take my eyes off these Beijing Red Guards. They all wore authentic-looking army uniforms and brown leather belts with brass buckles. They stood and walked with an aura of importance and confidence. Their hair seemed so sleek and trim, their complexions uncommonly smooth and white.

Going to See the Great Helmsman

I looked over our motley crowd, rumpled and covered with dust from the journey. At a glance, anyone could tell that we came from the countryside. The faces were bronzed, the haircuts shaggy, the clothing rough and shapeless. Some girls even wore traditional high-collared peasant jackets with buttons on one side. Most of these country bumpkins were squatting on their haunches and looking around with great curiosity. We were all like Liu Laolao, the old peasant woman in the novel *A Dream of Red Mansions*, when she went to the grandiose Grand Spectacle Garden to see her rich relatives. In fact, we were even more rustic than Liu Laolao; she at least knew how to ride in a sedan chair. Most of us would not know which side of the street to stand on to catch the bus.

I ambled over to the little door and looked inside. Two giant streamers hanging outside an auditorium bore the couplet that Little Bawang liked so much: "A hero's child is a brave man, a reactionary's child is a bastard." The Red Categories held sway here. I asked the gateman what kind of a school this was. He told me that the students were children of high-ranking army officers, division level and above. Yuanchao, with his division-level father, would be on the lowest rung of the ladder here.

"There is not a single student from the Seven Black Categories in this school," the old man said proudly. "Everyone's of the Five Red Categories. I'm sure that can't be true of your school." I told him he was right. He looked even prouder of himself. "If you wait until later this afternoon," he said, "you can see the long line of cars that come by to pick the students up."

As I peered into the little door again, a Red Guard inside gave the gate a violent kick with his shiny black boot. "Go away, you clods!" he shouted. As he stood at the door imperiously, his hands on his waist, I noticed that his armband was made of velvet. "Go away, you little bastards!" he shouted again, giving the gate another kick.

"You don't have to treat us like that," I said. "We're also Red Guards. Just look at our armbands. We're from Yizhen."

"Who cares about your dirty little village!" he shouted, with another kick. "I'm telling you to go away!"

"We came to see Chairman Mao," I said. "Why are you acting like a landlord in the old society?"

"Little bastard! Don't you dare compare me to a landlord!" With one stride, the lad was outside the small door and holding onto my collar. In another moment, some of my schoolmates were at my side. Seeing himself outnumbered by the country bumpkins, the Beijing student gave me a push and retreated with another stream of curses. "Who cares about staying at your lousy place?" I yelled after him.

After more waiting, we learned that indeed we would not stay at this elite middle school. Chairman Deng had negotiated for several hours with the leaders of the school, but they refused to accommodate us. The trucks returned to take us on another ride.

"Tiananmen Gate!" someone shouted. We strained our necks to see. It did not look quite right. Too small. Grass growing among the tiles on top. And where was the huge square?

It was not Tiananmen Gate; it was the Drum Tower, and we were to stay at Drum Tower Middle School, down a small lane, where ordinary people's children went. After dinner in the dining hall, we went to sleep on straw mattresses on the floor of the school auditorium. We would be staying here until we got word of Chairman Mao's next reception. Meanwhile, we would have time to explore the city, read dazibao on other

The author at Tiananman Square, Beijing, December 1966

campuses, and exchange revolutionary experiences with Beijing Red Guards.

Early the next morning, we received cards entitling "revolutionary students and teachers visiting Beijing from all parts of China" to ride the buses without charge. Little Mihu, Erchou, a few others, and I caught the bus from the Drum Tower to Tiananmen Square. Although we had seen it in countless pictures, its immensity impressed us as no picture could. Standing solidly on the north side of the square was Tiananmen Gate—the very place where, in October 1949, Chairman Mao had proclaimed, "The Chinese people have

Going to See the Great Helmsman

stood up!" Chairman Mao's picture hung over the gate's central arch. Beyond the gate glistened the yellow-tiled roofs of the Forbidden City.

We walked across the square to the Golden Water Bridge, where Chairman Mao had talked with the first group of Red Guards. Little Mihu suggested that we pay our respects to Chairman Mao as we saw other Red Guards doing. We stood in a row on the bridge, took out our little red books and held them against our chests, and bowed to the giant portrait several times.

We crossed the bridge and came to the foot of the gate. Visitors had scribbled revolutionary slogans on the maroon wall: "Long live Chairman Mao!" "We wish Chairman Mao a long, long life!" "Follow Chairman Mao to make revolution forever!" I rubbed my finger along the wall, leaving a light line. The maroon paint came off on my finger. I wanted to save this precious color forever. Taking my diary out of my pocket, I used my maroon finger to write the place and date.

Tiananmen Gate was the first of a succession of gates leading into the Forbidden City. We walked through to the third one, the Noon Gate, where the emperors had mandarins who had offended them beheaded under the noonday sun. A stone tablet on the back of a tortoise instructed all officials, civilian or military, to dismount from their horses and sedan chairs before entering the inner sanctum of the imperial palace. To our disappointment, the Noon Gate was barricaded. Whether one's intentions were to smash the Four Olds or to sightsee, no visitor could get through.

When we returned to the Golden Water Bridge, Little Mihu used his belt to lower his canteen into the canal and hauled up some of the stagnant green water to take back to his village. We gazed across the great square. In front of us ran East-

Is-Red Boulevard, whose name just two weeks earlier had been Perpetual Peace Boulevard. I had never imagined that so many buses and trucks and cars existed in all the world. They flowed along three lanes in each direction. Bicycles streamed along a fourth lane by the curb. A traffic policeman stood on a platform in the middle of the boulevard, brandishing a red-and-white baton with precision and grace.

Students at Drum Tower Middle School had told us that the Beijing Red Guards had made some revolutionary changes in traffic regulations during the movement to smash the Four Olds. They demanded that vehicles should stop at green lights and go at red lights, since stopping at red was counterrevolutionary; and that traffic should travel on the left side of the street, as in Britain, since the right side was not proletarian. The city had abandoned these changes after only a few days, because they had caused too many accidents.

From time to time, passing cyclists flung handfuls of handbills over the sidewalk. A group of Red Guards pedaled by, singing everyone's favorite song about Chairman Mao:

Sailing the seas depends on the helmsman,
All things on earth depend on the sun;
Moistened by rain and dew, young crops grow strong,
To make revolution, we must rely on Mao Zedong Thought;
Fish cannot leave water, nor can melons leave vines,
The revolutionary masses cannot leave the Party,
To make revolution, we must rely on Mao Zedong Thought!

Red Guards were going in and out of the pine grove on the south side of the square. Among the trees, we discovered a brisk trade in Chairman Mao badges. Most were like Yuanchao's, the size of a one-fen coin. Some were a bit bigger, like a two-fen coin. I inquired whether anyone would sell me a badge. "We are not speculators," said one boy. "We only trade. Two small ones for a big one." What if I did not have any badges to trade? "You can use Chairman Mao photos instead. Ten photos for one badge."

I had seen youths on the sidewalk selling photos of Chairman Mao receiving the first group of Red Guards. A pack of ten cost eight mao, which seemed rather expensive. But the idea of returning to Yizhen with a Chairman Mao badge captivated me. Better yet, I should get two and give one to Yuling. I ran off to find a photo dealer, came back with two packs, and bartered them for two small badges. I pinned one on my chest and the other inside my pocket. I was sure I could feel Chairman Mao's radiance burning into me.

My classmates and I had lunch in a restaurant crowded with Red Guard sightseers. It was the second restaurant I had ever gone to. The first was in Shimen. That was in 1960; the collective dining halls had just closed, and Grandpa had taken me to Shimen to get a new bellows for the stove. He was sitting at the table eating, and I was standing by his side, when a waiter came along, rapped on my head with a bundle of chopsticks, and said, "Get out, you little beggar!" Grandpa had to explain that I was his grandson.

This restaurant greeted us with a sign at the door: "Revolutionary comrades, as part of the campaign to smash old habits and customs, we restaurant workers have decided that customers should serve themselves." We served ourselves bowls of hot Sichuan noodles from the service counter, found a table, and sat down. A slogan on the wall next to us read "Resolutely oppose the rotten bourgeois lifestyle." When we were done, we followed the instructions of another sign above one of the sinks: "Revolutionary comrades, please wash your own bowls and chopsticks."

We rode a bus westward along East-Is-Red Boulevard to

the Military Museum. An American U-2 spy plane shot down by the Chinese air force sat on the lawn outside like a giant crow. Then we rode back across the city to the shiny new Beijing railway station. The terminal had two escalators, one going up and one coming down. We rode them over and over until we felt satisfied. When we got back to Drum Tower Middle School late that night, the auditorium was humming with talk of the day's adventures. Some students had gone clear across Beijing to the Summer Palace in the northwest suburbs. Others had taken the bus on the wrong side of the street and gotten lost.

On our third morning in Beijing, we all rode the public buses to the northwest edge of the city to visit Beida. The campus seemed a city in itself, a blend of traditional and modern architecture set among gentle landscaping. Despite the tranquil setting, the place was like a beehive. People swarmed over the paths and lawns, talking and arguing, listening to impromptu speeches, studying posters. The dazibao were everywhere, spread over walls, tacked up on bulletin boards, hung on clotheslines between trees and utility poles. Red Guard contingents from all over the capital were selling their own newspapers for two fen a copy. Every so often, a snowstorm of handbills materialized, and hundreds of hands reached up to grab them.

I joined a crowd at the Beida sports ground, where Beida's former Party secretary and vice-secretary, Lu Ping and Peng Peiyun, were scheduled to appear before a struggle meeting at 10:00 A.M. Most of the spectators were bumpkin types like myself. Perhaps Beida's own Red Guards had gotten bored with struggling against Lu and Peng. The culprits, a man and a woman, were marched out. Around their necks were cardboard signs labeling them anti-Party elements. They kept their heads bowed. A Red Guard made a brief speech listing their crimes. Another Red Guard interrogated Lu:

"Did you oppose Mao Zedong Thought?"

"No."

"Didn't you suppress the students at Beida?"

"Yes, I did. I made mistakes. But I didn't oppose Mao Zedong Thought."

The interrogator repeated the same thing with Peng, and she gave similar answers. The Red Guards shouted some slogans and led the two disgraced officials away.

I spent the rest of the day studying dazibao. The most popular new poster quoted a recent speech by the old army marshal Ye Jianying, revealing that Chairman Mao's physician had given him a checkup, pronounced him very healthy, and predicted he would live to be a hundred.

A number of posters debated the Tan Lifu Line. Tan Lifu, a Red Guard leader whose father was a high-ranking cadre, was credited with originating the "blood lineage theory," best expressed by Little Bawang's favorite slogan, "A hero's child is a brave man, a reactionary's child is a bastard." Tan Lifu's followers had set up a Red Guard organization called United Action, to which only children of high cadres could belong. Some people were beginning to criticize this theory as reactionary. My arguments with Little Bawang suddenly took on a new dimension. I began to copy down commentaries that might strengthen my position later on.

We went back to Beida the next day and to other campuses in the following days. We still had received no word of Chairman Mao's next reception. One day when we were at Qinghua University, Chairman Deng told us that the leaders of the Central Committee and Central Cultural Revolution Group were going to receive Red Guard representatives. He

Going to See the Great Helmsman

asked the Cultural Revolution group from each class to follow him to a line of buses parked on the roadside. The other students were not happy to be excluded, but Chairman Deng reassured them, "This is only a small reception. There will be a large reception soon enough. Everybody who is here will have the opportunity to see Chairman Mao." Unfortunately, the line of buses never moved. Late in the afternoon, Chairman Deng said the reception had been canceled.

A week passed and still no news. Some of the students from Yizhong had used up their grain coupons and money. Others began to complain about the lice in the straw mattresses. Our patience was nearly exhausted. In addition, we had overstayed our welcome at Drum Tower Middle School. More Red Guards were coming and they needed the space. Chairman Deng decided that we should return to Yizhong.

We tried to comfort ourselves by saying that Chairman Mao's two receptions on August 18 and 31 probably would be the only ones. Chairman Deng found an even better way to console us: he managed to buy a supply of Chairman Mao badges and gave us each one. We were trucked back to the station where the local trains stopped, and we boarded the train for Yizhen in high spirits, singing a song we had learned in Beijing:

> The hows and whys of Marxism,
> Tens of thousands of lines and threads,
> Come down in the last analysis
> To one single sentence, which is:
> To rebel is justified!

Going to See the Great Helmsman

Sending Off the Monsters

When we returned to Yizhong, I undid my bedroll and spent much of the day catching up on my sleep. In the afternoon, I went to find Yuling. I knew she would be happy about the Chairman Mao badge. I also could tell her that she need not be very disappointed, because we had not seen Chairman Mao after all.

Yuling's neighborhood had a strangely quiet air. Nearing her home, I saw paper strips over the courtyard door. I came closer and read the words on them: "Sealed by the revolutionary masses of Democracy Street." The message was dated the previous day. As I stood there wondering where Yuling and her grandmother could be, someone patted my shoulder. "Comrade Red Guard, what are you standing here for?" I turned around to see a youth about my own age, wiping his runny nose.

"I am looking for my classmate, who lives in this courtyard," I said.

"I'm sorry, you won't find her here anymore. She and her grandmother were ordered back to their hometown in Shanxi province. They left yesterday morning, escorted by two comrades from the Neighborhood Committee. I've been assigned to guard the courtyard."

"Why did they leave?"

"People said they were monsters and ghosts. They can't

stay in our town. They will work under the supervision of the poor and lower-middle peasants in their village."

The boy paused to wipe his nose again. "Every street in town has monsters and ghosts like this old woman. She had no job, no work unit to supervise her. This type of person could easily take advantage of these confusing times to conduct counterrevolutionary sabotage." I stared at the boy to see if he was making fun of me. He looked serious.

I headed back to school, taking the shortcut through the reed ponds. The catkins were going to seed. Their fluffy white heads waved noiselessly in the soft breeze. The sun was low in the west.

I unpinned Yuling's Chairman Mao badge from the inside of my pocket and looked at it glinting in the day's last light. I had been looking forward to giving Yuling her present and watching her face light up. I tried to imagine Yuling and her grandmother in the countryside. How would they survive? I had read a story in a Red Guard newspaper about villagers killing landlords and rich peasants. Would Yuling, as a child from a monster and ghost family, be safe? Would she ever return?

The questions piled up in my mind until my head was ready to burst. Tears came into my eyes. I sank onto a stone by the path and cried. The sun went down as I sat there, crying and crying. Only when the cold evening wind began to make me shiver did I stand up and stumble my way back to my dormitory in the dark.

Sending Off the Monsters

Defending
the Mountain Devil

In mid-September, Chairman Mao received Red Guards in Beijing for the third time. We Red Guards of Yizhong felt humiliated. Some students blamed Chairman Deng for sending us back to school too early. Others wanted to go to the capital again.

Chairman Deng was thinking of other things entirely. One of the Sixteen Points said participants in the Cultural Revolution should "grasp revolution to promote production." Moreover, Yizhong had a tradition of helping local peasants during busy farming seasons. The peasants were getting ready to plant the winter wheat crop. So all the students, Red Guards or not, were going to Perpetual Happiness Commune to work for a month. The monsters and demons would stay behind and do their labor in the school vegetable garden.

Perpetual Happiness Commune was an hour's walk from school, off the road leading to Lingzhi. It was made up of a dozen villages. My grade stayed with families in Xing Family Village. Half of the villagers had the surname Xing, and most of the other half were Liangs or Dongs. I slept on a kang with two other students and a vigorous patriarch named Xing Maishou—"ripe wheat" Xing. His arms were as scaly as old pine bark and his ribs protruded like bamboo scaffolding. A wooden coffin that his son had made him sat in his house. But when I asked him how his health was, he pounded his chest and exclaimed, "I am not old! General Huang Zhong of the Three Kingdoms could fight on horseback at the age of seventy, and I'm only sixty-eight!"

The Cultural Revolution had not ignored Xing Village. Former landlords, rich peasants, and other bad elements were under supervision, much as during Land Reform. Besides laboring in the fields, they had to get up earlier than everybody else to sweep the village streets. They were easily recognizable, for they all wore black armbands with their status described in white characters.

The peasants themselves had voted to abolish the last vestige of private farming, household vegetable plots. Now everything was grown collectively. The day's work began with recitations of Chairman Mao's quotations. Since many of the peasants were barely literate, we students read aloud to them. During rest breaks, we would sing revolutionary songs. Sometimes we picked out someone with a black armband and conducted a struggle meeting right on the edge of the field.

Xing Maishou was the best seeder in his production team. Using a primitive horse-drawn contraption that dropped seeds from a box, he could sow two rows at a time. He made it look no harder than strolling in a courtyard. I followed behind, pulling a stone roller to tamp down the soil.

One morning, as Xing Maishou squatted on the soft earth for a smoke and I sat down on the roller for a rest, I noticed that the paper strips the old man was using to roll his cigarettes were covered with writing. I picked up a strip and saw that it had been cut from a handbill. "Where did you get this paper, Big Uncle?" I asked.

"At the market in Yizhen a few days ago."

"Can you read, Big Uncle?"

"Read? Hah! I don't even recognize my name!"

Defending the Mountain Devil

"Do you often go to Yizhen on market day?"

"In the past I didn't, but now I go all the time since there are so many interesting things going on. And I can always get a big pile of paper, free of charge."

I watched for Xing Maishou after the next market day. Sure enough, he came home with a big pile of handbills under his arm. That evening, he asked me to help him make cigarette wrappers. As we cut the paper into strips, I thought how lucky Xing Maishou was to come from several generations of poor peasants. Just think what might happen to a former landlord or rich peasant who had the audacity to cut up revolutionary handbills!

After the fields were sown, I decided to go home, since I was already a fourth of the way there. When I got off the bus in Lingzhi and headed toward the center of town, I encountered dazibao spread over the buildings from foundation to eaves. The nearer I got to downtown, the more profuse the posters became. Almost all were about Papa. The majority seemed to be against him. In addition to the old label of "executioner" who had suppressed the student movement, the dreadful new title of "capitalist-roader" appeared.

One slogan splashed in meter-high characters across the front of the town department store read "Knock down the capitalist-roader inside the Party, Gao Shangui!" The last character had been altered, making Papa's given name into "mountain devil," which sounded similar to "mountain laurel," and two big red X's signifying the death sentence had been painted over the name.

I stopped to read another poster entitled "Expose Mountain Devil's Hypocrisy!" and signed by the Mao Zedong Thought Red Guards of Lingzhi Middle School. It said Papa's habit of smoking a pipe with a long bamboo stem was a hoax to make people think he empathized with the peasants. It claimed Papa really stuffed high-quality China-brand cigarette tobacco into the pipe bowl.

How absurd! Papa had always smoked tobacco leaves that he bought in the street, the same kind the peasants smoked. I had even helped him toast the leaves over the stove. Papa put out cigarettes only for guests. If he sometimes broke apart the leftover butts and put the tobacco into his pipe bowl, it was because he could not stand waste. How could these students make such ridiculous accusations?

"It's really unfair!" I said aloud. The few people passing by paid me no mind. Students with red armbands no longer were a rarity in these streets. The more I looked at this poster, the angrier I got. I pulled out my pen and jotted in the margin, "Sheer fabrication! Go to hell!" Of course, I did not sign my name.

Another poster by Thought Guards said they had commandeered a truck and sent a truckload of representatives to the prefectural government in Shimen to demand Papa's dismissal. It sounded like Papa's attackers were on the offensive. The last I had heard, the local peasants were rallying to Papa's support. Where were his defenders now? Why had they fallen mute?

At home, I found Grandpa reading one of his medical books. His look of serenity calmed me a bit. Perhaps the family's situation was not so bad. But Grandpa did not have much news. Papa, as far as he knew, was making rounds of the villages.

Mama stopped in briefly. Her hair, which she had always worn cropped short, had grown down to her shoulders, and

Defending the Mountain Devil

129

white threads were visible among the black. She told me Papa was in the countryside and had no time to deal with the students' complaints.

I asked Mama why Papa did not at least refute the false charges against him. "It's useless," she answered. "The students won't listen to a word. Papa doesn't want to waste his time. He even stops the people who want to defend him. He says it's better to let the students make havoc for a while, that when they're tired they will quiet down on their own." When I mentioned the poster that reported the Thought Guards' mission to the prefectural government, she said the Ism Guards and some villagers had blocked the truck. However, Papa himself had told his supporters to let the Thought Guards go, saying he would not be afraid to lose his official's cap if the authorities deemed him unqualified.

After Mama left, I began to worry about myself. Sooner or later, my schoolmates would find out about Papa. Then they certainly would exclude Weihua and me from making revolution. Grandpa seemed to read my mind. "Your father's case is different from the monsters and demons," he said. "He is a veteran revolutionary. And he is still the county head. Nobody's stopped your brothers and sisters from making revolution at primary school. Little Yiyuan, in fact, is a star dancer in her school's Mao Zedong Thought Propaganda Team."

The four younger children came home from school looking happy and unperturbed. I questioned them closely about the political situation in town, and particularly about the Thought Guards. "They don't have the people's support," Zhihua said, sounding very grown-up. "They're all bad eggs," said Xinghua. "Don't worry, Papa will win," said Meiyuan.

Defending the Mountain Devil

"Most of the Thought Guard sympathizers in our school have been locked up by their parents!" Yiyuan said.

Their confidence cheered and emboldened me. While Grandpa was chopping vegetables, I told them I wanted their help in a very important task. They could not let anyone know, not even Grandpa or Mama or Papa. They all agreed to my plan. After dinner, I led my commando team downtown. Only a few dim streetlights lit our way through the deserted streets. When I gave the order to advance, the five of us charged to the nearest wall and began tearing down dazibao. We went from one building to the next, ripping paper furiously. When we got to the department store, I found the poster about Papa's pipe, shredded it, and trampled the pieces into the dusty ground. After half an hour's work, I called a retreat. We did not want to get caught and charged with sabotaging the Cultural Revolution. I led my team on a diversionary run through the lanes to shake any possible tails. We slipped home under cover of darkness.

The next morning, I went downtown to see the reaction. Several Thought Guards were angrily writing more posters, accusing the Ism Guards of vandalizing the earlier ones. I bought stewed beef and sesame buns from a peddler. When my commandoes came home from school for lunch, I rewarded them with beef-stuffed sesame buns. Grandpa inquired about my generosity, and I could not resist telling him about our adventure. He put on a stern face and told us not to do such a thing again, but his eyes were gleaming with delight.

When I boarded the bus for Yizhen that afternoon, I began to think about how paradoxical my life had become. At school, I was a revolutionary, a rebel, a Red Guard. At home,

Defending the Mountain Devil

131

I had turned into a counterrevolutionary, a royalist, an anti–Thought Guard commando leader. The contradiction did not bother me for long. I worked out a theory that explained everything: if I did not defend Papa and instead let him get knocked down, I would become a Black Category person. Then I would no longer be able to contribute to revolution. So my actions were justified. To rebel against unjustified dazibao was justified!

The Carpenter-Spy

On our return to school, tan and muscular from nearly a month in the countryside, Yizhong's Preparatory Committee instructed us to compile dossiers on the teachers. Each class was to review evidence from posters and other materials and either verify or discard the charges. The purpose was to identify as many "comparatively good" teachers as possible. They would be allowed to make revolution with us.

Sitting in the classroom reading our file on Teacher Li, I came across a report signed by Little Bawang and Little Mihu charging that Li had deliberately distorted the piece he read to us about a woman Communist going to the execution ground. According to my two classmates, the original text said the woman had gone "with her head up, the evening breeze blowing back her gray hair," but Li had described her as "shivering in her shoes." They said that Li had deliberately defiled the Communist heroine because of his deep-rooted

hatred of the Communists, which stemmed from his own reactionary background.

I remembered that class vividly, how Teacher Li's voice had
broken and tears had brimmed up in his eyes. His reading
had dramatized the woman's bravery in the face of death. I
was sure that it had contained no such phrase as "shivering
in her shoes." I would talk to my classmates and set the record
straight. I did not have to wait long for Little Bawang. He
swept into the classroom waving a big red flag, and announced, "We're setting up a new Red Guard organization,
the Red Inheritance Red Guards. Only children of revolutionary military officers can join. I'm going to declare my independence from class 85!"

"It's fine with me if you want to imitate the Beijing aristo-
crats," I said. "I just read your report about Teacher Li. I'm
afraid your memory is faulty." Little Bawang lost his temper.
Waving the flag even more vigorously, he said, "Our memories are clear. You should examine your class stand. Why do
you want to protect that reactionary Kuomintang officer? Is
it because you were a teacher's pet? I'm not even going to
listen to you!" He turned and strode out.

Perhaps Little Mihu would be easier to convince. I found
him engrossed in a contest with a few other students to see
who could swallow the most hot water. They sat in the hot
sun, shirtless, eating salted turnip between gulps. Little Mihu's belly was already round. I asked him if he really remembered hearing Teacher Li smear the Communist heroine. He
gave me an embarrassed look. "Little Bawang said we
shouldn't show mercy to the enemy, so I signed. I don't really
remember what happened in class." "If that's the case, you
can come with me and cross your name out," I said. "We can't

The Carpenter-Spy

make things up, no matter how bad the person may be." Little Mihu docilely followed me back to the classroom.

Before the day was out, the Red Inheritance Red Guards had emerged, with headquarters in an empty classroom. The new organization drew its membership from nearly every class. Yuanchao joined and was elected deputy commander. Little Bawang was not accepted because his father's rank was too low. He would not talk to anyone for several days. Then, full of disdain for the army children who had shut him out, he set up his own Red Guard contingent, called the Safeguard Mao and Lin Red Guards. Ten of our classmates joined him.

Our class Cultural Revolution group was losing its authority. We could do nothing to prevent Little Bawang's secession or to keep others from following suit. Congfang founded the Perpetual Red Red Guards, and Caolan set up the Mao Zedong Doctrine Red Guards. Finally, Shuanggen and I collected the undesirables and set up the Central and South Seas Red Guards, named after the place in Beijing where the Central Committee and State Council members lived. We had a dozen members, including Erchou, the tomboy Huantian, and a few others who had been excluded from the original Red Guards.

Huantian was especially happy to be in our organization. Her upper-middle-peasant origins had worked against her since the start of the Cultural Revolution. Little Bawang had even accused her of having a counterrevolutionary name, saying that "changing heaven" indicated a desire to overthrow the new society. I had come to her rescue, pointing out that she was one of the oldest students in the class and had been born right before the founding of the People's Republic in 1949. Her name in fact celebrated the imminent arrival of the new society.

The Carpenter-Spy

We set up our Central and South Seas headquarters in an unoccupied dormitory room. Organizational tasks kept us busy for several days. First, we had to formulate and mimeograph our founding statement. Our guiding principle was, "In the spirit of the Sixteen Points, unite all those who desire to make revolution under the banner of the Central and South Seas Red Guards, to carry the Cultural Revolution through to the end." That settled, we stenciled new red armbands with gold dye, and ordered an engraved seal and silk for a flag from the Preparatory Committee. None of the splinter groups had declared independence from the Preparatory Committee, since everyone depended on it for logistical and financial support.

Our next step was to develop a plan of action that would earn us a reputation and new recruits. Huantian came up with the best idea. She had heard a rumor that strange noises resembling a wireless transmission often came out of the school carpentry workshop. "Let's keep watch on Carpenter Zhang," she proposed. "If we can catch him at something, our organization will gain nationwide fame."

Carpenter Zhang, a friendly man in his fifties, lived and worked in a cavernous building behind our headquarters. He repaired chairs and desks and made furniture. With classes suspended and all of us embroiled in revolution, nobody was supervising his activities. It would be easy for him to make counterrevolutionary mischief. We adopted Huantian's plan by unanimous vote.

For a couple of days, we kept watch on Carpenter Zhang's door from the rear window of our headquarters. We discerned no suspicious activity. We decided to conduct a night reconnaissance mission. After midnight, Shuanggen, Huantian, and I climbed a ladder to the roof of the building,

The Carpenter-Spy

opened a skylight, let down a rope, and slid into the carpentry workshop. Carpenter Zhang's bedroom was down the hall. We tried the door and found it latched. "I bet he's working his wireless under the quilt," Huantian whispered.

Agreeing that Carpenter Zhang might panic and do something drastic if we broke in, we looked for another way. One possibility was climbing into the space between the ceiling and the rafters, as we did in our classroom when the electric wiring needed repair. We made our way back down the hall, trying the doors until we found an unlocked one. Shuanggen stood on a table, removed a ceiling panel, and boosted Huantian and me up into the hole. He would stand guard at Carpenter Zhang's door. Should anything go wrong, he could storm in to help us.

Huantian and I crawled our way over the ceiling to Carpenter Zhang's room. We lay on our stomachs, pressed our ears to the boards, and tried to peer through the cracks. We could see and hear nothing, but we felt the warm air and smelled the odor of human habitation below. We lay under the rafters for a long time. As we were contemplating retreat, we heard a rustling sound. "He's going to send a cable to Taiwan!" Huantian whispered excitedly. Then came the distinctive ring of pissing into a chamber pot.

The rustling noise resumed. "This time, he's really doing it," Huantian said. More rustling, and then a creaking sound, as if the bed were moving back and forth. We held our breath and listened. Suddenly, there was a burst of noise, a mixture of moaning, groaning, and panting. It sounded like somebody suffering. It sounded like a woman. "What's going on? Where did the woman come from?" Huantian whispered. "A female spy, come to contact him?" I pinched her to silence her. There was another burst of groaning, this time in a man's voice. What could they possibly be doing down there in the middle of the night?

In a flash, I thought of a paragraph in the revolutionary novel *Primrose* describing a counterrevolutionary adultery scene. So that was it! I could feel the blood rush to my face.

A soft murmuring rose from below. "What are they doing?" Huantian asked. I whispered to her, "They've been fucking." Huantian shuddered, making the ceiling boards creak. "What's that noise in the ceiling?" the woman's voice called from below. "Nothing but mice," said the man. "This building has lots of mice. Tomorrow, we can get some poison to kill them. Are you tired? I'm tired. I have to make a cabinet for the Preparatory Committee tomorrow, and you have to travel back to the village. Let's go to sleep."

Huantian and I did not dare move until we heard Carpenter Zhang snoring. Then we crawled back into the hole we had entered by. A groggy Shuanggen sat below. "I almost fell asleep," he said. "I waited outside the door and didn't hear anything, so I came back here. What did you discover?" "The old fellow was fucking a woman in the middle of the night!" Huantian announced. "Really? I wish I had gone with you. Although I've often eavesdropped on newlyweds in the countryside, I've never really heard anything. You two didn't waste your time!"

We groped our way to the front door, opened the latch, and slipped out. When we got back to headquarters, Shuanggen insisted that we imitate the sounds we had heard. Instead of going back to our dormitory rooms, we stayed in our headquarters and slept on the tables and chairs, using dazibao paper as blankets.

The Carpenter-Spy

In the morning, we gave the rest of the Central and South Seas Red Guards a report on our mission. We were satisfied that Carpenter Zhang was not sending cables to Taiwan. The question now was whether to make further investigation into his morals. We decided that the woman probably was his wife, and even if she was not, the case lacked political significance; so we let it drop.

After the meeting, I went to the Preparatory Committee office to get the silk we had ordered for our flag. Chairman Deng had turned into a one-man distribution center for all the little Red Guard groups that were springing up like bamboo shoots after a spring rain. He was an amiable man and did not seem to mind. He measured six meters of red silk with a wooden ruler, tore it off the bolt, and handed it to me with a smile. "Wishing you great success!" he said.

Reply from a Socialist-Roader

A handbill posted on the classroom blackboard revealed what I most wanted to hide. Someone had drawn a chalk circle around it, with an arrow and the words, "Look at the latest news from Lingzhi." I did not have to go any closer to know what the handbill said. I had a good idea who had put it there. A few of my classmates were at their desks, reading files on teachers. Nobody looked at me. The silence was suffocating.

I took a walk to Rear Lake, where I sat down under a willow and wrote a letter to Papa. I did not begin with "Dear

Papa." It was better, under the circumstances, to be more formal.

Comrade Gao Shangui,

I have not seen you for several months. The last time I was home, you were in the countryside.

Many changes have taken place at our school. We went to Beijing to see Chairman Mao in September, but unfortunately missed the chance. We spent a month sowing wheat. I learned how to use a harrow while holding onto the mule's tail. I enjoyed it very much. You have always told me to learn from the peasants, and I am glad to say that I did.

Recently, handbills from Lingzhi found their way to Yizhen. They have caused some disturbance in our school. I feel that an invisible force is trying to push me off the revolutionary road. I am compelled to make a choice.

I have one question to ask you, a very important question on which my political future depends. Do you still believe you are a revolutionary? Please give me a certain answer, either yes or no.

Salutations in the name of the Great Proletarian Cultural Revolution!

Jianhua

I went to the gatehouse to buy an envelope and stamp, and dropped the letter in the mailbox outside the South Gate. Then I tried to prepare myself psychologically to be shunned by the whole school.

To my surprise and relief, events turned in my favor in the next few days. Rebels in the Yizhen county government, inspired by the activism of Yizhong's Red Guards, put up dazibao denouncing the county leaders. Among other things, they claimed that the leaders had collaborated with the former Party secretary of Yizhen, Han Rong, in persecuting Papa, whom they described as "Revolutionary Cadre Gao Shangui." This charge appeared all over Yizhen, and my

Reply from a Socialist-Roader

schoolmates could not possibly miss it. Not even Little Bawang suggested that I be barred from making revolution.

We finished our review of teachers' records and sent the files to the Preparatory Committee. As a result of the reevaluation, two-thirds of the faculty were classified as "comparatively good." The rest remained monsters and demons, including Li and Shen. The most active Red Guards began struggling against these unlucky teachers all over again.

Little Bawang's Safeguard Mao and Lin Red Guards interrogated Li and Shen at least once a day, until an accident occurred. According to Little Bawang's account, the students had slapped Teacher Shen on the face a few times when he lunged at them like a madman. Somebody—nobody would say exactly who—had plunged a javelin into Shen's body in self-defense, killing him.

The Safeguard Mao and Lin people had to report the incident to Chairman Deng. He said that he would conduct an investigation, but he never did. He did not even make a public announcement. Instead, he quietly had the body sent to the burial ground outside the north city wall where Vice-Principal Lin Sheng and the drowned student lay. Nobody wanted to get involved with a dead spy.

The atmosphere at school seemed stifling. I yearned to get away. The newspapers were full of reports about Red Guards traveling around the country to exchange revolutionary experiences. There was even a special new term for this travel—*chuanlian*, or "joining the great circuit." The Central Cultural Revolution Group had paved the way for chuanlian on a massive scale by decreeing that Red Guards could ride the trains free.

The Red Inheritance Red Guards were the first group at

Yizhong to leave on chuanlian. Weihua informed me he was going on chuanlian with three comrades from his small Red Guard group, the Red Brigade. They planned to head for Sichuan province in the southwest. I had never been south of Shimen. To be exact, I had never been south of the glassware factory in Shimen, where we had gone on a school field trip. I told Weihua that I was thinking of leaving, too. He advised me to find a few companions and travel in a small group.

I knew that if I raised the matter at a Central and South Seas meeting, everyone would want to come along. So I took Shuanggen aside and asked him to travel with me. We went to Chairman Deng to get a letter of introduction addressed to Red Guard reception centers at all the cities we wanted to visit. We also persuaded him to give us several blank letters of introduction stamped with the Preparatory Committee's seal to use in case of emergency.

Since Teacher Shen's death, my liking for Chairman Deng had diminished. When I asked him whether he really would investigate Teacher Shen's case, he gave me a soothing look and said, "The Sixteen Points make it very clear that the revolutionary masses are bound to make mistakes. If we pick on the masses too much, we'll also be making a mistake."

The day before Shuanggen and I were going to depart, a letter addressed to me in Papa's bold scrawl arrived. Papa seldom wrote to me, and when he did, his letters were only a few lines long. This one was three pages.

Jianhua,
Received your letter. I just got back from the countryside. This year's winter wheat was very well sown, which makes me happy, in spite of all the troubles and disturbances.

I have been the head of Lingzhi county going on five years now.

Reply from a Socialist-Roader

My ties with some of these peasants go back to the Anti-Japanese War. This mountainous area was part of the Shanxi-Chahaer-Hebei Border Area under General Nie Rongzhen's leadership. During those days, the people here supported our troops and guerrillas with everything from the food they took off their tables to the lives of their finest children. We fought in the same ditches against the Japanese devils. We promised them that when we won victory and set up the new China, they would have a much better life.

Life here has improved greatly, but we are far from reaching our goal. Many people still don't have enough to eat. This vexes me all the time. I feel we have the obligation to fulfill our promise to better their lives. To show how this can be done, we are setting up a model brigade deep in the mountains. The place is called Tile Terrace. The project is going very well.

As long as I am the head of this county, I will do my utmost to help feed the people. I cannot bear to see people hungry. This is probably why I am always engrossed in rural work, sometimes to the neglect of other things. Lingzhi is an agricultural county, and the emphasis of the work must be in the countryside.

As for the movement unfolding throughout the country, not only I, but many people, find it hard to understand. Why does it come when we are still struggling to recover from the Three Difficult Years? In those days, whenever I saw my children's gaunt faces, I felt guilty about my inability to meet my responsibility as a father. But I felt even more guilty about my inability to feed the people in my county. It was with great effort that we finally emerged from the great hardships imposed on us by the Soviet revisionists, the imperialists and reactionaries, and natural disasters, as well as by our own boastfulness. We should now be riding with the favorable wind to improve our economy and rid ourselves of poverty.

Even though this movement is beyond my comprehension, as a faithful Party member I must follow the Central Committee's leadership. Other leading comrades oversaw the early stages of the movement at Lingzhi Middle School, since I was in the countryside. But I am acting Party secretary at present, so I bear responsibility for anything that went wrong.

Reply from a Socialist-Roader

I understand the anxiety this has caused you and your big brother. Other comrades and I have experienced many movements, but the momentum of this one stunned even us. You ask me if I still believe that I am a revolutionary. I can assure you that I always have been, still am, and always will be a revolutionary. I have devoted my life to the cause of the revolution. I joined the Party when I was nineteen, and founded the Party branch in my native village. I gave up my job teaching school to join the guerrillas in fighting the Japanese devils. I have always believed in Communism, in the leadership of the Party, and in Chairman Mao. Yes, I believe that I am a revolutionary. I know that I am not a capitalist-roader. I witnessed what capitalism brought to China before Liberation. How could I favor capitalism over socialism? On the contrary, I am a socialist-roader, and always will be.

I am hopeful that you will have faith in me. However, if for the time being you believe that I am a capitalist-roader, as some people charge, you may abandon me. I will not complain.

Your Father

For once, he sounded something like a real father. I folded the letter neatly and put it between the pages of my diary.

On the Road

Shuanggen and I left our Central and South Seas soldiers a note saying that we hoped to meet them on the road, and walked out Yizhong's South Gate before daybreak, bedrolls strapped to our backs, armbands on our sleeves, and Chairman Mao buttons on our chests. At the train station, our letter of introduction was enough to get us free tickets to

Shimen, where we changed for Wuhan. Every seat in the southbound express was occupied, and Red Guards sitting on their bedrolls filled the aisles. Shuanggen and I settled down by the door at the end of one car. We pressed our noses against the door window, watching the endless green carpet of wheatfields.

From time to time, our train had to stop or slow down to make way for freight trains bound for Friendship Pass on the Sino-Vietnamese border. The boxcars were covered with slogans in white paint—"Down with U.S. imperialism!" "Down with Soviet revisionism!" "Down with Johnson!" "Down with Brezhnev and Kosygin!" The flatcars carried army trucks, tanks, and antiaircraft guns for the Vietnamese. We could tell that some of the trucks were Russian by their square cabs. Despite ideological differences, we had agreed to let the Soviets send aid to Vietnam through our territory.

I had read our Central Committee's nine open letters to the Soviet Central Committee several times. They criticized the "three peaces and one less" doctrine—peaceful coexistence, peaceful transition, peaceful negotiation with the imperialist countries, and less support for the oppressed countries. I also knew about the Cuban missile incident, in which the Soviets had backed down before the U.S. imperialists. I had doubts about the sincerity of Soviet support for the Vietnamese.

Shuanggen did too. He had heard that the Soviets were sending run-down equipment to the Vietnamese, and that they secretly cooperated with the U.S. imperialists by providing directions for B-52 attacks on Chinese antiaircraft posts in Vietnam. It was said that the North Vietnamese tried to keep their Russian friends and their Chinese friends apart, because Russian and Chinese soldiers often got into fights when they met.

On the Road

I thought back to the days when the Soviets had been our big brothers. In primary school, I had corresponded with a pen-pal in Moscow named Natasha. In 1960, right before the Russian advisers left China, she had stopped answering my letters. "I used to dream of going to Moscow to see Red Square," I told Shuanggen. "No more. That's the place I least want to go!" Shuanggen said that he felt exactly the same way.

We slept curled against each other. When morning came, we found ourselves riding through gently rolling hills. The soil had changed from black to red. We had crossed the Yellow River during the night. By early afternoon, we reached Hankou and Hanyang, two of the trio of cities that made up Wuhan. Here, the Han River flowed into the Yangtze. The map of China we had drawn so often in geography class had come to life. As the train crossed the gigantic Yangtze River Bridge, Chairman Mao's poem "Swimming," set to music, burst over the loudspeakers: "A bridge flew across the river to span south and north, a deep chasm turned into a thoroughfare . . ."

The train came to a stop at Wuchang, the third of the triple cities. Red Guards were everywhere, meandering through the railway station and filling the plaza outside. The local Red Guard reception office sent Shuanggen and me to an agronomy institute on the outskirts of the city, where we joined a thousand other travelers on gym mats in the auditorium. The line to the dining hall at dinner was almost a kilometer long, but moved as fast as an assembly line.

Deciding to put revolution before tourism, Shuanggen and I bought a stack of blank paper for copying dazibao, and visited Wuhan's two big universities—Hubei University, in downtown Wuchang, and Wuhan University, whose majestic wooded campus sprawled over a suburban hillside. We stud-

On the Road

145

ied the salacious details of the crimes of Hubei province's top officials. One poster accused the provincial Party secretary of having illicit relations with a famous acrobat whose body was so flexible that she could coil up like a snake.

When our wrists ached, we went to the Yangtze River Bridge and gazed down at the junks and steamers. This had been the first bridge built over the Yangtze, with the help of Soviet engineers. It connected two rocky hills on either side of the river, one called Turtle, the other Snake. Another line of Chairman Mao's poem "Swimming" described the scene: "Turtle and Snake are tranquil, winds move the sails."

From Wuhan, we would head for subtropical Guangzhou in the far South. I was looking forward to eating bananas and pineapples. So were throngs of other Red Guards who waited on the railway platform for the Beijing–Guangzhou express. The train arrived two hours late, and so full that people had to use the windows to get on and off. Shuanggen boosted me through a window, and I pulled him in after me.

The air inside the car was warm and stale. Red Guards occupied every available space. Besides filling the seats, they sat on each other's laps, on the backs of the seats, and on the small tables that divided pairs of seats. Some squatted in the aisles, others lay on the luggage racks, and still others had squeezed into the lavatories. Shuanggen and I found ourselves sandwiched among several youths, one of whom had very bad breath. The conductor could not lock the door because people were standing on the steps. In addition, one boy had climbed to the top of the train and was refusing to descend. Police finally coaxed him down.

The train began to pull out of the station with an earsplitting screech, and immediately halted again. "Comrade passengers, little generals of the Red Guards," came a voice over the loudspeakers, "our train is much too overloaded. We hope some comrades will take the interests of everyone into account and catch the next train." The train attendants were unlocking the doors, but nobody was getting off. Everybody seemed to be waiting for somebody else. "Comrades, our great leader Chairman Mao teaches us to learn from Dr. Norman Bethune's Communist spirit, to be utterly devoted to others with no thought of ourselves. We should implement Chairman Mao's teachings, take hardships upon ourselves, and make things easy for others." Shuanggen and I looked at each other. This would not be a very comfortable ride. We edged out the door. Others were leaving too, crowding the platform again. At last, the train coughed and puffed out of the station.

The next train to Guangzhou left at midnight and probably would be equally crowded. We decided to take a boat down the Yangtze to Nanjing instead. We rode the ferry from Wuchang to the Hankou docks and got two free boat tickets.

Boarding the brightly lit *East-Is-Red No. Three* that evening, we discovered that our tickets were not the same. I had a third-class berth, while Shuanggen was in fifth class, down in steerage. My cabin had eight bunks that under ordinary circumstances would accommodate sixteen people. At least three times that many were there. I would have to share my lower bunk with a young couple who had arrived first. Still, the boat was far more comfortable than the train.

I left my bedroll at the foot of the bunk and went down to the steerage section. Hundreds of people lay on straw mattresses on the floor. The air smelled of fish mingled with sweat. Shuanggen did not mind; he was happy to have room to stretch out.

When I returned to my cabin, I found the young couple

had fallen asleep in each other's arms, leaving me no space. I spread my quilt on the floor by the bunk and went to sleep to the sound of the river smashing against the boat.

We spent most of the next day gazing at the scenery along the river from the main deck. The following day at dawn, our boat glided up to the Nanjing piers. The river here was broad and flat. The current, like a soldier tired after several days on a forced march, had slowed to a gentle eastward roll.

After reporting to our living quarters, a classroom at a primary school, we went to Nanjing University to read more dazibao. The villains here were the Party secretary of Jiangsu Province, who was accused of running a revisionist, anti-Party clique dubbed the Cool Summer Night Enjoyment Club, and the mayor of Nanjing, who was said to belong to the club. The members reportedly gathered at night to chit-chat, drink, and play cards. Red Guards from Beijing and Tianjin rode across the campus and through downtown in commandeered trucks installed with loudspeakers, encouraging the local Red Guards to overthrow the Provincial and Municipal Party Committees. Chiang Kai-shek's former presidential palace, now the seat of the provincial government, was overrun with Red Guards.

Our first sightseeing stop was the mausoleum of the leader of the 1911 Republican Revolution, Dr. Sun Yat-sen. The hall sat on a hilltop, reached by a long flight of steps. Looking up at the domed ceiling, I was surprised to see that nobody had covered up the emblem of the Kuomintang flag, a white sun on a blue background. It seemed that the Cultural Revolution had stopped at a pavilion halfway down the hill. Graffiti objecting to the care lavished on the memory of a Kuomintang leader covered the pavilion's marble walls. "Why is this tomb kept so majestic and resplendent, while tens of thousands of revolutionary martyrs killed by the Kuomintang at Rain Flower Terrace lie in the mud?" one commentator demanded.

Rain Flower Terrace, outside Nanjing's south gate, was our next stop. Maple trees in the scarlet of late autumn covered the stretch of gentle hills. The Kuomintang had executed more than two hundred thousand Communists and Communist sympathizers here. Four stone walls marked the spots where Chiang Kai-shek's firing squads had shot revolutionaries en masse. Posters strung from the trees accused the Provincial Party Committee of neglecting the site and called for the committee's overthrow.

As we followed a narrow path through the trees, we came across many people crouching on the ground hunting for "rain flower pebbles"—translucent stones of many colors, which according to local legend fell from the sky with the rain. It was said that every house in Nanjing had at least one bowl of these pebbles. Premier Zhou had dug pebbles for relaxation when he was in Nanjing negotiating with the Kuomintang in the late 1940's. These days, Red Guards used them to form slogans and designs on the hillsides. One person had written a poem in pebbles, about maple trees dyed red with martyrs' blood. Shuanggen and I dug some pebbles for ourselves and took them back to the primary school.

A group of middle-school students from Beijing was staying at the same school. One evening, one of them advised us to visit as many cities as possible before it was too late, because the Central Cultural Revolution Group had issued a new directive ending chuanlian by train and boat. Nobody else had heard of such a decision, but he insisted it was so.

"What a stinking instruction!" I could not help saying. The boy grabbed my jacket. "What did you say? Did you say the instruction from the center is a stinking instruction?" he de-

On the Road

manded. "Beat him, beat him!" some of his friends chanted. "He dares to smear the Central Committee!"

Shuanggen bravely challenged them. "You can't beat him! He's from a lower-middle peasant family."

The Beijing youth gave me a push before letting go of my jacket. When he and his friends had left, another Beijing student warned me to be more careful, because the same gang had beaten a boy to death for saying something that they considered counterrevolutionary. Shuanggen and I decided to leave for Shanghai the next day. To our dismay, however, the number of people on chuanlian had grown so astronomical that we could only get tickets for a week later. We roamed both the train station and the port looking for people who might want to trade tickets. Everyone we encountered was as eager as we were to head for new destinations.

Shuanggen suggested that we join the lines of Red Guards waiting to board the trains anyway. "There are so many people waiting that the ticket inspectors can't possibly check them all," he said. "We may be lucky enough to get on." I was dubious about the plan. Red Guards were supposed to conduct themselves well. It would be embarrassing if we got caught. Shuanggen told me not to be so timid. "You have to use these tricks when you travel so far from home," he said.

So we joined the long line for the train to Shanghai. We waited and waited. Feeling restless, I asked Shuanggen to hold my place and went out to the plaza, where Red Guards were trading Chairman Mao badges. One youngster was offering a large golden badge for two small ones. Excitedly, I traded him the two badges I had gotten in Beijing. Now I had a big one as well as the small one Chairman Deng had obtained. Walking among the haggling dealers, I stopped to admire a new design, consisting of a small red badge inlaid on a five-pointed gold star. The owner wanted ten small badges for it, an impossibility for me.

When I returned to the line, Shuanggen greeted me with an angry look. When I told him that I had been trading Chairman Mao badges, he got even angrier. "You're such a burden," he said. "It would be much easier to chuanlian by myself." I was taken aback. In all our days together, we had not argued once. "When did I ever depend on you?" I asked, forgetting for a moment that he had saved me from a beating the previous day. Shuanggen answered, "Fine. If you don't need me, I don't need you either. I'm going by myself."

"Here." I took one of the blank letters of introduction out of my diary. "Fill this in yourself and go wherever you want." Shuanggen took the letter and left without looking back. He vanished into the crowds. My pride prevented me from running after him. From now on, I would have to get along by myself.

The line finally began to move. I held out my ticket with the date facing down. The inspector did not even look at it. Waiting on the track was a freight train so long that I could not see the end of it. I clambered into a boxcar, sat down on the floor, and leaned against my bedroll, feeling terribly weary. The steel door slid shut, throwing the car into darkness. The train began to move. It stopped irregularly during the night to make way for passenger trains. At each stop, boys and girls would jump down from the cars to relieve themselves on the railroad tracks.

We reached Shanghai early in the morning. I joined the flow of people along Nanjing Road. The gray, smog-stained buildings that rose so high on both sides of the street made me feel that I was walking through a deep canyon. Dazibao in the street denounced the mayor and Party secretary as

On the Road

151

counterrevolutionary revisionists and capitalist-roaders. One poster reported that workers had hijacked a train to Beijing to complain about the municipal leaders. Other workers had stopped the train by lying down on the tracks. A fight had ensued and several people had been killed.

At the foot of Nanjing Road, I stood on the bund overlooking the Huangpu River and watched the ships in the port that foreign warships had once controlled. Over the next few days, I crisscrossed the city with my free bus pass, visiting factories and exhibition halls.

My accommodations in Shanghai were high-class compared with the other places I had stayed. I shared a room at a public security station with students from Tianjin and a teacher from Jiangsu province. We had real beds, and each one of us even had a nightstand with a drawer.

One evening, the teacher asked me if I had any Chairman Mao badges to trade. He showed me a badge he had just acquired. It was just like the one I had admired at the Nanjing railway station. He wanted five small red badges or two gold ones for it. I told him that I only had the small red one I was wearing and a gold one. I opened the drawer of my nightstand to get the cloth bundle that contained most of my money and grain coupons, and unpinned my gold badge from the cloth. I had heard Shanghai had a lot of pickpockets, so I did not carry my valuables on the street. After examining the gold badge, the teacher agreed to trade. My collection now consisted of one five-pointed star badge. It seemed like a good deal, even though the star's edges were a bit worn and Chairman Mao's face was scratched.

Two days later, I planned to go downtown to buy some cheap radio parts. When I took out my cloth bundle, I was stupefied to find my money and grain coupons gone. Stolen, right here at a public security station! I did not know what to do. I needed the money to continue my trip. I needed to eat. I went to the people in charge of receiving Red Guards at the station, but all they could offer me were some comforting words and a few days of free meals.

My Tianjin roommates came back after dark, but the teacher from Jiangsu province did not return, although his cotton-padded jacket was still on his bed. It brought to mind one of the Thirty-Six Stratagems, "Leave the molting cicada's shell behind." Late that night, one of the Tianjin students offered to go with me to the railway station to look for the man. We picked our way through the crowds, knowing that we would never find the thief.

I already had my ticket for scenic Guilin and had planned to visit Hangzhou and Guangzhou on the way. The student from Tianjin told me that many Red Guards were traveling without spending a single penny of their own. They borrowed money from the local government wherever they went. They did not even carry quilts, knowing that the Red Guard centers would take care of whatever they needed. There was no reason to abandon my trip.

I decided to follow his advice. Then word came of a new directive ending free transportation for chuanlian. That Beijing Red Guard who had almost beaten me up in Nanjing had been right. The directive said that Red Guards would only get tickets to return home, with no stopovers allowed on the way. It also encouraged chuanlian on foot, in the style of the Long March. Reception stations would continue to function for the long-marchers. I would have to go home like everybody else. The public security station people gave me bread for two days and a letter explaining that my money had been stolen.

On the Road

I took a passenger train to Nanjing, took a ferry across the Yangtze to Pukou, and rode in a boxcar as far as Dezhou, a small city where I could transfer for Shimen. It was late afternoon, with gloomy skies and a cold wind. The train to Shimen would not come through until morning.

The waiting room in the small railway station was full of dusty peasants. All the benches were occupied with people staring blankly or sleeping. All of a sudden, a large group of schoolchildren burst in with flags, gongs, and drums, and turned the center of the room into a stage. They performed a short opera called *Don't Forget Past Bitterness*. A little boy wearing a skullcap and robe played the landlord, a little girl in tattered clothing the peasant maiden. The landlord beat the maiden with a whip, and she sang mournfully, tears flowing down her cheeks. At the end, rebellious peasants knocked the landlord down on the floor and shook their fists at him. Then, as swiftly as they had arrived, the children filed out.

Feeling chilled and lonely, I undid my bedroll and spread my quilt on the floor in a corner where a stove was sending out some warmth.

Rocks Down the Well

It was morning when I walked into the courtyard in Lingzhi. Meiyuan sat at the doorway, pumping the bellows on the coal stove and singing a revolutionary song. She welcomed me with a scream that brought Zhihua and Xinghua out. Setting my grimy bedroll down in the courtyard, I entered the house. An object that resembled a balloon was hanging under the eaves. Meiyuan explained that it was a pig bladder filled with yellow wine and millet, prescribed by an herbal doctor to cure Zhihua and Xinghua of bed-wetting. They had to drink the wine and then roast and eat the bladder. They already had been through several, and the remedy seemed to be working.

Other than that good development, all the news at home was bad. Grandpa's health had so deteriorated that he was too sick to leave the kang, so my little sister Yiyuan was staying with Mama and the three other children were cooking their own meals. Their curriculum at primary school had dwindled to the study of Chairman Mao's three most-read articles, "Serve the People," "The Foolish Old Man Who Removed the Mountains," and "In Memory of Norman Bethune." Worst of all, the attack on Papa had grown fiercer, and Mama had been dragged in as well.

Papa's supporters had fled, given in, or defected to the opposition. Even Papa's aide, Qin Mao, had turned against him in a brazen display of ingratitude. Just a few years earlier, Qin Mao had been herding cows in a poor mountain village when Papa met him on an inspection tour. Papa had liked this honest, hard-working cowherd so much that he had arranged work for him in the county government. Now Qin Mao had written a poster claiming that Papa worked him like a serf in the old society. As an example, Qin Mao said that he had emptied Papa's chamber pot. He failed to mention that he had done so only once, and this of his own free will, at a time when Papa was ill.

My younger brothers described how the Thought Guards

had paraded a hundred cadres through the streets of Lingzhi, the vice-head of the prefecture in the lead, Papa second, and others behind according to rank, all the way down to the head of Lingzhi's peasant militia. The Thought Guards had dressed the highest cadres in official robes and caps seized from the county opera troupe and made everybody walk with his hands raised in surrender to the revolutionary rebels. Near the end of the procession walked Mama, her hands over her head.

The Ism Guards had fallen apart, some leaders running into the mountains and others surrendering to the Thought Guards. As for Papa's colleagues, most were concerned with protecting themselves. Papa's second in command, Mo Yin, a man known to bend like a blade of grass with the prevailing political winds, was cooperating with the Thought Guards. It was just like the old saying, "You fall down a well, only to have people throw rocks after you."

Papa was no longer acting Party secretary of the county. The actual secretary, after returning from his Four Cleanups assignment in another county, had used a clever ruse to fend off would-be critics. Since the secretary was also chief political commissar of the local Military Department, in accordance with Chairman Mao's principle that "the party commands the gun," he merely put on an army uniform, which scared the rebel students away.

Mama and Papa now lived in a single room at the county government headquarters because the Thought Guards had expropriated their three-room flat. I wanted to see Papa, but my brothers said I should wait until evening, since the Thought Guards kept him busy during the day.

I wandered through Lingzhi reading the tirade against

Papa: "Burn Mountain Devil!" "Shoot Mountain Devil!" "Bury Mountain Devil alive!" "Boil Mountain Devil in oil!" I walked all the way to the middle school and found it deserted. The dazibao covering the walls were faded and peeling. Almost all the windows were broken, and shattered glass littered the ground. A small boy who seemed to be the only person around told me that the Thought Guards had moved to the County Party Committee compound.

On my way back home, I saw a procession coming up the street. I felt sure that Papa must be among the men walking at the front with their heads bowed. As they came closer, I saw that the man at the lead was Mo Yin, Papa's vice–county head. The throng of people yelling slogans behind him were not middle-school students; they were members of Four Cleanups teams rebelling against their leaders. Mo Yin had helped supervise the Four Cleanups in Lingzhi county. The Cultural Revolution had been going on for half a year already, and these people were still preoccupied with the previous movement.

At dusk, I went to the government courtyard to find Papa. He was sitting at a desk in a sparsely furnished room reading the *People's Daily*. A cotton-padded coat was draped over his narrow shoulders. He was wearing reading glasses, which I had never seen him use before. He turned when I called. His face was as stern as always. "Jianhua, you're back. Is Weihua back too?"

"No, we didn't travel together. I went with a classmate, and we had a quarrel and separated. I came back alone."

"You should not break off with your companions. Unity is always better than division."

"Where's Mama?"

Rocks Down the Well

157

"She and Yiyuan went to visit a friend. They'll be back soon. She's under a lot of pressure these days, so I encourage her to go out and relax."

Papa lifted his long-stemmed peasant pipe from the desk, packed it with tobacco, and lit it. He drew forcefully and the pipe glowed. He breathed smoke out his nostrils. "That was an interesting letter you wrote to Comrade Gao Shangui," he said. "Your mother was outraged that you addressed me as Comrade." For a fleeting moment, his lips seemed to curl in amusement.

"Excuse me, Papa, I thought the letter might get intercepted. Thank you for your response. It came just before I left on chuanlian."

A box labeled *die da wan*—herbal pills for injuries from falls, fractures, contusions, and sprains—was sitting on the desk. "I hear they're harassing you a lot. Are you injured?" I asked.

"Nothing serious. Nothing compared to what we experienced during the Anti-Japanese War. However, I feel uneasy about the methods these people use, knocking down everyone in power no matter what kind of person he is. It can't be what the Central Committee meant. The Sixteen Points make it very clear that the majority of cadres are good or comparatively good. We can't all be capitalist-roaders."

"Did they force you to admit to being a capitalist-roader?"

"They tried to, and I told them I am not one. I am sure of myself on this point. I cannot yield. Rebels from the communes came to me to demand that I dismiss their leaders, and I told them I cannot do that either. The county government appointed those leaders. I can't recall them on my own. But these people don't believe me."

Rocks Down the Well

"How can they be so unreasonable? Papa, I think you should leave this county for the time being. You can go back to Shuiyuan, where your old guerrilla comrades will protect you. Or you can go back to Yizhen, where you are still considered a revolutionary cadre."

"Jianhua, I'm not crazy about being an official. But the state assigned me here and I have to do my job. I can't desert my post."

"Why can't you resign? In feudal society, when officials fell from favor, they simply took off their caps and went home to become ordinary villagers. If feudal officials have such freedom, why don't Communist cadres in a socialist society?"

"There is quite a difference between us Communist cadres and those feudal officials. Our aim is to serve the people. As Chairman Mao said, we are like seeds, to be sown among the masses, to draw sustenance from the masses, to take root, blossom, and bear fruit among the masses. We should welcome criticism from the people and correct our errors. We can't run away. I am prepared to be tempered in this furnace. In the end, everything will be clarified—good from bad, white from black, truth from falsehood."

How stubborn Papa was! All his life, he had devoted himself to the revolution, even to the neglect of his family. What had he gotten in return? Curses, misunderstanding, and maltreatment. I wanted to cry out: "Papa, for your sake and ours, you can't go on like this!" But when I looked at Papa's weathered face and met his resolute eyes, the words froze on my lips.

Rocks Down the Well

A Long March, by Hook
or Crook

The bare winter trees seemed to have taken command of Yizhong. Not a soul was in sight as I walked through the half-destroyed marble entrance. I found only three of my classmates on campus—the tomboy Huantian; the dark-skinned, curly-haired Nkrumah, so nicknamed after the president of Ghana had visited Beijing; and Delta, named for the Greek letter we had learned in algebra because of the triangular shape of his eyes. They were in a dormitory room cooking sliced sweet potatoes on top of a stove. The others in class 85 were either on chaunlian or at home.

These three all came from upper-middle-peasant backgrounds. Nobody had wanted to travel with them, and they were afraid of meeting trouble if they went alone. I chided them for their cowardice and offered to go on chuanlian with them if they were willing to go on foot. Three pairs of eyes lit up with excitement. We decided to set out the next day for Beijing, since they had been excluded from our school trip there.

I repeated what the Tianjin student had told me after I had been robbed: we did not need to take our quilts because the reception centers would provide bedding, and we could borrow money and grain coupons from local governments along the way. It turned out that we would not have to borrow. A new directive made long-marchers eligible for an allowance of four mao a day. Chairman Deng gave us a letter of introduction and twelve yuan apiece, enough to last 30 days.

Weihua returned to school that night with a trophy from the South, a large bag of glutinous rice. Unable to resist buying it when he saw it selling so cheaply in Chengdu, the capital of Sichuan province, he had carried it for thousands of kilometers. This type of sticky rice was hard to find in the North. It was a main ingredient in both *babao fan*, eight-jewel pudding, a concoction with nuts and dried fruit eaten on the eighth day of the twelfth lunar month, and *zongzi*, dumplings wrapped in bamboo leaves or reeds made during the Dragon Boat Festival in the fifth lunar month. He would bring the bag to Lingzhi to cheer up the family.

Our long-march team of four started out before dawn, walking alongside the railroad tracks that led to Beijing. Huantian set a vigorous pace in front, holding a flag on a bamboo pole. Several times an hour, the headlights of a locomotive illuminated the endless track. The train would speed by with a tremendous clatter, and we would edge farther from the tracks to avoid being sucked under the wheels. Then it would recede, leaving behind the sound of our flag snapping briskly in the breeze.

The sun rose, tinting the wheatfields orange. Now that we were visible, from time to time a mischievous engineer would engulf us in a burst of locomotive steam. We stopped for breakfast at a small station and then continued on even more energetically. By midafternoon, we had covered 30 kilometers. But difficulties now arose. Delta was tired. Nkrumah's feet ached. They began to talk about hitching a ride. Huantian and I convinced them to go a bit farther. By evening, everybody was exhausted. When we saw some other Red

Guards scrambling onto the back of a truck at a station cross-ing, we joined them with a cheer.

The truck went only as far as the next station, and we found ourselves on foot again, this time in the dark. Three glum faces turned to me for a solution. I told Huantian to furl the long-march flag. We would catch the night train and be in Beijing by tomorrow morning. No need to worry about the expense; there were ways to get on a train without paying the fare, and the conductors seldom checked tickets at night. If a conductor came by, we could hide in the lavatory.

We boarded holding two-mao tickets for the next station. After several hours went by and no conductor had shown up, we relaxed and fell asleep. Early in the morning, we got off at a freight station in the southwest of Beijing, which was safer than trying to pass by the ticket inspectors at the main railway station. We walked in the direction of downtown. Street sweepers wielding twig brooms raised clouds of dust beneath the yellow street lamps. Joggers and shadowboxers came out. Shops began to open as bicycles and buses filled the streets.

A policeman directed us to the Red Guard reception center at a stadium on the south side of the city. Masses of young people were waiting in long lines that snaked through the stadium and several temporary buildings. Fellow long-march-ers told us that more Red Guards than ever were pouring into the capital, despite the end to free transportation for chuan-lian. So overtaxed were the reception centers, it was said, that Premier Zhou had vacated his own house to put up Red Guards. The latest rule was that visitors could stay in Beijing no more than a week. Furthermore, only those who came on foot would be received. Our letter of introduction posed a problem. It was dated December 1, just two days earlier. The

A Long March, by Hook or Crook

receptionists would never believe that we were as fleet-footed as the rebel messenger Dai Zong in the novel *Water Margin*, who could cover 400 kilometers in a day. If we got turned away, we would have no place to stay. We decided that our only way out was to alter the date on the letter. This was not hard to do, because the numbers were written in old Chinese style instead of Roman numerals. I used my pocket knife to scrape off one of the strokes in the number 12, for December, changing it to 11, for November. I added a few strokes to change the 1 to 21.

The letter passed scrutiny. We got free bus passes and were assigned to stay at the Philosophy Institute of the Chinese Academy of Social Sciences. We shared a room with fifteen other students. We needed neither quilts nor money nor grain coupons; the wheat-stalk mattresses were covered with clean sheets and new yellow blankets, and the meals were free. Best of all was the People's Liberation Army soldier assigned to our room, a friendly northeasterner, tall as a basketball player, who had seen Chairman Mao five times. His job was to answer our questions, help us with any problems, and make sure we left after one week.

We took the bus to Tiananmen Square. Beijing looked more revolutionary than it had four months ago. Billboards with Chairman Mao's quotations dominated the downtown street corners. Tall red characters reading "Long Live Chairman Mao" had sprouted atop office buildings and department stores. Many storefronts had fresh coats of red paint, and red flags flew everywhere.

Peeling slogans covered the reviewing stand in front of Tiananmen Gate, the balustrades of the Golden Water Bridge, and the two giant stone lions standing guard before the gate. "Smash the bourgeois headquarters inside the Party!" they

A Long March, by Hook or Crook

proclaimed. "Down with Liu, Deng, and Tao!" The surnames referred to Liu Shaoqi, the head of state; Deng Xiaoping, secretary-general of the Central Committee Secretariat; and Tao Zhu, a vice-premier. All three names were covered by red X's. How bold the Beijing rebels were to aim so high!

High-ranking leaders were under attack all over the capital. In some places, the rebels would march them out on a regular schedule for the benefit of out-of-town visitors. We went to the Central Communist Youth League headquarters for a look at the disgraced "two Hu's"—Hu Yaobang, secretary-general of the Youth League, and Hu Keshi, his assistant. Red Guards displayed them on a third-floor balcony every quarter-hour.

Beijing's Red Guards had split into three main organizations, each of which published its own tabloid newspaper. These papers were full of sensational stories about the decadent lives of high cadres. One regional Party secretary was said to dine on all sorts of delicacies, and Red Guards who searched his home had found four ox penises on the chopping board.

With free food, lodging, and transportation, my three comrades and I could afford to spend a few fen on a Red Guard paper whenever we liked. We also could afford snacks and souvenirs. Each of us bought a green cap and green canvas belt, for the fashionable military look. We bought Chairman Mao photos to exchange for more badges. We bought pigs' and goats' feet, ate them on the bus, and dropped the bones under our seats. We even spent eight mao apiece to have our pictures taken in front of Tiananmen Gate. The soldier in our room lent us his greatcoat to pose in. We also spent hours browsing through the department stores and saw a television set for the first time.

A Long March, by Hook or Crook

We were living an extravagant lifestyle at the Philosophy Institute. Since nobody had to pay for food, people often took more than they could eat. The dining hall floor would be strewn with leftovers at the end of each meal. One day, a poster appeared criticizing this waste. The poster said that we should learn from Premier Zhou, who ate steamed bread and stir-fried cabbage in the staff dining hall at the Great Hall of the People, and then poured hot water into his bowl and drank the thin soup. The situation improved dramatically after that.

Our roommates came from all over the country. They included several students from Guangdong province, who ran outside in amazement when a light snow fell over Beijing. There also were a few students from Inner Mongolia who disgusted the rest of us with their nightly hunt through their clothes for lice.

A week passed quickly. The four of us were given one-way tickets printed with the destination Shimen. We asked the soldier to help us stay, but he said he could not. We debated: should we go home by train, continue our long march on foot, or find a way to stay in Beijing? My comrades and I agreed that the last course was best. After the soldier escorted us to the train station, we returned to the Red Guard reception center and presented our letter of introduction again.

The ruse worked. This time, we were assigned to stay at the Beijing Children's Palace, behind Coal Hill Park. We discovered that the former coach of the world ping-pong champion Zhuang Zedong lived there. He played ping-pong with us at the very table where Zhuang Zedong had trained.

The food at the Children's Palace was delicious. The kitchen gave us free food coupons printed on green paper, which we turned in for meals. If we wanted seconds, we had to pay. Delta quickly figured out how to get seconds for free, using slips of plain green paper. You put a real coupon on top and a phony one underneath with just the edge showing, and told the server you were getting food for a friend. Nobody ever checked.

We put our bus passes to as much use as possible. We had a competition going to see who could ride all of the city's fifty-odd bus routes first. Often I would go out by myself in the evening, get on a bus, ride all the way to the last stop, change to another route, and so on, until it was very late. Sometimes I would fall asleep and the ticket-seller would wake me up at the terminal.

We investigated whenever we saw Red Guards conversing in little groups, for usually they were trading Chairman Mao badges. We accumulated the newest designs depicting revolutionary landmarks—Chairman Mao's birthplace, Shaoshan; the Jinggang Mountains, where the Communist Party had set up its base after Chiang Kai-shek's massacre in 1927; Zunyi, the site of a crucial Central Committee meeting during the Long March; and Yanan, the base area from the end of the Long March to the eve of Liberation.

The Red Guard newspapers kept us apprised of current events. Beijing rebels had captured Head of State Liu Shaoqi and his wife Wang Guangmei by holding their children hostage. "Red Guards Catch Liu Shaoqi by Stratagem" one headline read. We also picked up mimeographed copies of Chairman Mao's unpublished poems. One written to Wang Guangmei asked why she had erected a giant tombstone for her capitalist father, Wang Huaiqing.

The second week passed faster than the first. Again we were given tickets for Shimen and were escorted to the station. This soldier did not leave until we had boarded a southbound express. The train was no less crowded than the others I had been on. Delta and Huantian managed to squeeze onto a seat, while Nkrumah and I lay on the luggage rack, tied down with our belts so we would not fall out in our sleep. The train was bound for Guangzhou, and Huantian and Nkrumah agreed with me that it was too good an opportunity to pass up. We would go all the way, regardless of what our tickets said. Delta wanted to get off at Shimen but could not push his way to the door fast enough; so he ended up going too, against his will.

We had only a few yuan left. Our mouths watered at the sight of the roast chicken, fermented beancurd, and other local foods that vendors were selling on the station platforms. But we could not afford them and had to make do with cheap, crumbly cakes and boiled water.

We arrived in Guangzhou around midnight, three days and three nights after leaving Beijing. As we filed out of the station, sweating in the warm, humid air, we dropped our tickets for Shimen into a box as if we were Red Guards returning home. Anybody could have told by our padded clothes that we were northerners, but nobody bothered to look. The reception center did not question our claim to be long-marchers and assigned us to a building in downtown Guangzhou. We used our remaining money to buy bananas. We visited the municipal government office that dealt with Red Guard affairs to ask for a loan, only to find a crowd of other Red Guards with the same idea. The man in charge was giving nothing away. All we got were four tickets to the Guangzhou Trade Fair. We did not worry, however, since our lodging and food were free here too.

It was exciting to walk around Guangzhou just after dark, when local people did their shopping and dined out. We

A Long March, by Hook or Crook

167

peered into all the restaurant windows and read the menus. It was said that people here would eat anything with four legs except a table, and anything with two wings except an airplane. Some restaurants had terrariums full of live snakes and jars full of dried mice on display. Others offered the famous monkey brains, served at a special table that locked the monkey's head in place; the waiter would open the skull and the diners would eat while the body wriggled under the table.

In front of a department store by the Pearl River, we found a brisk night market in Chairman Mao badges. We held up packs of Chairman Mao photos and shouted: "Ten photos for one Jinggang Mountain badge! Ten photos for one Yanan badge!" Suddenly, we found ourselves surrounded by five youths who were wearing sunglasses even though it was dark. They snatched our photos, ripped them up, and scattered the pieces. "Those are pictures of Chairman Mao!" I protested. "How dare you tear them up! Counterrevolutionaries!" One of them knocked me down with a punch to the chest. Nkrumah and Huantian tried to help me up but got pushed down too. The buzz of bartering around us subsided for a few moments, but nobody came to our assistance. We started running. The youths chased us all the way to the bus stop, yelling curses in Cantonese. We leapt onto a bus and the doors closed behind us. It was time to leave Guangzhou.

Unfortunately, the Central Cultural Revolution Group had just issued a new document suspending the distribution of one-way tickets home. Red Guards who had set out on chuanlian by train were supposed to be home by now, and those who had set out on foot could get home on foot. We could not possibly buy return tickets, for we had spent our last fen on bananas. Without money, we could not even get a platform ticket to sneak back into the Guangzhou railway station. As for walking, we were more than two thousand kilometers from home. Delta began to cry.

After studying a map, we headed for a small train station on the city outskirts. We walked from the fields right onto the platform and boarded the first train that came through, a local full of peasants. Although we had taken off our red armbands to avoid attracting attention, one young woman attendant kept staring at us. She began to check tickets. We were caught, turned over to the head of the train crew, and evicted at the next stop. Rice paddies stretched all around us. We had not even left Guangdong province.

We decided to wait until dark and try to sneak onto a freight train. While my comrades napped in the waiting room, I wandered among the shops and stalls by the station, eyeing the heaps of fruits, nuts, and dried fish. I found the fish especially tempting. We had left Guangzhou with just two lunch tins of cold rice and a few steamed buns from the place we had stayed. Fish would be just the thing to round out the meal. The shopkeeper turned his back momentarily. My hand seemed to take on a life of its own, snatching two dried fish and shrinking back into my sleeve. I walked slowly back to the waiting room and put the fish into one of the lunch tins. My heart was pounding. I had never before stolen anything.

I awoke from a deep sleep to the sight of a policeman standing over me. I thought he had come to arrest me for stealing the fish. But he merely wanted to kick the four of us out of the waiting room. Perhaps he thought we were pickpockets. We argued that we were not bad people, but he insisted. We wandered out into the darkness.

Numerous trains chugged through the station without stopping. At last a freight train came to a stop. We hoisted each other into a low, open car and found ourselves sitting on

A Long March, by Hook or Crook

a thick carpet of coal dust. The next car looked cleaner, so we decided to move there. Huantian and I were still on the coupling when the brakes of the train released with a long hiss and the cars began to move. With Nkrumah and Delta holding onto Huantian's arms, I boosted her in, then struggled against the rushing air to climb in after her. The four of us rolled together on the floor of the car and laughed hysterically in the moonlight.

It was cold, a reminder that we were returning to midwinter. We huddled together in one corner of the car. The train stopped irregularly, sometimes for long periods. Maintenance inspectors would come along and hammer under all the cars, setting our heads to ringing. In the morning, we awoke to find ourselves blanketed by a light dusting of snow. Our faces were black with coal dust. We stretched our stiff bodies and took out our lunch tins. What a treat it was to have fish with our rice! I admitted my theft to the others, and they commended me.

The second night was even worse. We wrapped our faces in our towels and tucked our hands into our sleeves. Hunger and cold kept us awake. In the morning, I found my right hand stuck in a half-curled position. I tried to straighten the fingers with my left hand, but they curled up again like a chicken's foot. Delta said I must have contracted "chicken-claw madness," a disease that a man in his village had.

Soon after, the train stopped again, and we sat for a couple of hours. We were about to get up and look around when we felt a hammer striking the wheels right beneath us. A hand, a blue cap, and a weathered face appeared over the edge of our car. We were sure this railway worker would march us to the nearest public security station. However, he merely advised us to get off. As we clambered out, we realized that our car was one of five sitting on a railroad spur. The locomotive had abandoned us and disappeared.

The worker had not spoken in Cantonese, a good sign that we were out of Guangdong province. We learned that we were in Hunan, still only a third of the way back to Beijing. This was a small station on a feeder line, twenty kilometers from the Beijing–Guangzhou railway. We made a forced march to the nearest station on the main line, where the head of a freight-train crew, a sympathetic northerner, agreed to take us to the next big station. We sneaked onto several passenger trains in succession. Each time we were discovered and kicked off, we consoled ourselves with the knowledge that we were closer to Beijing.

Early in the morning, we arrived in Changsha, the capital of Hunan. Chairman Mao's birthplace, Shaoshan, was not far from here. It was a good place to leave the railroad for rest and revolutionary sightseeing. The Red Guard reception center sent us to the Hunan provincial stadium. Our first meal there, good white rice, stewed beef, and Hunan pickles, was the best food I had ever tasted in my life. We slept on the stadium floor for a full day and night without waking up. Then I reported to the stadium clinic with my chicken-claw hand. The doctor prescribed acupuncture and infrared treatment.

Changsha was full of landmarks of Chairman Mao's youth. We visited the teachers' college where he had studied, and saw the well where he had doused himself with cold water every morning. We took a ferry to Orange Islet in the middle of the Xiang River, which he had referred to in one of his poems. We would have gone to Shaoshan if we had had the money for bus fare. Instead, we settled for Shaoshan badges acquired at the local badge-trading spot.

A Long March, by Hook or Crook

We were in Changsha on Chairman Mao's seventy-third birthday, December 26. The stadium dining hall served noodles in celebration of his longevity—in spite of a Central Committee resolution, adopted just after Liberation, that said people should not celebrate leaders' birthdays.

The rules for long-marchers were changed again. Once more, Red Guards could get free tickets home to rejoin the struggle against the capitalist-roaders. We registered immediately for four train tickets to Shimen. We soon got them, but they were not direct; we would have to change in Wuhan.

We arrived in Hankou at midnight on the last day of 1966, penniless and hungry. The next train for Shimen was the following afternoon. Leaving my three companions sitting on the waiting room floor, I bravely set out alone for the Municipal Party Committee headquarters to beg for some help. An official there put me to bed in a room with other Red Guards. The next morning, he gave me breakfast, eight yuan, and eight jin worth of grain coupons.

Elated, I took a bus back to the railway station. My comrades were not in the waiting room. I spotted them on the sidewalk talking to a policeman. Delta was showing the policeman a Jinggang Mountain badge and saying, "We haven't eaten for a day. Please trade us a little money and a few grain coupons for this badge. Normally it's worth ten or twelve small badges." The policeman led them into a restaurant and ordered three bowls of noodles. I appeared at the table. Proudly, I offered to repay the policeman for the food. He refused. I unpinned my prized golden Chairman Mao badge from my chest and insisted he take it.

A Long March, by Hook or Crook

Spring Festival Visitors

North China peasants had a ditty about Counting Nine, the nine periods of nine days each that followed the winter solstice.

> In the first and second Nine Days,
> The cold makes you tuck your hands into your sleeves.
> In the third and fourth Nine Days,
> You can walk on the firm ice.
> In the fifth and sixth Nine Days,
> You go to the river to see the willow buds.
> In the seventh Nine Days rivers thaw,
> In the eighth Nine Days geese fly back.
> During the nine days of the ninth Nine Days,
> The oxen plow the fields.

It was midway through Counting Nine when I returned from the South. Huantian, Nkrumah, and Delta went home to their villages, and I went to Lingzhi to join my family for Spring Festival, the lunar new year. The town was preparing for the ancient holiday as it always had. Regardless of the campaign to smash the Four Olds, this was one occasion that people would never give up.

On street corners all across town, white steam rose from cast-iron cauldrons two meters across as butchers sharpened their knives. People might eat gruel the rest of the year, but for Spring Festival they would have pork. "Sichuan peppercorns, clove, cinnamon, fennel, anise; stew your spring festival meat with five spices!" the spice vendors called as they ground out their fragrant brown powder.

I stopped to watch a butcher slaughter a pig. Its feet were tied tightly together and it was squealing madly. Although everyone around wore cotton-padded clothes, the butcher was shirtless, with a bloody apron tied around his waist. His face was flushed as if he had been drinking. Smiling, he forced the pig down with one knee, grasped the snout with one hand, and with the other drove his knife up to the handle into the throat. A good butcher was supposed to pierce the heart with one such deep thrust. He withdrew the knife with a swift twist. The blood flowed into a basin. Salt was added to make it coagulate faster.

The butcher cut a small opening in one of the pig's hind legs and maneuvered a long steel tube in and out beneath the pig's skin. He put his mouth at the opening and blew the pig up like a balloon. Several men heaved the pig into the cauldron for a scalding. Then the butcher shaved off its hair with a razor and chopped off its head. The headless pig was hung from a hook. He split open its belly. The intestines and everything else came out intact. Everything was cleaned. Finally, the butcher cleaved the carcass neatly in two. The two halves lay across a wheelbarrow, the flesh trembling. The butcher was drawing on a cigarette as if nothing had happened. His audience had a new appreciation of the saying "Fame portends trouble for men just as fattening does for pigs."

Several old scholars had set up calligraphy stalls in front of the county theater. For a small fee, they would produce Spring Festival couplets for peasants shopping in town. The best calligrapher was a white-goateed man with six fingers on his right hand. In past years, he had written things like "Amid the popping of firecrackers, we bid farewell to the old year; tens of thousands of households put up new peachwood charms against evil." This year, he had abandoned such superstitious nonsense for statements like "Drinking water, don't forget the one who dug the well; living in happiness, don't forget Chairman Mao" and "The spring wind turned the mountains and river green; Mao Zedong Thought turned our hearts and the country red."

Behind the calligraphers, fresh slogans adorned the theater wall: "Down with the agent of the bourgeois headquarters inside the Party, the capitalist-roader and counterrevolutionary revisionist Mountain Devil!" and "Knock the capitalist-roader to the ground, put a foot on him so he'll never get up, and let his name stink for ten thousand years!"

The rebels now charged Papa with saying that class struggle had died out, an opinion he had voiced at a meeting years before. They also charged that he had followed Liu Shaoqi, who was now known as China's Khrushchev, in pushing the capitalistic Three Frees and One Contract—private plots, free markets, independent enterprises, and household production quotas. Papa had been working in the steel plant in Shimen when that policy was adopted. He had not opposed the measures after his rehabilitation because he thought they would help tide the peasants through the Three Difficult Years.

Papa and Mama still made their home in that little room. Yiyuan told me that Red Guards from the middle school and the county government showed up at all hours to take Papa off for interrogation. Once they had come at midnight. Mama had helped Papa climb out the back window and told them that another group of rebels already had led him away. Sometimes the rebels took both Mama and Papa for questioning, leaving Yiyuan behind. She had numerous "aunties" and "uncles" now—friends who adopted her when Mama and Papa were gone.

The Thought Guards had grown even bolder. Their leader was a student called Daba, "big scar"—people said he had fallen on a rock and gashed his face while running across a field with a stolen watermelon. His followers were instigating rebellion in villages and factories all over the county and were on the verge of wresting power from the County Party Committee and government. Rebels already had grabbed the seals at the prefectural level, following the lead of rebellious workers in Shanghai who had seized power from the municipal authorities in a campaign termed the January Storm.

My younger brothers and sisters were on winter vacation. Grandpa's condition had grown still worse. Zhihua and Xinghua took care of themselves pretty well, but Meiyuan was becoming a little street urchin. In the daytime, she played outside with other little devils. In the evening, she hung around the theater, hoping to get in for a glimpse of the new revolutionary opera, *The Red Lantern*. One night, I found her near the theater playing a crude country game with her playmates. Lined up against a wall, they would squeeze toward the corner formed by another wall as they shouted, "Hey, hey, squeeze for warmth! Hey, hey, squeeze for warmth!" When the one getting squeezed into the corner could not stand it anymore, he would slip out and go to the other end of the line. Was there any stupider game in the world? Angrily, I ordered her home. The next night I found her there again, doing the same thing.

I usually brought my younger brothers firecrackers when I came home for Spring Festival, but I had no money left after my travels. I browsed through the town firecracker mart, where dealers with cartloads of explosives competed noisily for customers and even had price wars. One salesman was demonstrating his "throwing firecrackers" by tossing them against the wall of a pigsty. Another showed off his "rising fire," a rocket that hissed into the sky, leaving a blue trail, before exploding in an orange spray. A man with a distinct Yizhen accent stood on the back of a horse-drawn cart and shouted:

> One part nitrate, two of sulfur, three of charcoal,
> Firecrackers bring a new year prosperous and grand.
> Since gunpowder's invention in the Tang dynasty,
> Yizhen's firecrackers have earned fame across the land!

Another man in a cart across the way responded:

> From Nanjing you travel all the way to Beijing,
> The very best firecrackers are from Shandong!

Each man lit a long string of red firecrackers with his cigarette and held it aloft on a bamboo pole. The firecrackers crackled like machine guns, sending bits of paper and blue smoke in all directions. The smell of gunpowder filled the air. Children scrambled in the midst of the explosions, trying to trample firecrackers that had not yet ignited so they could get away with a few free samples. I was watching two particularly active boys, who had put on gloves and pulled the earflaps of their hats around their faces for protection, when I realized that they were Zhihua and Xinghua.

"Don't you know how dangerous that is?" I scolded them after the strings of firecrackers had burned out and their frenetic dance had ended. "Mama won't give us money to buy firecrackers," Zhihua said petulantly. "Sometimes she doesn't even give Grandpa enough money to buy medicine." My brothers would not be happy until they had some firecrackers. I suggested we raise some money by picking up trash in the street to sell to the salvage station. One jin of wastepaper could bring three fen. A good "two-kick" firecracker that exploded in the air cost only five fen.

Xinghua had an even better idea: we could collect the scrap metal and other junk left behind by the Thought Guards when they had smashed the classrooms at Lingzhi Middle School. We went to the school and filled two big baskets with treasures—crushed aluminum bowls, bent keys, smashed locks, tangled electrical wiring, broken light switches, tin toothpaste tubes, empty bottles—and sold everything to the salvage station for more than five yuan. We bought firecrackers, a new bottle of opium-licorice pills for Grandpa's coughing, and sesame buns with beef.

We carried on this lucrative business for quite a few days. When we had scavenged through all the ransacked buildings we could find, we began collecting paper. If people were around, we just picked up rubbish from the street. If we were alone, we would peel posters from the walls, where the paper was ten layers thick. One day, a group of Thought Guards caught us peeling away their latest pronouncements. They confiscated our baskets and pushed us down, giving Zhihua a bloody nose. That was the end of our venture.

Weihua did not come home until a few days before the lunar new year. He had left school again to make a long march to Yanan. He sent us a photograph of himself standing on the Great Wall. On the back, he had written a line of Chairman Mao's poetry: "You are not a hero until you have scaled the Great Wall." He arrived in Lingzhi looking lean and brown, with a bag of Yanan millet and a bottle of Shanxi province's famous vinegar. He spent a whole afternoon making a Spring Festival lantern from sorghum stalks and colored paper. When the candle inside was lit, the heat made a wheel with paper cutouts of the ancient generals of the Three Kingdoms spin merrily.

When Weihua and I went out the next morning to buy food for our new year's feast, we found the following notice posted on every street corner downtown:

Under the wise leadership of our great commander Chairman Mao and the Central Cultural Revolution Group, the January Storm is spreading with the force of a thunderbolt throughout our sacred land of seven hundred million. The revolutionary high tide of grand revolutionary alliance, grand seizure of power, and grand struggle is surging forward. The clarion call has been blown, and the militant drums have sounded. Amid this excellent situation, we revolutionary rebels of Lingzhi county have determined that the time is ripe to seize power from the bourgeois, counterrevolutionary Party Committee and government. To accomplish this great historical task, we are calling a countywide rally on the eve of Spring Festival to dismiss the agent of the bourgeois headquarters inside the Party, the counterrevolutionary revisionist and capitalist-roader Mountain Devil, from his posts both inside and outside the Party. The rally will be held on the drillground of Lingzhi Middle School. All revolutionary rebels are invited to attend. This great event will give the people of Lingzhi a wonderful, revolutionary Spring Festival.
Salutations in the name of the Cultural Revolution!

The announcement was signed Mao Zedong Thought Red Guards of Lingzhi Middle School, Revolutionary Workers Rebel Headquarters of Lingzhi County, Revolutionary Peasants Rebel Liaison Station of Lingzhi County, and Revolutionary Rebels of Departments of the Lingzhi County Government.

"How ridiculous," I exclaimed. "The Thought Guards can't run the county. They may claim to have a grand revolutionary alliance with the workers and peasants, but in fact they're just a bunch of students."

"Ridiculous or not, these people are in dead earnest," Weihua said. "Red Guards everywhere are following the example of the Shanghai workers."

"How can they have a big struggle meeting on the eve of Spring Festival? It will ruin the holiday!" I shouted.

The streets were full of last-minute shoppers—peasant men in bulky black padded coats with white towels around their heads, housewives with long braids of garlic draped around their shoulders, grannies with bound feet sitting in wheelbarrows beside halves of pigs, children eating sticks of candied hawthorn fruit. A startled old peasant stopped to stare at me.

We went home without doing our shopping and told Grandpa about the notice. He stroked his wispy beard and said, "I never expected this movement would last so long. Never mind. If they dismiss your father from office, we can go back to our hometown. Remember Tao Yuanming? He was a county magistrate during the Jin dynasty. He couldn't stand being an official, so he went home. Or Bao Longtu of the Song dynasty, the prefectural official who fell into disfavor after executing a relative of the emperor for wronging the peasants? He was allowed to go home too. And of course, there's Hai Rui . . ."

"I've already told Papa he should go home, but he can't," I said. "Grandpa, times have changed. Even if Papa's removed from office, the rebels won't let him quietly slip away."

"They want to destroy him politically, mentally, and physically," Weihua said. "It's like riding on the back of a tiger: the only way to get off is to be eaten."

Grandpa thought awhile in silence. Then he said, "They have to give us a way out. They have to let us live."

On the last day of the old year, Grandpa took several opium-licorice pills and got off the kang to cook for the first time in weeks. He prepared a big pot of soup with pork, bean-curd, seaweed, cabbage, and bean-starch noodles. The tantalizing smell filled the courtyard.

Mama had brought Yiyuan home the night before and rushed out with hardly a word. I dished out a bowl of soup for my little sister with as little liquid as possible. We called her "the girl who eats the thick" because she only liked the good part of the soup. Since she was the baby of the family, we let her have her way.

We were about to start eating when a group of people with red armbands rushed into the courtyard. "Is your mother here?" one of them demanded. It was Papa's aide, Qin Mao, the former cowherd. Now he was head of the rebels in the county government, since he had been the most "oppressed."

"No." I did not want to talk to this traitor.

"No? Didn't she bring your little sister here last night? She said she would return to her room, but she never did."

"What do you want my mother for?" Weihua demanded.

"None of your business. Just tell us where she is."

"Don't waste your breath on them!" Thought Guard Chief Daba, the scar on his cheek gleaming scarlet, pushed his way to the front of the group. "These little bastards of the capitalist-roader only listen to force! Search the house! Mountain Devil's stinking wife cannot have grown wings!" The intruders poured through the doorway, sweeping the bowls off the

Spring Festival Visitors

181

table and sending Grandpa's delicious soup all over the floor. "What's this piece of trash?" Daba slashed at Weihua's lantern with a stick until it fell to the floor, where it was trampled to shreds.

"Weihua! Jianhua!" Grandpa looked at us, his eyes intense behind his glasses, wordlessly warning us to stay calm. Another boy took a mirror off the wall and held it up to show the others the picture of the ballerina on the back. "Look, they still harbor such obscene bourgeois stuff." He smashed the mirror on the floor. Yiyuan began to cry. "Stop barking, you little dog-cub!" Daba yelled. "Are you barking because your dog of a Papa is losing his official cap?" Yiyuan cried even harder.

The intruders kicked the furniture about. They flung open the wardrobe, ransacked the drawers, and rummaged through the cardboard cartons where we stored outgrown clothes and shoes. Those who searched the back room emerged triumphantly with a stack of well-worn books: *Romance of the Three Kingdoms*, *A Dream of Red Mansions*, the biography of the peasant rebel Li Zicheng describing how he overthrew the Ming dynasty, and a Qing novel about corruption and injustice, *Witnessing the Twenty Weird Years*. They were the books that Grandpa had raised us on. "Confiscate them as evidence!" Daba ordered. Grandpa had a look of alarm in his eyes but said nothing. The rebels left with the books, swearing angrily over their failure to find Mama. "Bandits! Hoodlums!" Weihua and I cursed once they were out of sight.

The Capless Official

Not until evening did Grandpa tell us that Mama had been hiding just next door. An old lady who was on very good terms with Grandpa lived there. Papa had told Mama that he could not evade the rally, but perhaps she could. On new year's eve, she had left their room just before the rebels put sentries at the door, brought Yiyuan to us, and gone next door. For a night and a day, she had lain on the neighbor's kang with a quilt over her head.

The old lady's son, who had joined the crowd of ten thousand at the middle-school drillground, described the rally to us. Thought Guards had dragged Papa onto a makeshift stage and ordered him to kneel down. Papa refused, saying that he had never knelt down in front of anybody, not even his parents, and that he did not know how. The Thought Guards kicked him behind the knees and pulled his hair to force him down. He was held in a jet-plane position for two hours. The rebels took turns holding his arms up like wings and planting their feet on his back. Qin Mao and other rebel leaders made speeches denouncing him as Lingzhi county's biggest capitalist-roader. Finally, they put a feudal-style official's black cap from a Beijing opera costume on Papa's head and then took it off to symbolize his removal from office. When the rally was over, Papa could not walk. He had to be carried offstage.

Grandpa, my two sisters and three brothers, and I sat

around the table in silence, listening to the account. After our informant had left, Grandpa swallowed more opium-licorice pills and tried to cheer everyone up. "Don't be upset, children," he said. "When you take off the official cap, your whole body feels light. Papa can breathe easier now. They want to ruin our Spring Festival, but let's not give them the satisfaction. Come on, let's make *jiaozi*!"

Making jiaozi, steamed dumplings, had always been our central Spring Festival ritual. "Nothing is more comfortable than lying in bed; nothing is more delicious than jiaozi," the saying went. We would wrap them late on new year's eve, put them out in the courtyard to freeze, and boil them on new year's morning. Zhihua, who was becoming an accomplished cook, prepared the dough and set it aside. He chopped the pork into fine shreds, while I minced the scallions and cabbage. Grandpa combined the ingredients with just the right amounts of soy sauce and sesame oil. Zhihua rolled the dough into long ropes, which he cut into slices to be flattened into circles. The rest of us folded in the filling as fast as he could supply us with wrappers.

Mama arrived when we were almost finished, her eyes swollen, her hair uncombed. "Papa has bruises and a backache," she said in a flat voice before we had even asked. "I've sent for a doctor. Otherwise, everything is all right. Yiyuan can come back with me." As she led my little sister out the door, she added, "Don't offend the other kids when you go out to play. On second thought, you'd better just stay at home."

At midnight, we lit our firecrackers outside the house. We fell asleep to the staccato of firecrackers popping all over town and awoke to the same sounds. Weihua and I ate our jiaozi in haste and headed for the government courtyard. Two red paper lanterns and a sign saying "Happily celebrate Spring Festival in revolutionary style!" hung over the front gate.

Papa lay in bed, covered with two quilts. Mama and Yiyuan sat at his side. The top of the desk looked like a pharmacy shelf. "Papa, we brought you jiaozi," Weihua said, holding out a tin lunchbox.

Papa raised himself with difficulty. "Have you eaten yet? How are they this year? Mutton or pork?"

"Pork," I said, looking over the bruises on his face. "We got a whole quarter of a pig."

"Good, good. Put them there on the stove. When I get hungry, I'll eat."

"Papa, are you in much pain?" Weihua asked.

"Not much. When we were fighting the Japanese, our medics sometimes operated on wounded soldiers without anesthesia. The men would pass out from the pain. That you could call pain."

Papa's haggard face took on a glowing expression. "How I miss those days!" he said. "We all had one goal: to drive the Japanese out of China. Nobody cared about rank or personal gain. Everybody was ready to lay down his life. When we had one corn pancake, we all shared it. Where is that spirit today? Why are we conducting these endless struggles?" He lay back on the pillow again.

"Papa," Weihua said, "take care of yourself. Maybe you should be a little more flexible in dealing with these people."

"I know they would be easier on me if I went along with them. But I have my principles. I never gave up my principles to the Japanese or the Kuomintang. I didn't give them up to

Han Rong. Why should I give up my principles to these students who don't even know what revolution is?" He lifted himself up again in agitation. "They're not making revolution, they're just making havoc! They're luring more and more young peasants out of the fields, and the farmland's going to waste."

Mama put a restraining hand on Papa's arm and slid another pillow under his head. With a weak smile, she said,. "Don't worry about these things. You are now an overthrown capitalist-roader. You have joined the ranks of the ordinary folk. Take advantage of it. Have a good rest. Forget about politics and work."

"How can I forget about it? In a month, it will be time for spring plowing. Tractors, fuel, fertilizer, transport—all these things require planning. What are they going to do about next year's crops?"

"When Butcher Zhang dies, do you think people will eat pork with the bristles?" asked Mama. "They'll find a way."

"When you take off your official cap, your whole body feels light," I added, quoting Grandpa's words.

"Where did you learn such a feudal idea?" Papa asked, the hint of a smile on his lips.

"In school," I lied.

Yiyuan suddenly shouted, "Look, it's snowing!"

Papa winced as he lifted himself up again to look out the window. Snowflakes were falling like goose feathers, clinging to the leafless trees. "Good," he said. "A timely snow promises a good harvest!"

The Capless Official

Smears and Skirmishes

Weihua and I usually stayed home until Lantern Festival, two weeks after Spring Festival. But life in Lingzhi was becoming unbearable. When my little brothers and sisters went out to play, other children would mock, "There go the dog-cubs of the capitalist-roader!" These rude country kids were beginning to recognize Weihua and me as well. When Weihua caught one and slapped him, it only made things worse; now they hurled stones and clods of dirt along with their taunts. We decided to go back to school just a few days into the lunar new year.

I was the first student in class 85 to return from the holiday. I cleaned my dormitory room, spread out the new cotton mattress I had brought from home, and lit the stove. I sat on my bed and began to plan my next chuanlian, for rumor had it that free transportation would resume in the spring. In my diary, I sketched an outline map of China—the hen with two eggs that we had drawn so many times in geography class. With a red pencil, I drew triangular pennants at each place I had visited and traced a new itinerary that would take me through the remaining provincial capitals, famous cities, and scenic spots. I even included Lhasa and Urumqi. I calculated that if I spent one to three days at each place, the whole trip would take two months.

As I was admiring my map, the door opened and Fangpu walked in. He had put on some weight and gained some color in his face. A soft brown fuzz had sprouted on his chin. We greeted each other, and I asked him how his chuanlian had gone. "Excellent!" he said. "I spent more than a month in Beijing and saw Chairman Mao three times. How about you? Did you see Chairman Mao? How many times?"

"Not even once," I said.

"Really? What a pity. I thought everybody had seen Chairman Mao."

"I went to the South. I thought I could come to Beijing and see Chairman Mao when the crowds had thinned out. But when I got there, he was not receiving Red Guards." I did not want Fangpu to think that I was unenthusiastic about the idea of seeing Chairman Mao.

"You're planning another trip?" Fangpu had noticed my map. "It looks more thorough than Confucius's lecture tour during the Spring and Autumn period. Don't get your hopes up. A campaign against money-worship is just getting under way. The Preparatory Committee already stopped giving out chuanlian allowances. I don't think we'll be going on chuanlian again."

"Then what shall we do?"

"What shall we do? Are you afraid of becoming a hero with no place to display your prowess?" Fangpu smiled and patted me on the shoulder. "Little Brother, join our East-Is-Red Corps. We're about to kick aside Chairman Deng, dismantle the Preparatory Committee, and take power into our own hands. We're stepping up our propaganda efforts right now. We plan to launch a newspaper, *Battlefield News*. Wouldn't you like to join us as a reporter?"

I hesitated. I admired Fangpu as a poet, but did I want him as my political leader? I stalled. "For the time being, maybe I can be a free-lancer," I replied. "If I think of something inter-

esting to write, I can contribute it to your *Battlefield News*."
An angry look passed over Fangpu's face. Then he smiled and
patted me on the shoulder again. "Fine, Jianhua, you can sit
back and observe for a while before you make up your mind."

Fangpu had officially resigned from the Preparatory Committee and set up the East-Is-Red Corps with several other
seniors during the Spring Festival holidays. They made their
headquarters in a house in the bell-tower courtyard, and announced their presence with posters accusing the Preparatory
Committee of "leniency toward capitalist-roaders, monsters,
and demons." Three days in a row, they hauled out Ding Yi,
made him limp across campus, and held struggle meetings
against him. They also found some new culprits, including a
young teacher who had written a poster criticizing Liu
Shaoqi, with three red X's over every reference to Liu. In one
place he had put three red X's over Chairman Mao's name
too, something nobody would do deliberately. Nonetheless,
the East-Is-Red Corps people branded him a counterrevolutionary and locked him in a small room.

The East-Is-Red Corps swelled as students returned after
Lantern Festival. Almost all of my classmates joined. The
campus resounded with their cries: "Kick aside the Preparatory Committee and dethrone Chairman Deng!" and "Thoroughly expose and criticize the Preparatory Committee's
bourgeois reactionary line!" Eventually, Fangpu and his followers stormed Chairman Deng's office and declared him
overthrown. They chopped the Preparatory Committee's seal
into pieces. Deng surrendered without protesting. Because he
had offended nobody, the East-Is-Red Corps people let him
go without bothering to hold a struggle meeting. They announced their great victory over the school public-address
system, which they now controlled.

Smears and Skirmishes

Just as the East-Is-Red Corps seemed to be reaching the pinnacle of power, a small group emerged to challenge it. The manifesto of the Lu Xun Commune, posted in the bell-tower courtyard, promised to carry on in the "hard-boned spirit" of Lu Xun, the great critic of feudalism and reaction in Kuomintang days, whose satirical style we all tried to imitate. "We will recruit men and buy horses to redirect a revolution that has been misled," the manifesto said. Among the nine signatures at the bottom was my brother Weihua's.

Although the new organization chose its words carefully and did not attack the East-Is-Red Corps by name, Fangpu and his followers could not tolerate even a suggestion of dissent. They put up a statement declaring the Lu Xun Commune a "royalist faction" run by "hooligans." They ransacked its headquarters, burned a stack of fresh handbills, took away the mimeograph machine, smashed the furniture, and posted more accusations on the walls.

A smear campaign soon followed. Anti-Commune rumors spread like wildfire across campus. The *Battlefield News* reported that the Commune was a "hodgepodge of social dregs" whose members were not pure red. Weihua, "dog-cub of a capitalist-roader," was cited as an example. The Commune's leader, Mengzhe, a lad from a peasant family, was said to have a "wild pheasant" for a mother and a "vagabond" for a father. The evidence given was that he came from Railway Station Village on the other side of the railroad tracks, a place described as "notorious for its vagrants and harlots." The loudspeakers blared threats against the Commune all day long in the shrill voice of Baimudan, "white peony," a girl in Weihua's class.

Worried that Weihua was getting too entangled in school politics, I went to his dormitory room to look for him, only to learn that the East-Is-Red majority had evicted him. His roommates had written threatening slogans on the wall by his bed, then splashed ink on his bedding and thrown it out the door. He had moved into another room with his comrades-in-arms. When I got there, students wearing East-Is-Red armbands were posting a couplet around the doorway that read: "Small as the temple is, the demon wind blows strong; shallow as the pool is, the turtles are many." There was no worse insult than to be called a turtle.

Little Bawang turned around and leered at me. "Jianhua, are you planning to become a turtle too?" he asked sarcastically. Little Mihu was there also. His puckish little face reminded me of a submissive Pekingese dog. I gave him a stern glare, and he tried to shrink out of sight behind another student. I went into the room and slammed the door behind me. The Lu Xun Commune members were writing posters. Weihua was drafting a commentary that criticized the East-Is-Red Corps for arrogance. He agreed to stop and come out for a walk with me. As we left, he laughed at the couplet around the door. "Such insults will only increase our support," he said.

"Weihua, you shouldn't get so deeply involved in political controversy," I admonished him. "You know that the East-Is-Red Corps can crush your little group. Papa's situation makes you even more vulnerable."

"I didn't take this step lightly," Weihua said. "I joined the Lu Xun Commune because of its progressive stance. The East-Is-Red Corps follows the ultraleftist line of riding rough-shod over everyone and overthrowing everything. We will unite with everybody who wants to make revolution, regardless of family origin or political problems. We also believe that the majority of teachers are good or comparatively good, and we will unite with them too. We oppose using brute force against anyone, even Ding Yi. We have to struggle to prevent the East-Is-Red Corps from rampaging through Yizhen like the Thought Guards in Lingzhi. We're not worried about being in the minority. Our leader, Mengzhe, is a careful strategist. He often studies Sun Zi's *Art of War*. We intend to win over the majority step by step, through propaganda and education. In the end, we'll prevail."

Weihua assured me that the rumors about Mengzhe's parents were false, that Mengzhe came from an honest, hardworking peasant family. As for Mengzhe himself, Weihua seemed to adore him. He listed Mengzhe's fine qualities and talents: kind, fair, peaceable, foresighted, an honors student, a versatile technician who liked to tinker with radios, cameras, and clocks, an accomplished shadowboxer and sword dancer. I soon was convinced of the righteousness of their cause. "Weihua, should I join the Commune?" I asked.

"Not for the time being. It would complicate matters. Two dog-cubs of a capitalist-roader would give them twice the ammunition to suppress us. However, you might set up your own organization to lend us support." I mulled over the idea as I walked back to my dormitory.

A new slogan had appeared on campus: "Down with Mengzhe!" For the first time, students were attacking students. I found a freshly inked message on the wall above my bed:

> It's criminal to be a royalist,
> And the crimes warrant ten thousand deaths.
> If the royalist dies, serves him right,
> And if he doesn't, we'll bury him alive.
> Jianhua is a dad-protecting factionalist!

I decided to leave before I got driven out. With my belongings rolled up in my mattress, I wandered around in the dusk looking for a place to stay. I found an empty room outside the back gate of the bell-tower courtyard. I put newspaper over the broken windows and went to sleep on some chairs.

The next day, I swept out my room and brought in a bed, desk, stove, and electric bulb borrowed from other vacant rooms. Now I had a clean, cozy home. With a few dazibao on the walls, it would make a fine headquarters for a Red Guard organization. Taking a clean sheet of white paper, jet-black ink, and a big brush pen, I wrote the name of my new one-man organization in my finest calligraphy: Skirmisher.

The membership expanded to three before the day was over. Two errant boys from another class, whom I did not know very well, wandered in and took a liking to my head-quarters. Ours was an informal, almost underground group whose main activities were scattering handbills produced by the Lu Xun Commune and writing anonymous dazibao attacking the East-Is-Red Corps.

One day when I was distributing handbills in downtown Yizhen, I ran into Yuanchao and his little sister Kangmei. He carried a kite and she was holding the string. They had been playing out in the fields. I was surprised that Yuanchao had not returned to school to continue making revolution. "We got back from chuanlian on Spring Festival and are still worn out," he said. "We visited almost every revolutionary site through my father's connections. Some of Papa's old com-rades-in-arms even sent cars for us." Yuanchao was no longer wearing his Red Inheritance Red Guards armband. He told me that the group had disbanded. "It's only natural that we go our separate ways," he said. "The Cultural Revolution is deepening, and our members' parents have various points of view."

The movement was even splintering in the Army Hospital,

Yuanchao said. "Is there much disorder?" I asked. "Of course, great disorder, great chaos!" he said. "It's almost as chaotic as at school. Some people are even writing posters against my father. Isn't it ridiculous? Papa is a Red Army veteran with great deeds to his name."

"I know how you feel. My father's been dismissed from office by the rebels in Lingzhi county. But I'm sure army officers are safer than civilian officials."

"Not necessarily. The rebels in Beijing are attacking everyone but Chairman Mao and Lin Biao. Even the old revolutionary generals and marshals are on the hot seat. According to Papa, several of them went to see Chairman Mao and told him to stop the Cultural Revolution right away, but he refused to listen. They got so angry that they cursed at him. Zhu De pounded the floor with his cane. Xu Xiangqian struck the table so hard with his hand that he broke his wrist. They shouted and quarreled for quite a few hours, to no avail."

I invited Yuanchao to join the Skirmisher. He said he was not ready to go back to school yet. He would stay at the hospital to look out for his father.

Spring Buds

The East-Is-Red Corps would not let anyone forget my brother's status as the son of an accused capitalist-roader, since this was the strongest evidence that the Commune was a "royalist" organization. Weihua's membership was becoming a contentious issue within the Commune. Some members felt that his presence alienated would-be sympathizers. Weihua submitted his resignation twice, but Mengzhe would not accept it.

A *People's Daily* editorial calling on Red Guard organizations to rectify their ranks brought the matter to a head. The Lu Xun Commune announced that it would hold an open-door rectification session on the question of Weihua's membership. Onlookers of all persuasions filled the Commune headquarters. Latecomers gathered at the door and outside the windows. The nine founders sat at desks arranged in a semicircle, my brother in the middle. Mengzhe opened the meeting with a quotation from Chairman Mao about reaching unity through criticism and self-criticism. He said the Commune had decided to hold this meeting to help Weihua in the spirit of this principle.

Weihua sat erect, allowing no emotion to show on his face. When Mengzhe asked him to state his case, he began to read a self-criticism in a soft voice. He also started by quoting Chairman Mao, saying that if thousands of martyrs had laid down their lives for revolution, we ought to be able to do something as simple as correcting our mistakes. He went on to admit that he had undertaken some "dad-protecting" activities in Lingzhi. He said that he lacked understanding and still had some petty bourgeois ideas. He ended by saying he was willing to resign to atone for his mistakes.

The other Commune members took turns criticizing him. Mengzhe invited comments from the audience. East-Is-Red Corps people took the opportunity to attack the "royalist." Mengzhe summed up the session by saying that Weihua had displayed great sincerity in admitting his past mistakes. Therefore, in accordance with Chairman Mao's teachings, the Commune would allow him to remain a member in good standing. "Our policy is to unite with anyone who can be united with and who desires to make revolution," Mengzhe concluded.

When the room had emptied, I congratulated Weihua. "How did you stay so calm before so many people?" I asked. "Do you think we were really conducting a rectification?" he said with a grin. "It was just a performance to silence the East-Is-Red Corps and impress the nonaligned. We rehearsed it several times. It was all Mengzhe's idea."

The tactic seemed to have its desired effect. After the meeting, the East-Is-Red Corps propaganda against the Lu Xun Commune temporarily subsided, and nonpartisan students began to take a stand. New organizations popped up like the buds on the willow trees: Daybreak, Dawn, Sunrise, Wild Grass, Spring Wind, Hard Bones, Toward the Sun, Cold Eyebrows, Beacon Fire, Great Wall, Catch the Old Dragon. Many of the names came from Chairman Mao or Lu Xun. These new groups declared themselves neutral, which implicitly meant support for the Lu Xun Commune and defiance of the East-Is-Red Corps. One, led by the talented clapper performer Leiting, was so daring as to call itself the East-Is-Red Commune. "'East Is Red' is not an East-Is-Red Corps monopoly," Leiting explained during his recruitment drive. "We can't let them monopolize everything."

"Why don't you people who oppose the East-Is-Red Corps simply join the Lu Xun Commune?" I asked Leiting. "Why set up all these little independent kingdoms?"

"In terms of Chairman Mao's military theory, this is called using the countryside to surround the city. Many small groups together seem greater in strength and impetus. And this way, we can all be king of the hill!" He snapped his fingers as if they were clappers. "Jianhua, why don't you join us? Your Skirmisher is too lonely with just the three of you."

"You cunning king of the hill! Do you want me to give up my kingdom? Although I have only two followers, I am king. Why should I give up my throne to be your servant?"

"What if I appoint you propaganda minister?" Leiting said. "You can run our newspaper."

I was beginning to like this joker more and more. I accompanied him back to his headquarters in the old recreation building, called the Cross Building because its two hallways formed the shape of a cross. Two ping-pong tables sat in the middle of the room, forming a giant conference table. New bookshelves lined the walls. The library consisted of a four-volume set of Mao Zedong's *Selected Works* and a copy of *Quotations from Marx, Engels, Lenin, Stalin, and Lu Xun*, a handy reference work compiled by Red Guards in Beijing. A red paper sun covered the window. My headquarters looked shabby by comparison. I decided to merge the Skirmisher with the East-Is-Red Commune.

Leiting had recruited twenty followers. Every day, we held strategy meetings, wrote commentaries and news stories, and posted dazibao. We pooled money to buy a silkscreen frame and collected stenciling equipment from abandoned offices. The ink and paper came from the school Logistics Office, which somehow continued to operate free of any faction's control. Our newspaper, *Spring Thunder*, began to roll off our crude press.

The East-Is-Red Corps could not stay silent in the face of these new challenges. Fangpu lashed out at the Lu Xun Commune and the new organizations with a poem entitled "My Feelings About the Current Situation." Students crowded outside the dining hall to read it.

Spring Buds

A black wind rippled across Yizhong,
Attempting to smother the bright spring;
A buffoon designated himself a king,
Wrapping himself with Lu Xun's tiger skin;
The revolutionary current no one can tame,
While the buffoon will perish in body and name;
Thousands of boats will sail by his corpse
   rotting on the river bed,
And victorious heroes will see the east turn
   brilliant red.

Fangpu sounded desperate to hold onto the mountaintop. He should have learned from Wang Lun, a rebel leader in the novel *Water Margin*, whose narrow-mindedness had earned him the nickname "White-Robed Scholar." Having occupied Mount Liang, Wang Lun could not stand the idea of sharing his territory with other rebels and tried to murder them. In the end, he himself was killed by another rebel leader, who developed the mountain into a great stronghold of rebellion.

I wrote a poem entitled "In Response to Comrade Fangpu" and posted it beside his:

Delicate flowers struggle to emerge,
Springtime moans while cold winds surge,
Sweeping across the frozen land, strangling life,
Declaring itself victorious by purge.
But purple and green will fill spring's vase,
For no one can conquer nature's laws;
A revolutionary should have a magnanimous heart,
A white-robed scholar can never lead a great cause!

My poem attracted an equally large crowd, until East-Is-Red Corps members tore it down and accused me of using "the rubbish of feudal culture" to attack their leader. I resurrected the poem on the front page of our newspaper, *Spring*

Thunder. The day that issue came out, Little Mihu stopped by the East-Is-Red Commune headquarters and handed me an envelope. Inside was a four-line poem from Fangpu:

> Boiling beans over a beanstalk fire,
> Beans are crying in the cauldron:
> Both of us are red descendants,
> Why torture each other so eagerly?

It was a revised version of a famous poem by Cao Zhi, son of the fierce and ambitious Cao Cao, who had ruled the kingdom of Wei during the Three Kingdoms period. After Cao Cao's death, his eldest son Cao Pei had become king of Wei. Suspecting Cao Zhi of wanting to usurp the throne, Cao Pei had him arrested and ordered him to compose a poem in the time it took to walk seven steps, or face death. Cao Zhi quickly came up with a poem so moving that Cao Pei released him.

Under his revised version, Fangpu had written, "Little Brother, I am saddened by what has happened between us. I often think of our first meeting over wild vegetables. I hope our friendship will not perish." I did not waver. Our roads were diverging irreversibly. Our common love for poetry was not enough to bind us. I modified another ancient poem and sent it to Fangpu.

> Eager to make revolution,
> I walk the fields in late afternoon;
> A sunset of boundless splendor
> Heralds the approaching dusk.

Fangpu did not write back.

Arrival of the Cadets

In March, the director of Yizhen county's Military Department came to Yizhong to tell us the army was in charge. He said the armed forces were assuming a new administrative role all over the country. Power seizures by rebel organizations were hereby declared invalid; only "three-in-one" revolutionary committees with representation from the army, revolutionary cadres, and revolutionary rebels were legitimate. A prerequisite to forming such a committee was a grand revolutionary alliance of all factions. To achieve that goal, the army was undertaking a Three Supports and Two Militaries campaign—support for industry, agriculture, and revolutionary leftists, and military control and training. A People's Liberation Army platoon would come to Yizhong to carry out the Two Militaries.

There were various conjectures about the army's new role. Some people said it was to help the rebels consolidate power. Others said it was to restore order in places paralyzed by factional fighting. Still others said it was to curb rebel activity and prevent incidents like the one in Qinghai province where rebel students had tried to storm a district army headquarters and the commander had ordered machine-gun fire on the mob.

Whatever the reason, the army came. Thirty-six soldiers with field packs on their backs marched into Yizhong. The first thing they did was to order us to return to our original class groups. All the organizations had to abandon their headquarters and split up. Reluctantly, I moved my mattress and belongings back to my old bed. The writing on the wall that had driven me out was still there.

All of class 85, minus Yuling and Yuanchao, sat together in our classroom for the first time since before chuanlian. Everyone had stories to tell. Most of my classmates had seen Chairman Mao. Zongwei had traveled to Urumqi and stayed two months, painting pictures of the minority peoples. He claimed to have barely escaped betrothal to a beautiful Uighur girl who had fallen in love with him. Sanxi had spent a month hunting bears in the virgin forests of the Northeast. Erchou's tale was the most exciting of all: he and several schoolmates had gone to North Vietnam! They had planned to go all the way to South Vietnam to help fight the U.S. imperialists, but Vietnamese militiamen had sent them home after they crossed Friendship Pass. As proof of his adventure, Erchou had brought back a broad-brimmed Vietnamese hat.

Most of us were impressed, but Little Bawang accused Erchou of crossing the border illegally. To be safe, Erchou hurried downtown to report the trip to the County Military Department. The director assured him that, though going to Vietnam with the intention of fighting the American imperialists was a slight breach of discipline, it was not a serious offense.

A man named Niu was assigned to our class. From the four pockets on his jacket, we knew that he was an officer. In fact, nobody in the platoon wore the two pockets of a common soldier. As senior cadets from the Missile Engineering Institute outside Shimen, officially known as People's Liberation Army Unit 901, they were already junior officers.

Since early in the Cultural Revolution, we had grown used

to making our own schedules, going to bed late and getting up late. The 901, as we called them, brought a new routine to our school. Bugle music roused us before dawn to march to the sports ground, where we practiced drill formations. We spent the rest of the morning in the classroom, studying Chairman Mao's works. Niu went over every sentence again and again to make sure we all knew it by heart. Sometimes he had us recite articles in turn, each student rattling off one sentence. In the afternoons, we returned to the sports ground to practice bayonet drill or antiaircraft defense.

One day, Niu distributed copies of an article from the Party journal *Red Flag* that criticized Liu Shaoqi. It did not mention Liu by name, but we all knew who "China's Khrushchev" and "the high-ranking official who has taken the capitalist road" was. Under the 901's direction, we began to write posters attacking Liu.

A series of films classified as "poisonous weeds" gave us more ammunition. We saw the documentary *Liu Shaoqi Visits Indonesia*, which showed Liu, his wife Wang Guangmei, Foreign Minister Chen Yi, and Chen's wife, accompanied by President Sukarno, watching topless Indonesian dancers. Wang Guangmei wore a skintight qipao and a necklace. The revised subtitles said that Liu had "flirted with bourgeois ruler Sukarno" and pointed out how decadent his wife was. We also saw *Prairie Fire*, about the famous Anyuan coal miners' strike organized by Liu Shaoqi. The commentary said that Liu had betrayed the workers and sabotaged the strike by compromising with the capitalists. Each time Liu's face appeared on the screen, the auditorium resounded with cries of "Down with Liu Shaoqi!"

There were other films too—one that glorified the reformist emperor Guangxu as a great patriot; another about a poor peasant who collected money by begging to build schools for poor children; another about two actress sisters, one of whom married a capitalist while the other took the revolutionary road. These films were said to perpetuate imperialist versions of history, or encourage servility, or advocate class compromise. I thoroughly enjoyed them all, for the chance to see any movie at all was a rare treat.

Unfortunately, the poisonous-weeds film festival only lasted two weeks. We turned our focus to Liu Shaoqi's *How to Be a Good Communist*. The slim volume, first published during the War of Liberation and reprinted in 1962, had been reissued again. Embossed on the cover, beneath the title, was a line in parentheses: "For the purpose of criticism." Soon Yizhong was papered with dazibao that condemned Liu for opposing Mao Zedong Thought, pushing the feudal ideas of Confucius and Mencius, and "peddling sinister revisionist trash."

It was a fine show of unity against a common enemy. However, the currents of antagonism between the East-Is-Red Corps and the Lu Xun Commune still ran deep. The 901 itself became yet another divisive factor. The East-Is-Red Corps people resented their loss of power to the military and opposed the policy of equal treatment for all. They especially disliked the soldiers' allowing all but the worst monsters and demons among the teachers to take part in military training. The Lu Xun Commune people and their supporters liked the 901.

By the end of April, Fangpu and his followers had regrouped. They declared a boycott of military training. They put up dazibao that accused the 901 of supporting the "conservative" Lu Xun Commune instead of the "leftist" East-Is-Red Corps, and spread rumors that the 901 had joined a counterrevolutionary conspiracy against the Ministry of Defense. "The 901 are royalists under cover of the People's Liberation Army!" they charged. The Lu Xun Commune and many small organizations resurfaced to counterattack with slogans of their own: "Learn from the People's Liberation Army! Salute the People's Liberation Army!" "To oppose the People's Liberation Army is counterrevolutionary!" "We'll fight anyone who dares to oppose the People's Liberation Army to our last drop of blood!"

The month of military practice that had drilled each class into a well-oiled marching team came to naught. We fell into disarray once more. Most of the former East-Is-Red Corps members joined the attack on the 901. I decided to start fresh with a new organization, which I named Uniquely Beautiful View after a line from Chairman Mao's poetry. Leiting agreed to let me withdraw from the East-Is-Red Commune, in the interests of broadening the front against the East-Is-Red Corps. I won over two recruits, Erchou and Zongwei.

I tried to convince Little Mihu to join too, without success. "I have three reasons to remain loyal to the East-Is-Red Corps," he said. "First, Fangpu is a long-standing revolutionary rebel, while Mengzhe is a royalist upstart. Second, the 901 does not represent the glorious tradition of the People's Liberation Army. Fangpu says they're nothing but a group of college students in uniform. Third, I want to go with the majority."

"Truth often rests with the minority," I said. "Marx, Lenin, and Chairman Mao were all in the minority at the start of their revolutionary careers."

"I've already thought it over. Fangpu is very nice to me. I'm his messenger. I like the job."

The East-Is-Red Corps quickly rebuilt its strength and soon

claimed a membership of seven hundred—ten times the membership of the Lu Xun Commune and Leiting's East-Is-Red Commune combined. Meanwhile, support for the Lu Xun Commune continued to grow among the nonaligned students, and Fangpu's followers made some tactical mistakes that drove more students into the opposing camp.

One tactical error involved the officer Niu. When Niu was making a last attempt to organize class 85 into a political-study session, my East-Is-Red Corps classmates surrounded him, backed him into a corner, and taunted, "901 royalist! Get out of our school!" Niu held his little red book high in the air as if to fend them off. I took Niu by the arm and led him outside, followed by cries of "Jianhua is a royalist! Jianhua is a dad-protector! Fish like fish, shrimp like shrimp, turtles get along with tortoises!" On the path, Niu let out a cry of pain and put his hand to his face. Somebody had let off a stone from a slingshot and hit him in the eye. Erchou and I brought him to the clinic, where Dr. Yang dressed the wound before sending him to the Army Hospital.

My group promptly put up posters to publicize this East-Is-Red Corps crime. The other minority organizations joined the protest. The East-Is-Red Corps leadership issued a statement claiming that the Lu Xun Commune itself had stoned Niu to arouse the anger of the 901. The situation in my dormitory room was so tense that Erchou, Zongwei, and I decided to move to a room in the Teachers' Building.

The director of the County Military Department came to Yizhong again and criticized the East-Is-Red Corps for using violence against the 901. A few days later, the 901 men packed up and left. The Lu Xun Commune and allied organizations cheered the cadets as they marched out the South Gate, while the East-Is-Red Corps, over the public-address

Arrival of the Cadets

system, hailed their departure as "a great victory for Yizhong's revolutionary leftists."

Besides gaining new recruits among the unaffiliated students, the Niu incident also caused some East-Is-Red Corps defections. Sanxi came over to our Uniquely Beautiful View. Our four-man organization started a wall newspaper on the porch outside our headquarters. We changed the essays daily, and Zongwei illustrated them with cartoons. Our rival classmates came by almost every morning to curse us as we wrote.

The Grand Alliance

In June, the conflict between the East-Is-Red Corps and the Lu Xun Commune moved beyond the school walls and into the streets of Yizhong. Each side lobbied for support among the local populace. My band of four liked to scramble up the pagodas and scatter handbills over the crowds on market day. Organizations and work units in town began to align themselves with one faction or another. The County Military Department came out in support of the Lu Xun Commune. The county opera troupe and Light-Industry Bureau also had pro–Lu Xun Commune majorities. The East-Is-Red Corps was dominant in the Army Hospital, the Hydrology Institute, the Public Security Bureau, the People's Procuratorate, and the People's Court, and had a slim lead at the normal school.

Our struggle took on a new dimension when news came that the 901 cadets were involved in sharp debate with the

93rd Army, a field army stationed in Shimen. The 901 had openly denounced the 93rd Army, accusing it of suppressing a revolutionary leftists' organization in Shimen called the Madman's Commune—named after Lu Xun's famous story, "A Madman's Diary." The cadets had formed an organization called the 901 Revolutionary Rebel Corps and proclaimed themselves protectors of the Madman's Commune. Their main slogan was "Down with Li Tongmao and liberate Shimen!" For quite a few days, we assumed that Li Tongmao ran the 93rd Army. Later, we learned he was deputy commander. The cadets had focused on him because he came from a landlord family, whereas the commander was a Long March veteran with an unblemished background.

We Lu Xun Commune supporters could not help feeling thrilled at the boldness of the cadets. At the same time, we wondered how a thousand missile-engineering students could stand up against a powerful army that boasted tens of thousands of troops, not to mention tanks and artillery. We worried about whether the Lu Xun Commune and other small organizations at Yizhong would get into trouble for supporting the 901.

The questions grew more urgent when a 93rd Army engineering battalion moved into Yizhen and started building what were said to be missile silos on the edge of town. The soldiers turned Yizhong's sports field into a construction yard, where dump trucks delivered piles of gravel, cement, and steel bars, and stone crushers and cement mixers ground away. Once these troops found out that the East-Is-Red Corps opposed the 901, they openly sided with our adversaries.

The propaganda war being waged on campus and in town had become full of references to 901, 93rd, Madman's Commune, and other factions in Shimen. The situation was growing more and more confusing. In Shimen, the 93rd Army had supported a moderate Red Guard faction while suppressing the radical Madmen. At Yizhong, the 901 had favored the moderate side, the Lu Xun Commune, over the East-Is-Red Corps. In other words, the 93rd and the 901 had acted alike. But now they were enemies. Yizhong's moderate Lu Xun Commune had become linked to Shimen's suppressed Madman's Commune, since both were favored by the 901; and the Lu Xun Commune also was linked to the attack on the 93rd Army by virtue of its support for the 901. The East-Is-Red Corps was proclaiming itself "pro-army," while labeling the Lu Xun Commune and its supporters "anti-army madmen." The Lu Xun Commune, meanwhile, reiterated its unflagging support for the 901 and criticized the 93rd Army's repression of the revolutionary Madmen.

I could not sort out the logic of the situation. I found Weihua mimeographing handbills at Lu Xun Commune headquarters and asked him why we middle-school students at Yizhong were getting involved in the complex factional struggles of Shimen. "Circumstances are forcing us to take a stand," he said. "The 901 helped us when we were in a difficult situation. We should support them when they need us."

"The 93rd is a powerful army," I pointed out. "They could easily crush us."

"Not so easily. First of all, a field army is not supposed to take part in political struggle. The cadets have the advantage of being students; they can do whatever students at other schools can do. Second, the 901 is directly under Army General-Staff Headquarters. The 93rd is only under the Beijing Military District. So the 93rd is afraid to attack the 901 directly. Third, the 901 has broad support. A number of famous rebel organizations have issued statements supporting the

Madman's Commune and the 901—such as New Beida, Jing-gang Mountains of Qinghua, Red Flag of the Beijing Aviation Institute, and August 18 of Tianjin University. We should have confidence."

Weihua's self-assured air made me feel better. I helped him run off the last of the handbills. They invited all pro-901 students to a rally to denounce Li Tongmao, to be held at the Missile Engineering Institute the next day.

The cadets sent five trucks to pick us up early in the morning. No sooner had we climbed aboard than hundreds of East-Is-Red Corps members appeared. They linked arms and blockaded the South Gate. "Firmly oppose the Lu Xun Commune and all its running dogs from joining the 901 to oppose the People's Liberation Army!" they chanted. "Paper tigers, paper tigers!" students on the trucks responded. "Go ahead, go ahead!" we urged the drivers.

As the first truck rolled slowly toward the blockade, several East-Is-Red Corps members dropped to the ground beneath the front bumper. Their chants changed to "Defend the People's Liberation Army to the death!" and "Fight to the last drop of blood to defend the Great Wall of the People's Liberation Army!" We railed at our opponents for an hour, but they would not budge. We got down from the trucks and began arguing face to face: "We are going to Shimen! It has nothing to do with your East-Is-Red Corps! Well water and river water shouldn't mix; you mind your business, we'll mind ours!"

"We want to stop you from colluding with the 901 against the People's Liberation Army!"

"We do not oppose the People's Liberation Army. We only oppose Li Tongmao, who carried out a bourgeois reactionary line and suppressed the revolutionary leftists in Shimen!"

The Grand Alliance

"If you oppose Li Tongmao, you oppose the 93rd Army, and hence you are opposing the People's Liberation Army!"

"Your reasoning is absurd!"

"You are absurd!"

Sanxi and Erchou grabbed the arms of a girl who was lying under the truck bumper. It was our classmate Xiangyun. She kicked at them ferociously, screaming, "Don't touch me, you scoundrels! I'd rather die here than yield to you!" Xiangyun's brother Xiangsheng, who had a clubfoot, limped over and spit in her face. "You family traitor!" he said. She kicked him too. Students began to shove each other, and fists shot out.

At this point, Mengzhe leaped to the back of a truck and called a retreat. "All revolutionary students, listen to me!" he shouted. "People with ulterior motives are inciting the masses to struggle against each other. We must not fall into this trap. I hereby announce the withdrawal of the Lu Xun Commune and other revolutionary groups." The East-Is-Red Corps people cheered as we fell back and let the trucks roll out of the gate, empty. It was noontime and the 901 rally must have nearly ended.

Erchou, Sanxi, Zongwei, and I decided to go to Shimen on our own to lend support to the cadets' movement. Pro-901 college students gave us a place to stay. For several days, we roamed the city, reading dazibao and discussing the revolutionary situation with members of the Madman's Commune whom we met in street parades. The Madmen were easy to recognize because their flags and armbands bore the two characters for "madman," written in a wild scrawl. Once my Uniquely Beautiful View team felt familiar with the local situation, we began to put out a newsletter from our base at the college, calling for the overthrow of Li Tongmao. We stayed up a whole night to produce an extra edition about a debate between two sound trucks, one pro-93rd and the other pro-901, which had gathered a crowd that blocked traffic for hours at the intersection in front of the office of the Shimen Military Control Commission. When dawn came, we had two thousand neatly mimeographed papers to distribute. Our top story was headlined "Pro–Li Tongmao Faction Meets Setback in Great Debate!"

In the evening, the four of us returned to the same intersection pushing a handcart laden with dazibao supplies. We planned to return to Yizhen the next day and wanted to make a final contribution to the local propaganda war. We were pasting slogans on a wall when a man in blue coveralls interrupted us. "What does this mean?" he demanded. A number of other people were watching us as well.

"It's very simple: down with Li Tongmao and liberate Shimen. Can't you read?" Sanxi said.

"You have written a counterrevolutionary slogan against our great leader, great teacher, great supreme commander, and Great Helmsman, Chairman Mao," the man said.

"What are you talking about?" Sanxi said. "If there is any counterrevolutionary slogan to be found, it must have been written by you!"

"Look at the way you wrote Li Tongmao. The third character should be the *mao* for 'exuberant,' but you have written the *mao* for Chairman Mao's surname. Your slogan says *Da dao Li tong Mao*—'down with Li and Mao.'"

"I wrote that *mao* to mean 'hair,' not the surname," Sanxi protested, "because *mao* for 'exuberant' is too nice for Li Tongmao. And *tong* here doesn't mean 'and'; it's just part of Li Tongmao's name."

The man was not swayed. "You could have chosen another *mao*. The fact remains that this *mao* is Chairman Mao's surname. No doubt about it, this is a counterrevolutionary slogan."

"That's ridiculous! We're all Chairman Mao's Red Guards. We wouldn't slander him. Let these other people judge." Sanxi looked around pleadingly.

"Counterrevolutionary, definitely counterrevolutionary," one of the onlookers said.

"Let's take this group of counterrevolutionaries to the Public Security Bureau," suggested another.

"The Public Security Bureau is not functioning. Let's take them into the Military Control Commission," the man in coveralls said. A few youths stepped forward and marched us toward the commission office.

The night guard in the office said the matter would have to wait until morning. The man in coveralls turned us over to the youths, who taunted us all night as we sat on the curb. Early in the morning, they finally let us go. We trudged back to the college, our cart still half-laden with slogans.

After we got back to Yizhong, a second scuffle broke out between East-Is-Red Corps members and Lu Xun Commune supporters. Someone had climbed the pole atop the Principal's Building and unscrewed the amplifiers from the loudspeakers that carried Baimudan's shrieks through the air. Her cries of dismay, even unamplified, brought students running from all directions. "There's the thief! Don't let him go!" Baimudan, her face smeared with tears and dust, was pointing at Qiude, who had succeeded me as Leiting's newspaper editor. His clothes were disheveled and his shirt was torn. "False accusation!" he yelled back. "Hooligan!" Baimudan shouted. "Harlot!" Qiude retorted.

Two boys sprang out of the crowd and punched Qiude. Two more jumped out. By the time I realized they were Weihua and Leiting, they had pummeled the first two to the ground. More fistfights erupted. When a blow landed on my back, I hit back at the nearest person wearing an East-Is-Red Corps armband. This time, Fangpu and Mengzhe both arrived to stop the fight. Fangpu accused the Lu Xun Commune of sabotage. Mengzhe denied it and accused the East-Is-Red Corps of inciting violence. "Struggle by reason, not by force," he quoted from the Sixteen Points.

My three comrades and I retired to headquarters to assess the situation. Sanxi and Erchou had been kicked in the crotch, and Zongwei hit in the head. We agreed the fight would not be the last. "Chairman Mao says that armed struggle is the highest form of political struggle," I observed. "When people can't solve their contradictions, they naturally resort to struggle by force."

The big question before us was how to prepare for the fighting to come. We decided that absolute pacifism was not a practical option. "Chairman Mao says we will not attack unless we are attacked, and if we are attacked we will certainly counterattack," said Zongwei. "The East-Is-Red Corps has attacked, and we must be ready to counterattack."

Erchou suggested that we practice Shaolin boxing. Still, it would be four of us against seven hundred of the enemy—and we doubted whether we could hone our skills as finely as the legendary eighteen monks of Shaolin Temple. We concluded that the best defense would be for all the small groups to unite under centralized leadership.

Many of our allies were considering the same idea. At a unity conference, Leiting formally proposed a grand merger of the Lu Xun Commune, the East-Is-Red Commune, and all the small supporting groups. Almost all the groups endorsed it. We joined forces in a big unified organization called Red

Rebel Headquarters, with Mengzhe as commander-in-chief. Qiude was named editor of the newspaper, *Red Rebels*. Xiaomei, "small plum blossom," the school's best soprano, headed the Propaganda Performance Team. Jinfeng, "golden phoenix," was general staff secretary. We recruited a number of teachers: my old homeroom teacher, Wen Xiu, helped run the newspaper, and physics teacher Feng played accordion for the performance team. More East-Is-Red Corps members defected to our side, including one of their lower-ranking leaders, a girl named Yulan, "magnolia." Leiting headed the first brigade, which included his original East-Is-Red Commune, my Uniquely Beautiful View, and a few other groups, totaling 70 people. We exchanged our old armbands for our new Red Rebel insignia.

Scores of us took the train to Shimen for another 901 support rally, this one called by the United Workers Rebel Headquarters. The United Workers were strong on the east side of the city, where textile mills and other factories were concentrated. They had chosen a stadium on the west side of the city, just a few blocks from the Military Control Commission, to deliver their challenge to the 93rd Army. The thousands of workers who crowded the stadium looked as if they had just left their looms and assembly lines. The men's coveralls were stained with grease, the women's caps decorated with cotton fluff. Hundreds of red flags, many bearing the frenetic calligraphy of the Madman's Commune, fluttered in the morning breeze.

A couplet flanking the stage set up at one end of the playing field read "We dare to go up to the ninth layer of heaven to pluck down the moon; we dare to plunge down into the five oceans to catch the turtles." Sanxi and I went over to admire the huge loudspeaker fixed on the sound truck. The opening of the big horn was two meters across. Ten amplifiers were clustered at the other end like multiple warheads. This was the famous 901 loudspeaker that could be heard in downtown Shimen from the Missile Engineering Institute fifteen kilometers out in the western suburbs.

"Where did they buy such a giant loudspeaker?" Sanxi asked.

"You can't buy such a loudspeaker," said a Madman student who was also admiring it. "The 901 people designed and built it themselves. For people who design missiles, making such a loudspeaker is like doing first-grade math."

A cadet tested the speaker, drawing cheers and applause from the audience seated on the playing field and in the stands. Rebel dignitaries mounted the stage. The rally was about to begin. Just then, another truck, mounted with four large speakers, rolled onto the field. "Firmly smash the anti-army conspiracy!" it blared. "Smash the black United Workers!" People in army uniform on the truck hoisted a flag. They were from Shimen's Army Computer Engineering Institute.

In rolled two more trucks blasting slogans. Amid deafening noise, a United Workers leader stepped to the podium and announced that the rally would proceed as planned. His voice, amplified by the Missile Institute's giant loudspeaker, could be heard even over the three sound trucks from the rival school. Then a long line of trucks and jeeps mounted with speakers entered the stadium and drew up in a semicircle before the stage. Sanxi and I counted 24 vehicles. The big 901 speaker was drowned out.

Workers, Madmen, Red Rebels, and other spectators began to scramble down from the stands. Paper parcels flew across the playing field and burst into yellow puffs as they hit the intruding trucks. Within a minute, hundreds of these dirt bombs were hurtling through the air. Sanxi and I joined the assault, scooping up handfuls of the sandy clay that covered the stadium ground, wrapping it in handbills, and throwing it toward the mouths of the enemy speakers. The air became opaque as sound trucks fell silent. Dirt bombs continued to explode. People began to cough and choke, and then to push and shove. Sanxi had disappeared in the thick yellow dust.

Making out the shape of a truck, I unscrewed the gas cap and dumped in a handful of sand. As the dust settled, I could see that the stage was deserted and the giant 901 speaker had been robbed of its amplifiers. Some people were engaged in fistfights; others pressed toward the exits. Three enemy vehicles were still working. I hurled a final sand bomb toward one. Before I knew what was happening, two people grabbed me by the hair, twisted my arms behind my back, and forced me to walk. With a push, they sent me running through a human corridor formed by two lines of men. I ran as fast as I could, covering my head with my arms to ward off the blows. I collapsed at the other end. Sanxi burst into view, his face red and dirt-streaked. "Fuck their mothers!" he said. "Fortunately, my muscles are strong from working in the fields. Otherwise, I would be chopped meat!"

Uncommon Laughter

The showcase outside the Lingzhi county theater that had once displayed pictures of scenes from plays was now filled with photographs of rebel struggle meetings against Papa and other leaders. Weihua swore angrily as we walked by.

Our brothers and sisters told us that they had attended some of these meetings with their schoolmates. "We even shouted slogans," Yiyuan said proudly. "We shouted, 'Down with Gao Shangui!'"

Weihua became furious. "How dare you go to struggle meetings and shout slogans against Papa? Hasn't he suffered enough? Does he need his own children to denounce him?" The more he yelled, the angrier he grew. He grabbed Yiyuan, turned her upside down, and shook her by the ankles. "Are you going to do that again? Speak!"

"No, I'll never do it again!" Yiyuan cried, flinging her arms about in the air, her eyes wide with fright. "I'll never go to another meeting! I'll never shout slogans again!"

It was my turn to lose my temper. "You bully!" I shouted at Weihua. "Are you a bandit?" I ran out of the house and down to the riverside, where I let the cool evening breeze blow on my face.

When I got back to the house, Weihua and Grandpa were sitting on the stoop. Weihua was crying. Grandpa was telling him, "Your brothers and sisters are under a lot of pressure. Being in Yizhen, you don't know what they have to suffer here. All the ignorant kids in the street curse and abuse them. Their schoolmates watch their every move. They have no choice but to attend these struggle meetings. Both your mother and I agreed to let them go. These days, the problem is how to survive, not whether to keep your honor or save face."

Weihua's deep, grief-stricken sobbing affected all of us, for he seldom cried. The younger children began crying too. I joined Weihua on the stoop and said softly, "Big Brother, I'm sorry. Please don't cry anymore." His sobbing diminished, but he did not lift his head for a long time.

Uncommon Laughter

Papa was touring the countryside now under a Thought Guard escort. The rebels had vowed to lead struggle meetings against him in every village in the county. Mama was visiting our old hometown, Shuiyuan, and was expected back any time.

I was home with Grandpa the evening Mama returned. I was eager to hear whether the old courtyard where we had spent our first years was just the way we had left it—with the big cypress tree Grandpa had tended and the well Grandpa had once gone down to rescue a duck. But Mama was even more brusque than usual. After greeting me, she turned to Grandpa and began talking in a low voice.

"Dad," she said. I could not remember ever having heard her call Grandpa "dad." "I have bad news for you. Big Uncle died. He hung himself." Big Uncle was Grandpa's older brother. Big Uncle's son had died of hunger and disease on a reservoir construction site during the Three Difficult Years.

After a long silence, Grandpa asked, "Why?"

"After my cousin died, he raised a lot of complaints. When the Cultural Revolution came along, people put up dazibao accusing him of attacking socialism. He got scared."

Grandpa heaved a loud sigh.

"Dad, don't be too upset. Uncle was too weak. As a teacher, he should have been more philosophical."

I felt like a shadow in the room. I wanted to know more, but sensed that I was not even supposed to be hearing this much.

"Another thing," Mama continued. "Rebels ransacked our ancestral burial mounds to look for treasures. They dug up Grandpa's and Great-Grandpa's cypress coffins and used the wood for tables for the production brigade."

Treasures in that old cemetery? I could picture the place in

Uncommon Laughter

my mind, with its grass-covered mounds shaded by pines. Grandpa had taken Weihua and me there to sweep the ancestor's tombs. Mama's family had always been middle peasant. All they owned was a five-room house in a courtyard inlaid with pebbles. Only landlords took treasures to the grave.

"Some good villagers objected to the grave robbery," Mama said. "They said the Fu daughter was a revolutionary cadre even before Liberation, so my family's ancestral plot should not be violated this way. I did not want to get involved, for fear of bringing more trouble to the family. I merely collected the bones in an urn and let my nephews rebury them in the original place. My nephews are very poor now. I told them not to get involved in politics. They said that in fact they are not even given the chance."

After Mama had left, Grandpa sat on the kang looking downcast. When Weihua came home, I related the conversation to him. His questions were the same as the ones on my mind: "Is it possible that Mama's grandfather and great-grandfather were landlords? Are Grandpa and Mama landlords?" We did not dare ask.

Weihua returned to Yizhong before me, thinking that Mengzhe might need him. I stayed a few days longer because rumor had it that Papa would come back from the countryside sooner than expected. The day he arrived, I went to see him. Some beans he had planted outside the door of his single room had grown up to the windowsill. The door was unlocked, but nobody was there. Instead of medicine bottles, a neat stack of paper sat on the desk. Beside the paper rested Papa's long-stemmed pipe. The bowl was still warm. Papa could not be too far away.

I looked at the top sheet of paper to see what document Papa might be drafting. "My Self-Criticism, by Gao Shangui," it said. I turned to the next page, and the next, and the next. The self-criticism was divided into ten parts, and ran almost two hundred pages. Part 1 was entitled "I Failed to Hold High the Great Banner of Mao Zedong Thought." Part 2 was "I Neglected to Grasp the Enemy, Ourselves and Our Friends, and Only Paid Attention to Grain, Cotton, and Oil." The third part was "I Did Not Comprehend the Great Significance of the Cultural Revolution." The fourth part was "I Chose Appointees with Serious Historical Problems." Hurriedly, I scanned page after page of small, neat characters, searching for any serious admission, such as opposing Chairman Mao or the Party. Most of the other capitalist-roaders in the county government already had pleaded guilty to such things. Papa had not. His self-criticism fell short of total surrender.

I had barely restacked the pile when Papa appeared at the door, wearing his usual white cotton peasant shirt and a straw hat. "Jianhua, how are you? I went out to see the wheat fields. It's only two weeks from Grain in Ear, the time to cut wheat." Papa removed his hat. His hair had been shaved to a stubble.

"You got a haircut, Papa?"

"Yes, it's cooler and saves me the trouble of shampooing. It's also hard for them to pull hair that's so short."

"How are things in the countryside?" I searched Papa's face, finding no sign of cuts or bruises.

"Not bad. The common people make their own judgments. They treat me no differently than when I was county head. A few of the Thought Guards even changed their minds after seeing how people treated me. They found their consciences."

"The Thought Guards let you come back to town?"

"They didn't want me to come back. But the 93rd Army

tank regiment stationed in this county ordered them to let me come home for a rest. The regiment commander also restored my full salary, which had been cut in half. These army men have very good sense."

I wondered how much Papa knew about the 93rd Army. "Papa, what do you hear about the 901 Missile Engineering Institute in Shimen?" I asked.

"I know the Thought Guards are dissatisfied with the tank regiment and have contacted the 901, trying to get their support. But the 901 have never been to this county, so I'm not familiar with them."

New questions whirled through my mind. Might our faction in Yizhen be linked to the Thought Guards through the 901? Were Weihua and I indirectly supporting my father's persecution? I opposed the Thought Guards and would never do anything to support them. I also opposed the East-Is-Red Corps and would never dream of joining them in order to support the 93rd Army just because the tank regiment supported Papa. Thought Guards, East-Is-Red, Lu Xun, 93rd, 901 . . . I felt more confused than ever.

"Jianhua," Papa called sharply. "Whatever you do, do not join a faction that opposes the army. The army is the pillar of the country. The country cannot do without the army. Whoever opposes the army will come to no good end. Do you hear me?"

"Yes, Papa." The names were still spinning around in my head.

The atmosphere at dinner was cheerier than it had been in a long time. Under Grandpa's guidance, Zhihua had made noodles that came out thin and even. Everyone praised him. Mama came by in a buoyant mood and stayed to eat with us, a rare event. "Papa had some wonderful experiences with the

Uncommon Laughter

Thought Guards in the countryside!" she said. She related several anecdotes of his trip that were already making their way around on the town's grapevine.

Once when the Thought Guards were walking Papa from one village to the next, they met an old peasant pulling a cart up a long slope. Papa went over to help him. The Thought Guards scolded Papa, saying, "For all you know, you might be helping a landlord!" The peasant got angry. "Why scold this good comrade? I'm a poor peasant three generations back!" he said indignantly. The Thought Guards warned the old man, "You'd better not call him comrade; he's the country's biggest capitalist-roader, Gao Shangui." The peasant stopped his cart and invited Papa to ride. Of course, Papa declined the offer and walked with the Thought Guards to the next village.

When the Thought Guards brought Papa to Tile Terrace, the model brigade that he had helped set up and that was his favorite place in the whole county, they were enraged to find the peasants cooking him good things to eat. When a Thought Guard found a woman preparing jiaozi for Papa, he shouted at her, "Don't you know what he's here for? He came to be struggled against as a capitalist-roader, not to be entertained like an emperor. Where is your class stand? Why don't you entertain the Red Guards with jiaozi, instead of giving us wotou?" The woman replied, "We are afraid that jiaozi may turn you revolutionary Red Guards revisionist, so we only give them to the capitalist-roader. Meals that help you recall past bitterness are better for you."

We all laughed so heartily that clods of dirt fell down from the ceiling.

"I have more good news," Mama went on. "The rebels in the county government have split with the Thought Guards after learning that the Thought Guards have sided with the 901 in Shimen to oppose the 93rd Army tank regiment. The Thought Guards have never been so isolated."

"What's the 901?" Xinghua asked.

"A batch of rotten eggs, like the Thought Guards," Mama said. I suppressed the urge to argue with her, not wanting to ruin her high spirits.

Victory Fish

Virtually the entire populace of Yizhen, old and young, men and women, workers and peasants, housewives and peddlers, had taken sides. Either you were pro-901 or you were pro-93rd Army. In the town where Zhao Yun of the Three Kingdoms had once been the favorite topic, the numbers 901 and 93 now were on everyone's lips. Once-harmonious families were breaking up. Siblings refused to talk with one another, or communicated with curses and fists. Once-loving husbands and wives were filing for divorce. Best friends had become enemies.

In mid-June, both pro-901 and pro-93rd forces held rallies in downtown Yizhen to show their strength and proclaim countywide alliances. Our side formed the Red Revolutionary Rebel Headquarters of Yizhen County. I spent the night before our founding rally in the chemistry lab with Teacher Feng, dropping zinc into bottles of hydrochloric acid to make hydrogen for the hundreds of balloons that we would set afloat over the town the next day.

At Yizhong, fistfights between Red Rebels and East-Is-Red Corps members had become everyday events. We interrupted each other's meetings and stole each other's equipment in broad daylight. Around the clock, we fought amplified propaganda battles against the East-Is-Red Corps. Our platform was to unite all those who could be united with. All but one of the teachers who were not monsters and demons joined our side. East-Is-Red Corps defections grew from a trickle to a torrent. The Red Rebel ranks expanded to seven hundred, while the East-Is-Red Corps dwindled to four hundred.

One morning, the enemy newspaper, *Battlefield News*, announced that the East-Is-Red Corps had taken three of our comrades prisoner for attempting to steal their amplifiers again and had sentenced them to five days in custody. "Anyone who dares to undertake such sabotage in the future will be subject to more serious punishment," the paper warned. We quickly established that the main prisoner was Haozi, "mouse," a daredevil of a boy who had often been assigned to risky tasks. He and his two accomplices, after being interrogated all night, had blamed Mengzhe for engineering this plot to steal the amplifiers, as well as the previous amplifier theft. It was a great propaganda coup for the East-Is-Red Corps and a heavy blow for us.

I was writing a commentary for our paper, *Red Rebel*, accusing the other side of holding hostages, when Sanxi burst in with more news: "Jianhua, come on! We've caught the spy responsible for the kidnapping of our comrades!" I followed Sanxi to the bell-tower courtyard, where he rapped on a door. Someone opened it just enough to admit us. "Don't let anybody else in," someone else said.

The windows were covered with quilts. Only one dim bulb was on. When my eyes had adjusted to the dark, I recognized a group of boys from the first grade who had joined the Red Rebels in the recent wave of defections. Their leader was Dusu, whose father headed Yizhen's trade-union organization. I also discerned a figure sitting on a chair in a corner. Going a few steps closer, I saw that it was Yulan, whose defection we had hailed as a major conquest. She was bound to the chair with ropes. Her white blouse was torn and her hair fell loosely over her face. Her eyes were full of hatred.

"This afternoon, we saw Fangpu's personal messenger, Little Mihu, loitering around Rear Lake," Dusu said. "We put him under surveillance and found him receiving notes from a Red Rebel member outside the city wall. Little Mihu fled, but we caught this girl. The bitch was eavesdropping on secret meetings at headquarters. She is responsible for the arrest of our commando team."

Dusu ordered the other boys to pull Yulan's chair into the middle of the room and unbind her. "Yulan, did you send information to Fangpu about the loudspeakers?" he asked her.

"Yes," Yulan said. "Now you can wail over the sad fate of your thieves."

"Stop slandering our comrades," Dusu replied sharply. "Fangpu planted you as a spy in our headquarters, didn't he?"

"I came by myself because I hate you conservative royalists," Yulan said.

One of the boys slapped her in the face. "You stinking bitch, don't you dare slander us! Confess how you were planted. Otherwise, we won't let you go."

Yulan held her head high and whispered, "Stinking executioner."

The boy hit her several more times. She stayed erect, saying nothing. In a moment, the others had joined in. They hit her

Victory Fish

on the head and back, kicked her legs, and slashed her cheeks with willow branches. She pressed her lips firmly together and held onto the seat of the chair. She reminded me of the heroine in the novel *Red Crag*, who had been tortured and executed by the Kuomintang and American imperialists in Chongqing's prison.

"Stop!" I yelled at the boys. Yulan had toppled from the chair and was curled on the floor. The boys looked at me with puzzled expressions. Sanxi's smile of pleasure also gave way to a look of perplexity. "Stop beating her," I said.

"What are you talking about?" one of the boys said. "We can't show mercy for this venomous snake. She brought suffering upon three of our best comrades." The boys resumed slashing Yulan with the willow branches.

I rushed out of the room and headed for Red Rebel headquarters, where I interrupted a leadership meeting to tell Mengzhe about the maltreatment of Yulan. He dispatched Leiting to stop the boys. Then he proposed that the Red Rebels offer to trade Yulan for the three captives held by the East-Is-Red Corps. The motion passed unanimously. Within a few minutes, the offer was broadcast over the Red Rebels public-address system. Half an hour later, the East-Is-Red Corps loudspeakers announced acceptance.

The prisoner exchange was conducted late that night in the bell-tower courtyard. A line of East-Is-Red Corps members faced a line of Red Rebels in the darkness. Red Rebels carried Yulan on a bedboard to a point midway between the lines and set her down. East-Is-Red Corps people carried Haozi, also on a board, to the midway point. His two partners walked under escort. Each side took its own back. Then both sides melted into the night.

Moments later, the East-Is-Red Corps loudspeakers broke

the silence. "Down with the Red Rebels! Protest the Red Rebels' cruel atrocities! Make Mengzhe pay the blood debt!" Our speakers barked back, "Down with the East-Is-Red Corps! Protest the East-Is-Red Corps' cruelty! Make Fangpu pay the blood debt!"

I stayed up all night working on a revised commentary for *Red Rebel* and helping Qiude put the paper to press. At breakfast, the dining hall seemed unusually empty. Not a single East-Is-Red Corps person was there. Witnesses reported that they had seen the enemy march out the South Gate at dawn, carrying Yulan on her board. We soon found out that they had gone to petition the County Military Department to punish the boys who had beaten her. Mengzhe instructed the Red Rebels to follow them. "We should put up a reasoned struggle," he said. "No violence is allowed. Wear down our adversaries through argument and debate."

Row upon row of East-Is-Red Corps members were sitting on the ground in the courtyard of the County Military Department. Yulan lay on the board at the front of the group, covered up to the forehead by a sheet. Fangpu stood beside her, leading the crowd in slogan-shouting. A petition posted on the courtyard wall demanded three things of the military authorities: first, retribution for the beating; second, withdrawal of any form of support for the Red Rebels; and third, a self-criticism to the people of the county, apologizing for having supported the Red Rebels and pledging to support the East-Is-Red Corps instead. If the department did not respond by noon, the East-Is-Red Corps would go on a hunger strike in protest.

As Red Rebels filed into the courtyard, the East-Is-Red Corps people began to moan and cry as if they were in a funeral procession. I saw my classmates Caolan, Congfang,

Victory Fish

and Xiangyun sitting together, tears running down their faces. Huantian was there too, but she was not wailing.

Sanxi stood in front of our classmates and shouted, "What are you crying for? Are your parents dead?" "Hooligan! Everyone in your family is dead! And you won't live long!" Caolan shouted back. She resumed her sobbing. "With justice on your side, you can go anywhere; without it, you can't take a step," Sanxi said. "You may rant and rave, but you'll get no sympathy from the people." Caolan stopped crying again to respond. "Executioners! You beat Yulan so badly that she urinated blood! How could you do such a terrible thing?"

"Tell me this," interjected Zongwei. "Who started the beating? Who beat Haozi and his two comrades? Who planted the spy in our headquarters?" "Who sent thieves in the night to steal our amplifiers?" Caolan countered. "Who spread vicious rumors and slander via loudspeaker?" Zongwei said.

So the arguments went, on and on until noon. Then the county military director appeared to say that his department would investigate the incidents under dispute. He went back inside without addressing the three points in the petition. "In view of the County Military Department's complete bias in handling our grievances, we hereby launch our mass hunger strike," Fangpu announced. Yulan was carried off on her bedboard to recuperate, her face still covered by the sheet.

Having no desire to miss lunch along with the hunger strikers, our side returned to school. With Mengzhe's approval, some of us decided to offer our adversaries food. If they refused, it would illustrate to the townsfolk that they were suffering on their own accord, not because of us. The whole first brigade marched through the streets of Yizhen carrying bamboo steamers full of wotou. Leiting led us, carrying a big pot of summer squash. As we entered the courtyard, Baimudan stood up to conduct a Chairman Mao quotation song:

> We must have resolve,
> And not fear to sacrifice our lives;
> We must overcome ten thousand hardships,
> And go all out to win victory!

Leiting took a pair of bronze clappers from his pocket, cleared his throat, and chanted a response:

> Comrades, listen to me,
> Chairman Mao has said that we
> Should avoid unnecessary sacrifice
> And above all conserve our lives
> To make revolution!
> In order to make revolution,
> You must be in good condition,
> And in order to be healthy,
> You must eat heartily
> For the revolution!
> Good health is the capital of the revolution,
> So eat, comrades, eat,
> And don't abuse your stomachs!

I opened the top rack of a steamer and offered Xiangyun a wotou. She knocked it out of my hand, saying, "Who wants your stinking food?" I offered one to Little Mihu. He puckered up his face and turned away. I tried Little Bawang. Turning his head in disdain, he said, "Since when does the weasel pay respect to the hen?"

"If you're too embarrassed to eat in front of us, you can do so after we leave," I said, setting the steamer on the ground. "When they're hungry, they'll eat," said Sanxi. "There's no horse that doesn't eat grass."

Victory Fish

We left the steamers in the courtyard all afternoon. The wotou were cold and untouched when we came to take the steamers back to school. After dinner, we brought fresh food. This time, the hunger strikers threw dirt into the cauldrons.

I stayed up late writing a report for *Red Rebel* about our kindness. Then I returned to the courtyard. The weakened strikers were leaning on each other or lying on the ground. A girl's mournful voice began to sing:

> Lifting my head, I see the Big Dipper,
> Deep in my heart, I miss Mao Zedong;
> In the black night when I think of you,
> Brightness floods into my heart;
> When I feel at a loss, I think of you,
> You illuminate my way like a beacon . . .

Gradually, others joined the wailing soloist, until all the strikers were singing, many with tears flowing down their cheeks. They repeated the song over and over until they were exhausted.

Just before midnight, a soldier emerged with a radio. He had not come out to discuss the petition. Instead, he said that an important message was expected on the central radio station's midnight news. He turned up the volume so that we could all hear the broadcaster announce China's first H-bomb explosion.

The next day, the hunger strikers again refused the food we brought. They would not even drink water. By the third day, they were all lying on the ground. Several got sunstroke and had to be carried away. Still, the military department gave no response.

Parents of East-Is-Red Corps members came to the courtyard hoping to persuade their children to eat. Xiangyun's brother Xiangsheng came with their father, a retired army officer, who entreated Xiangyun to abandon the strike. She listened passively with her eyes closed. Then she sat up and declared, "You did not fear death when you were making revolution, nor do I when I am making revolution!" Xiangsheng gave her a kick with his good foot. Their father gave him a slap for abusing his sister. Then he left, cursing Fangpu for leading his daughter astray.

On the third night, a group of men slipped into the courtyard like shadows and began hauling the strikers away. At first, the strikers struggled and screamed, saying that they would rather die than leave without victory. But they soon quieted down and let the men carry them out. In fact, the intruders were other people from the pro-93rd Army faction who had orchestrated a way to save the strikers from losing face. The drama unfolded smoothly, and the courtyard was empty within half an hour. Our first brigade followed the rescuers to the County Commerce Bureau, where the pro-93rd Army forces had a majority. Through the windows, we watched people feeding our adversaries bowls of gruel.

The East-Is-Red Corps students did not return to school for a week. When they came back, it was only to get their quilts. They were making what they called a "strategic retreat," which they compared to the Red Army's departure from the Jinggang Mountains to escape Chiang Kai-shek's fifth Encirclement and Annihilation Campaign. Our paper *Red Rebel* called it "fleeing helter-skelter," the way that Chiang Kai-shek had fled to Taiwan.

The whole campus now belonged to us. Mengzhe felt we would be vulnerable to surprise attack if we remained scattered, so we all moved into rooms around the bell-tower courtyard. I shared a room with my three closest comrades—Sanxi, Zongwei, and Erchou.

Since no girls remained in Vatican City, the four of us decided to explore that forbidden place. The dormitory rooms were in disorder, piled with scrap paper, old clothes, broken glass, split bedboards, and overturned chairs. "Look, a horse-riding cloth!" Sanxi exclaimed, snatching a sanitary belt off a clothesline. "This should be used to cover Fangpu's mouth!"

Erchou was gathering old toothpaste tubes. "There's a lot of good junk here," he said. "It's a pity to let it go to waste." As an experienced garbage-picker, I wholeheartedly agreed. Soon the four of us were earning a modest but steady income by scavenging. We made two or three yuan a day selling toothpaste tubes and worn-out shoes to the town salvage station, enough to keep us well supplied with popsicles.

Life seemed free and easy. We did not even have to wash our dishes after meals. The East-Is-Red Corps students had left their tin bowls and lunchboxes behind in the dining hall, and we helped ourselves to them whenever we ate. When we were finished, we threw the bowls and boxes onto the rooftops or crushed them underfoot and sold them along with the toothpaste tubes and old shoes.

When we tired of going to town and eating popsicles every day, we turned to carpentry. We expropriated tools from Carpenter Zhang's workshop, dismantled dilapidated tables, and used the wood to build boxes and cabinets. Wood shavings and sawdust covered the floor of our room. When we tired of carpentry, we turned to fishing, using needles bent over candle flames for hooks. Rear Lake was teeming with carp because the school had missed the annual fish-catch the year before, so we caught quite a lot, even with only turnips and squash for bait.

Victory Fish

News that the lake was overstocked spread quickly after other students saw us grilling fish over a campfire. The Red Rebel leadership decided to organize a thorough catch. We dragged a large net the length of the lake, trapping mounds of jumping carp. After scaling and cleaning them on the banks, we steamed them in washbasins. Everyone got as much as he or she could eat. What made this feast especially delicious was the fact that the East-Is-Red Corps people were missing it. "If Little Bawang and the others could see us, they would die of anger," Sanxi said.

The First Martyr

Our life of leisure within the school walls could not last forever. As the oppressive July heat spread over the North China plain, the battles between our allies and our enemies spread through the town of Yizhen. Whenever we went downtown for popsicles, we heard stories about the latest escapades of the East-Is-Red Corps. Fangpu's people had moved into the Hydrology Institute on Perpetual Victory Street, an anti-901 stronghold. Every night, they would pour across the street to the Army Hospital to help the anti-901 Dr. Bethune Battle Team fight the pro-901 Red Medical Soldiers. The encounters were fierce ones, conducted with stones, bricks, and slingshots. Before long, the Red Medical Soldiers were forced into a corner of the hospital compound. Their leader was kidnapped, tortured, and released near death. It did not come as a surprise when Mengzhe ordered us to move to the Army Hospital to reinforce our beleaguered comrades.

We joined the Red Medical Soldiers in what had been the tuberculosis ward; the patients had gone home to avoid the fighting. Luckily, this section of the hospital had a dining hall and a contingent of friendly cooks. Beds were plentiful. It was the first time I had ever slept on a bed with springs, a thick mattress, and mosquito netting. Yuanchao was the only one in my class who even owned a mosquito net. When he had put it up in our dormitory room, the rest of us had persuaded him to take it down, saying it was not in the Communist spirit to divert mosquitoes from his bed to ours.

Yuanchao showed up soon after we moved in, and joined our organization. We were glad to have him, for he would make a good guide through the hospital's maze of buildings and courtyards. Although Yuanchao's father no longer actually ran the hospital, he still was its nominal head. The anti-901 people had made him wear a signboard and stand before a few struggle meetings, but did not dare treat a Long March veteran too harshly. Now he was resting at home. Yuanchao warned us not to go anywhere at night alone because we might get taken hostage.

It took only a few nights for our side to battle its way out of the corner. Taking advantage of the abundant supply of broken bricks and rocks on the ground around our ward, we pushed the front all the way to the old Catholic church, which now served as an auditorium, in the center of the hospital complex. The church and the area around it became a no-man's-land. When darkness fell, both sides would creep up to throw stones and bricks at the opposing shadows.

Mengzhe decided to form a Night Tiger Team that could strike deep into enemy territory under cover of darkness. He picked 36 fighters from among the volunteers, including Wei-hua, Leiting, Sanxi, and Erchou. A boy as agile as a monkey, Lushuang, was appointed head of the team. I became the official *Red Rebel* correspondent assigned to cover the team's maneuvers. Armed with a slingshot and a pocketful of pebbles, I followed along with my notebook.

Each night was much the same as the one before. We crept out after nightfall, clambered in and out the windows of unfamiliar buildings, skirmished with an enemy we could not see, and sometimes got lost. All night long, muffled running, the twang of slingshots, the sound of bouncing stones, and occasionally the crash of shattering glass punctuated the darkness.

One night, team members captured an army nurse from the Dr. Bethune Battle Team. They carried her struggling and screaming like a tied pig to our ward and jailed her in an empty office. Sanxi, Erchou, and I went to look at the captive. A group of boys were shouting at her, "What's your battle plan? When will your night troops come out? If you don't speak, don't plan on getting out of here alive!" The nurse answered the questions with a sneer.

Sanxi strode up to her and tore the red star from her army cap. "Are you qualified to be People's Liberation Army?" he demanded. "Fascists!" she replied. Another boy slapped her across the face. She stubbornly kept her head high. I left the room, not eager to witness another beating.

I could not sleep that night. Sometime early in the morning, I got up and walked softly back to the room where the nurse was jailed. The sentry guarding the door had fallen asleep. I pulled out the nail holding the latch and went in. The nurse also was asleep. Shaking her awake, I whispered, "Don't be afraid. Go, quickly." She looked at me in surprise

The First Martyr

before rising and slipping out the door. The next morning when the escape was discovered, the Red Rebels could do nothing but curse the sentry for sleeping on the job. Of course, I let him take the blame.

Weihua was our first casualty: a sharp rock hit him in the forehead. Sanxi and Erchou helped me move him back to the ward, where a doctor put him to bed and wound a white bandage around his head. Afterward, Lushuang and Leiting obtained hardhats made of willow twigs to distribute to our fighters. "A fall into the pit, a gain in your wit," Leiting said as he tossed me one. "As Chairman Mao would say, we are learning about warfare from engaging in warfare."

"Is this strong enough?" I put my hat on the ground and jumped on it, thinking it would collapse, but it did not. "Don't look down on willow twigs," Leiting said. "These are soaked in water and dried in the sun. This is the best protection against bricks and stones." Sanxi and Erchou walked proudly back and forth with their helmets on. On the front of Sanxi's was the red star he had taken from the captured nurse.

The pattern of skirmishes by night and relative calm by day changed when the East-Is-Red Corps abducted one of our members, a mild boy everyone called Heping, "peace." He had defected from the East-Is-Red Corps because he thought it too prone to violence. He was always arguing against force. Even some of us thought he was too much of a pacifist. According to Mengzhe's scouts, Heping had been tied to a post in the courtyard of the Hydrology Institute for interrogation. He had reprimanded his captors and refused to answer any questions. Mengzhe called an emergency meeting and said the heroic Heping must be rescued at any cost.

Hundreds of Red Rebels assembled outside our ward, with

The First Martyr

helmets on and pickax handles and a variety of other clubs in hand. We began to jog across the hospital grounds toward the front gate. Mengzhe halted us at the church for another announcement: Heping had just been put into a jeep and driven out of the Hydrology Institute gate. Mengzhe's informants suspected the jeep was headed for Shimen.

Mengzhe instructed the Night Tiger Team to chase the jeep, telling everyone else to return to the ward and stay on alert. I climbed onto the back of a truck with the team. Mengzhe came too. The truck sped out the south gate of town, forded the Hutuo River, careened down a country road, and stopped by a poplar grove along the main road to Shimen. Here we would wait behind the trees and watch for the jeep. Mengzhe estimated that it would come down the road in ten minutes. The truck would drive out to form a roadblock so the team could attack the jeep and rescue Heping.

Ten, fifteen, twenty minutes passed, and no jeep arrived. We waited nearly an hour before returning to the hospital, where someone told Mengzhe that the jeep had detoured through the mountains to the west before going to Shimen. We had no more word of Heping until four days later, when a notice appeared at Yizhen's main intersection saying he had died of sunstroke in a jeep on the way to Shimen. The notice was stamped with the seals of the county Public Security Bureau, People's Procuratorate, and People's Court, all agencies under anti-901 control. The last sentence of the notice was "The revolutionary masses must be vigilant to ensure that class enemies do not use this incident to stir up trouble."

Mengzhe called another emergency meeting. "Comrades, Heping has been cruelly murdered," he said. "According to our inside sources, Heping scathingly denounced his captors

The First Martyr

237

on the jeep ride. They tied his hands behind his back and stuffed dirty socks into his mouth. He suffocated to death. Only a devil would believe their story about sunstroke.

"Comrades, I knew Heping well. He was a nonviolent person. He argued with me and many others to repudiate violence. In the end, violence killed him. Comrades, we cannot be naïve about class struggle. We must defend ourselves by force! We must not let another Heping Incident occur!"

Our cries resounded throughout the ward: "Debts of blood must be paid in blood!" "Avenge the martyr Heping!" Over the next few days, ancient swords and spears that had rested for years in the households of Yizhen began to appear among our ranks.

The Red Revolutionary Rebel Headquarters of Yizhen County called a memorial meeting in Heping's honor. Thousands of people from as far away as Shimen stood with heads bowed before an outdoor stage covered with funeral wreaths and dominated by a large portrait of our martyr. After the ceremony, we wound through downtown Yizhen in a procession, carrying the wreaths and Heping's portrait. When we reached the Army Hospital, people battered down the steel gate, swarmed into the compound, and began throwing stones at windows. Members of the Dr. Bethune Battle Team who lived in the front buildings returned the fire with slingshots. The volleys continued until darkness fell.

The county's pro-901 forces guarded the hospital gate that night, sealing in the Dr. Bethune Battle Team and preventing the East-Is-Red Corps from coming across the street. The Night Tiger Team launched an assault from the rear of the compound, forcing the Dr. Bethune Battle Team to consolidate in a single building. This allowed us to push the battlefront past the church. I fell asleep on a pew to the sound of

The First Martyr

bouncing pebbles and breaking glass and awoke to the sight of the morning sunshine playing over Chairman Mao's face. Red Rebels were still on the rooftops, shooting stones at the Dr. Bethune Battle Team's stronghold. Not a single window-pane remained intact in any of the buildings around.

The Red Rebels were determined to capture the Dr. Bethune Battle Team's remaining building that day. In the afternoon, Night Tiger Team fighters climbed from a nearby wall onto the roof, took off the tiles, knocked a hole in the roof, and bombarded the occupants with tile shards from above. Meanwhile, our first brigade battered in the front door with a log. We poured inside, shouting "Surrender or face death!" A white sheet on a bamboo pole emerged from a window.

The defeated doctors, nurses, and orderlies filed outside. As army personnel, they all wore uniforms. A few had bandaged heads or their arms in slings. Most had their hands raised. Sanxi ran up to one young woman who did not have her hands up and pushed her to the ground. Another student took the red star from her cap and the red tabs from her collar. "Strip them all of their red stars and insignia!" Leiting shouted. "They disgrace the image of the invincible People's Liberation Army!" More Red Rebels ran up to collect the souvenirs. Some grabbed army caps and put them on their own heads.

While our prisoners of war were being herded into another building for interrogation, I wandered around the upstairs of their abandoned stronghold. Heaps of bandages, medicine bottles, quilts, books, and papers were strewn through the corridors. Upturned beds blocked the windows. Below each window were piles of stones and bricks, as well as shards of glass. Sunshine flooded through the hole in the roof. A shiny Chairman Mao badge glinting on a desk caught my eye. I

The First Martyr

picked it up and pinned it on my shirt. I also picked up a fountain pen. I came across a wallet. It had 25 yuan inside. I hesitated a moment before deciding that the money would make up for my loss to the thief in Shanghai. I put the bills in my pocket and tossed the wallet on the floor.

Mengzhe decided that we could better guard the captives at Yizhong. With the Dr. Bethune Battle Team enclosed between two lines of Red Rebels holding spears, we marched back to school. Yuanchao stayed behind; now that the Army Hospital had been liberated, he would go home and join the faction of the "free and unfettered," he said. Weihua, still recuperating from his head wound, left to visit relatives in Shuiyuan, our mountainous hometown where the summers were always cool.

After a few days, we got word that townsfolk were entering the unsupervised hospital and taking anything they could carry away. Mengzhe instructed us to return to evict the looters and restore order. In addition, we were to search the Hydrology Institute across the street. After our defeat of the Dr. Bethune Battle Team, the East-Is-Red Corps had fled to the Public Security Bureau. Mengzhe also granted our prisoners their freedom, on the condition that they go back to work and promise to refrain from anti-901 activities.

When we got to the hospital, we found not only townspeople but also peasants from surrounding villages rummaging through the buildings. Their numbers increased after dark. The Red Rebels posted a ban on looting. That night our people surprised several hundred offenders, ordered them to lay down their bundles, scolded them, and then let them go.

We combed through the booty for clothes, blankets, stretchers, medicine, rubber tubing to make catapults, and anything else that looked useful or interesting. We also searched the whole compound looking for things that the looters might have missed. I discovered a room full of army uniforms. The door had been pried open, and shirts, caps, socks, and shoes were scattered everywhere. Sanxi, Erchou, and I exchanged our ragged outfits for fresh white cotton underpants, white shirts, khaki trousers and jackets, socks, new rubber-tipped sneakers, belts, and caps. I stuffed my old shirt and shorts into the pocket of my smart new jacket. We left the building jubilantly, carrying several cartons of medicine bottles. Zongwei's eyes widened as he saw us. We directed him upstairs.

Mengzhe appeared as we were loading the medicine onto our truck of booty. He frowned at us and said, "We are revolutionary rebels, so we must obey revolutionary discipline. One of the main rules of discipline is to turn in all captured items. You must take off those uniforms and put them on the truck. The organization will dispose of the war trophies in a unified way."

"Can't we just wear them for a few days?" I begged.

"No. It will make a very bad impression on the masses."

There seemed to be no room for negotiation. I took off everything but my new underwear and sneakers, and put my old shorts and shirt back on.

"What about your shoes?" Mengzhe asked.

"I threw them away back there."

"Go get them."

"They're full of holes; otherwise I wouldn't have thrown them away."

Mengzhe paused. "Hand in those shoes after you buy some new ones." It was his way of saying that I could keep the army sneakers.

Zongwei came running out of the building in his new uni-

The First Martyr

241

form just in time to see Erchou, Sanxi, and me transformed into our shabby civilian selves. He quickly changed back too. The four of us joined the search at the Hydrology Institute just as Leiting was walking a motorcycle out of the gate. "Hurray, an electric donkey!" we cheered. Mengzhe had done even better: he drove up in a jeep. The best thing I found was a leather case containing a pair of binoculars stamped "Made in Germany" in English. I slung the case on my shoulder. Lushuang, the head of the Night Tiger Team, noticed it and made me turn it in.

Our victorious army marched through Yizhen, several trucks filled with booty rolling behind. When we got to the main intersection, Sanxi took a handful of coins from his pocket. "It's so hot, let's buy some popsicles," he said. "Where did you get that money?" I asked. "From a drawer. Zongwei said it wasn't worth taking, but I emptied the drawer anyway."

Sanxi took off his willow-twig helmet, dumped the coins into it, dipped into his pocket several more times, and took out several more handfuls of coins. He handed the money to an old woman selling popsicles and asked her to count it. It amounted to more than two yuan. "Give me two yuan worth of popsicles and keep the change," Sanxi said. The old woman put 40 popsicles into his helmet. They were quickly devoured by the Red Rebels lucky enough to be marching near Sanxi.

The First Martyr

Summons by Subterfuge

By the standards of Zhuge Liang, the great strategist of the Three Kingdoms, the Red Rebels were in a good position to take the offensive against the East-Is-Red Corps. Zhuge Liang had said there were three crucial factors in victory: opportunity, geography, and popular support. The Heping Incident had created a groundswell of popular support for our side. By mid-July, public sentiment in the city of Yizhen had turned decisively against the East-Is-Red Corps.

Those who still wanted to fight us had withdrawn to the isolated stronghold at the Public Security Bureau where Fangpu now made his headquarters. The rectangular layout of squat, interconnected buildings surrounding a series of three courtyards, with one taller building in the rear, made an ideal fortress. The East-Is-Red Corps had built brick battlements on top of the flat roofs on three sides, and installed its flag and loudspeakers atop the pointed roof in back.

East-Is-Red Corps people rarely appeared in public anymore. They had started a new round of struggle meetings against overthrown county officials in an attempt to divert people's attention from our criticism of them, but the tactic had failed utterly. They ceased holding meetings after one of their members stabbed a Red Rebel during a scuffle. Although our comrade survived, his wound gave us more reason to seek revenge. Our headquarters issued a statement saying that the new blood debt and the old one would have to be paid together.

To prepare for our offensive, Mengzhe set up a base at the local opera troupe's theater, just a block from the enemy camp. He sent the Night Tiger Team and the first brigade to occupy the theater, which we easily accomplished since the troupe supported us. We set up loudspeakers and installed giant catapults to shoot bricks into the Public Security Bureau compound. Sometimes the bricks fell onto the roofs of the houses between, but the residents did not dare complain. The Night Tiger Team went across the rooftops every night on scouting and harassment missions.

Our forces were becoming increasingly well armed. Lushuang had a gleaming sword, which he claimed dated from the Three Kingdoms period. Leiting had a samurai sword left over from the Anti-Japanese War. Xiangsheng, the clubfooted boy, had a whole set of marvelous weapons—an ancient spear, its finely forged head fixed on a white pole decorated with a brilliant red tassel; a sword whose hilt was inlaid with ivory, silver, and gold; and a steel helmet.

Mengzhe had assigned a group of students to mass-produce broadswords cut from steel plate under the supervision of several blacksmiths sympathetic to our cause. Erchou, Sanxi, Zongwei, and I, dissatisfied with these crude weapons, decided to make our own from high-carbon steel files. One of the blacksmiths softened each file in the furnace for us and held it steady on the anvil with tongs as we hammered it flat. The blacksmith said his family had made swords since the time of the Three Kingdoms. One of his ancestors had even forged Zhao Yun's Green Iron Sword, a task that had taken 81 days. When I asked him how much our headquarters was paying him, he became sullen. "I don't do this for money," he said. "No money could buy my skills. As a matter of fact, my usual work is hoes, scythes, and ladles. I haven't made a sword or spearhead in years. I came to help you only because I support the 901."

We made wooden hilts and leather sheaths for our swords. We also forged spearheads, which we fixed on sturdy wood poles. Later, we made body armor of thick pieces of leather. Some students even made armor from steel plate.

Sanxi, Erchou, and I slept side by side on benches inside the theater, marched through town with the first brigade every morning to show off our might, and joined the harassment missions against the enemy each night. Zongwei had decided to stay at school and work fulltime illustrating the *Red Rebel* newspaper. Although he did not say so, we knew he preferred struggle by words to struggle by force.

In early August, I got two telegrams in a row from Lingzhi telling me to go home because Papa was ill. I wondered if someone was playing a trick on me, for I had never received a telegram from home before. In any case, I did not want to leave my battle post. I put the telegrams aside.

I was helping to install two searchlights on the theater roof when somebody called from below to say that a man had come to see me. The man was standing outside the theater door with a motorcycle. I did not know him. "You're Jianhua?" he asked in a heavy Lingzhi accent. "Your father is seriously ill, and your mother asked me to pick you up. She said to tell you that you don't have to stay long; a brief visit will be enough."

Leiting agreed to give me leave but told me to come back as soon as possible. Half an hour later, after a dusty motor-

Summons by Subterfuge

cycle ride, I was home. Grandpa was chopping vegetables with the vigor I remembered from his healthier days. He gave me a broad smile. "Is Papa in the hospital?" I asked.

"Hospital? No, he's not in any hospital," Grandpa answered.

"Isn't Papa ill? Mama sent a motorcycle to bring me home to see him."

"No, he's not ill."

Indignation and anger welled up inside me. Had my parents lied to get me home? Had I left my important work in Yizhen for nothing?

"Papa and Mama are worried about your safety," Grandpa said. "Everbody's talking about the fighting in Yizhen. Weihua's safe in Shuiyuan. Maybe you should go there too. You could get killed in that fighting."

"Grandpa, you don't understand," I said. "We're defending Chairman Mao's revolutionary line. We have to fight. There's bound to be bloodshed and loss of life."

Grandpa looked at me quizzically. "I'm afraid I don't understand."

"Why did you lie to me?" I demanded when Papa and Mama came in with Yiyuan.

"We knew you wouldn't come home if we told you the real reason," Mama said. "We're very concerned about you. You've seen Weihua's terrible head wound."

"Papa, you've always taught me to be honest. How can you play such tricks?"

"It's for your own sake," Mama said.

"We're making revolution," I said. "Revolution!" I yelled. "Don't you understand? If everyone's parents lured their children off the battleground, who would be left to fight for Chairman Mao's revolutionary line?"

Summons by Subterfuge

"What revolution?" Papa suddenly roared. "Do you call what you're doing revolution? It's beating, smashing, and looting! I've heard plenty about your 901 faction's behavior from the tank regiment."

"The tank regiment is a unit of the 93rd Army," I said. "They naturally take every opportunity to smear us."

"Don't talk like that!" Papa said. "You must stop participating in anti-army activities!"

"The 901 is also People's Liberation Army."

"They're a bunch of cadets."

"They're officers under General-Staff Headquarters in Beijing."

"I don't care what you think. You may not go back to Yizhen. You must either stay here with Grandpa or go to our hometown like Weihua."

My anger erupted in a blind rage. "No wonder people call you a capitalist-roader!" I screamed. "You always try to suppress revolution!"

Papa's face turned red, while Mama's went white. Yiyuan began to cry. "Jianhua, stop talking nonsense," Mama said. "You sound no different from the foolish middle-school students here. Are you our son?"

"No, I'm not your son! I won't be a capitalist-roader's son! I'm a revolutionary! I want to make revolution!"

Papa picked up a feather duster and slashed at me. I jumped aside. Grandpa's cleaver was lying on the chopping board. I grabbed the cleaver, jumped onto the kang, and brandished my weapon in the air. "Unfilial son!" Papa roared, his face now almost purple. He slashed at my legs with the duster. "Attack by reason and defend by force!" I yelled, dancing about on the kang. "If you dare to attack, I'll counterattack!" Grandpa approached me and reached for the cleaver, murmuring, "Child, you must be mad, you must be mad." I refused to surrender my weapon.

Mama twisted the duster from Papa's hand and led him out, turning back to yell at me. "Go away! Wherever you go and whatever befalls you are of no concern to us!" Yiyuan followed them, bawling at the top of her lungs. I threw the cleaver on the floor, charged out the door, and ran toward the bus station. On the way, I passed a crowd of Thought Guards mixing it up with peasants. I did not stop to hear their arguments.

That evening, as I stood on the theater roof toying with the new searchlight, I began to feel sorry about the fight. How could I have called Papa a capitalist-roader? Would he ever forgive me? A shower of stones clattering down on the rooftop like hail roused me from my contemplation. It reminded me that we were supposed to replenish our ammunition stores. We worked late into the night, carrying stones and bricks onto the roof.

Storming the
Enemy Stronghold

In full battle regalia, we stood at attention and chanted in unison, "Be determined, defy every sacrifice, overcome tens of thousands of difficulties to win victory!" Chairman Mao's words would give us courage and strength for the all-out assault on the East-Is-Red Corps.

During the past few days, Mengzhe had moved our second,

third, and fourth brigades into the theater. We had set up catapults and heaped bricks and stones on the rooftops for blocks around, and stockpiled extra ammunition in the lanes. Now we tightened our helmets and armor, climbed onto the theater roof, and fanned out to our positions on the houses surrounding the Public Security Bureau. The Night Tiger Team, carrying two ladders, hid in alleys across the street from the fortified compound.

Our enemies would have one chance to surrender peaceably. At 7:00 A.M. sharp, the Red Rebel loudspeakers broadcast an ultimatum giving them ten minutes to give up. Their speakers replied with a barrage of denunciations, delivered in Baimudan's screeching voice.

At 7:10, we bombarded their fortress from the sides and back with stones and bricks. We were using one of the Thirty-Six Stratagems, "make a feint to the east and attack in the west," hoping to divert their attention so we could breach their defenses in front. Baimudan kept shrieking, but our speakers partially drowned her out with the "March of the People's Liberation Army."

Our strategy did not work as planned. Each time the Night Tiger Team tried to advance and set its ladders against the front walls, enemy fighters rose behind the battlements and pelted them with bricks and stones. Mengzhe sent some Red Rebels back to school for bedboards to use as shields. We intensified our cover fire as a line of boards advanced across the street, two people holding each board steady to protect two or three others. Several team members brandished long-handled hooks of the type local people used to recover buckets that had fallen down wells. With the hooks, they began to pry the battlements loose. As bedboard teams staggered, swayed, and fell, Leiting ordered members of the first brigade

Storming the Enemy Stronghold

down to the street to replace them. Erchou, Sanxi, and I took turns holding a board and wielding a hook. Before long, all the battlements in front had fallen. Fully exposed to the fire from adjacent rooftops, the enemy troops fell back.

The Night Tiger Team hoisted its ladders. We mounted them and advanced across the fortress roof, spears and swords poised for combat. Our adversaries ran in disarray toward the three-story building at the rear of the compound as we pelted them with ammunition from the piles of bricks they had left behind. The defense lines on either side of the fortress fell apart. More Red Rebels swarmed up, shouting "Charge! Rout the enemy! Charge!"

The enemy soldiers were running onto a porch and through a doorway on the third floor. "They have become turtles in a jar!" Sanxi yelled. "They have no place left to escape!" Baimudan's shrill voice was unrelenting. "Revolutionary comrades! The anti-army factionalists have lifted their execution-er's sword over us! We appeal to you to end this cruel and wanton persecution of the true revolutionary rebels!" she screamed. Several boys climbed the slanted roof of the three-story building, scaled the flagpole, and disconnected the speakers. "Hooray, we've finally shut that parrot up!" Sanxi said.

The Night Tiger Team repeated the procedure it had used at the Army Hospital, stripping the roof of its tiles, knocking a hole in the roof, and throwing the tiles down inside. Screams and other sounds of pandemonium rose from the building.

Suddenly, a window on the third floor opened and a figure appeared, holding a big red flag emblazoned with the name of the East-Is-Red Corps. It was Yulan. After recovering from her beating, she had become deputy chief of the organization.

"I'd rather die than surrender to you!" she shouted. Then she soared from the windowsill. The red flag furled halfway around her as she cried "Long live Chairman Mao!" She hit the ground. Her body lay perfectly still, enfolded in the flag. The silence seemed to last for an eternity. It was broken by the clatter of stones coming out of the building, a final, futile display of resistance.

A white shirt waving at the end of a spear poked out from a window. A door on the ground floor opened, and a line of East-Is-Red Corps students filed into the courtyard with their hands raised. My class monitor, Caolan, came out limping. Congfang and Xiangyun were bleeding from head wounds. Fangpu did not appear. We later learned that he and several aides, along with rebel leaders from the Public Security Bureau, the People's Procuratorate, and the People's Court, had left the fortress in Yulan's charge and gone to a commune outside town where the anti-901 faction was dominant.

A contingent of Red Rebels escorted our prisoners to Yizhong, where they would be shut up in classrooms until we decided what to do with them. Dr. Yang would treat their injuries. Mengzhe sped off by jeep to report our victory to the Red Revolutionary Rebel Headquarters of Yizhen County. The rest of us explored the enemy's last bastion. The third floor was a single large hall. I looked up at the three gaping holes in the roof. I looked around at the tile-littered floor, trying to picture how my frantic schoolmates had huddled under straw mats to evade the barrage from above. I looked out a window and saw Yulan's flag-wrapped body being carried away.

"Heavens!" Erchou said. I turned to see him holding a shotgun toward the ceiling. He pulled the trigger. The gun went off. "Heavens!" he said again. "This could have killed a lot of people. They didn't use it. They didn't dare fire the first gunshot." Erchou said that he was going to keep the gun for self-defense, in case anti-901 people came from Shimen to seek revenge. Sanxi and I looked around for more guns but found nothing better than a dagger stuck in a pillar.

Leiting was supervising the collection of spoils in the court-yard. We carried an amplifier, two cartons of crackers, sacks of wheat flour, a quarter of a pig, and two cases of raw eggs back to the theater, where the girls in charge of our backstage kitchen prepared a feast. Our cooks boiled the eggs and set them out in buckets on the stage. I laid down my spear, took off my willow-twig helmet and leather armor, and devoured fifteen eggs. By the time the next course was brought out, I had a terrible stomachache. I ran outside and vomited.

When Leiting discovered Erchou's shotgun, he led a group back to the enemy fortress to make a thorough search for firearms. We went through room after room of the Public Security Bureau until we found three Mausers, two revolvers, and several boxes of bullets hidden in a chest full of blankets. Leiting let me have a Mauser. He kept one gun for himself, gave two more away, and saved the last one for Commander-in-Chief Mengzhe. Additional search parties returned to the theater with swords and handcuffs. Xiangsheng brought back a rusty carbine, which he put in a basin of kerosene to soak.

Our leadership did not like the idea of Red Rebels walking around with guns and sent word that we should hand them all in. Mengzhe had to come to the theater in person to per-suade Leiting. We could hear them arguing up in the balcony. "The headquarters should be in charge of the guns," Mengzhe said. "They're likely to cause some bloody incidents if they stay in the hands of brigade members."

"The enemy killed one of our comrades and stabbed another," Leiting said. "They had a shotgun loaded and ready to shoot at us. They won't use stones and bricks the next time."

"Comrade Leiting, the situation is delicate. If we should provoke them into armed warfare, the 93rd Army's firepower could easily overwhelm us."

"What if they come to attack us with guns? Are we going to fight them with slingshots?"

"We are strengthening our fortifications. We have plans to make defensive weapons. If the time comes when you really need guns, we'll distribute them to you. For now, however, you must hand over the guns that you found."

"I cannot hand over the guns."

There was a long silence. Then Mengzhe said in a firm voice, "As Red Rebel commander-in-chief, I order you to hand over those guns immediately. If you do not obey my order, I'll expel you."

Silence again. Then Leiting began to cry.

Leiting finally stopped crying, came downstairs, and ordered us to give the guns to Mengzhe. The only exception was the rusty carbine in the basin of kerosene.

·

Spies in the Marketplace

On a hot, humid midsummer night, the Night Tiger Team had escorted a senior student named Chunfei to the railroad station, where pro-901 cargo loaders put him on a freight train to Beijing. At the invitation of Chen Boda, the head of the Central Cultural Revolution Group, pro-901 and anti-901 groups from Shimen had sent representatives to the capital to try to negotiate a truce. Mengzhe had decided to send an emissary to present our opinions on the situation in Yizhen.

Chunfei periodically sent back reports that the two factions were still at loggerheads. While their leaders bickered in the Great Hall of the People, their followers were continuing to battle each other in Shimen. The most encouraging message was that Chen Boda had recommended that the Madman's Commune of Shimen change its name to the Lu Xun Commune; "madman" was inappropriate for an organization in new socialist China, he said, since Lu Xun had written "A Madman's Diary" in the darkest days of Kuomintang rule. The leaders of the Madman's Commune had immediately agreed to the change. We Red Rebels, having evolved from the Lu Xun Commune at Yizhong, could not help feeling that Chen Boda's suggestion indicated implicit support for our side.

Following our rout of the East-Is-Red Corps, Chunfei returned to Yizhen with a disturbing update. The Central Cultural Revolution Group had been pressing Shimen's two factions to put aside their differences and form an alliance. Instead, the Lu Xun Commune had joined a new province-wide organization of rebellious college students called the August Fifth Storm, a name that commemorated the date of Chairman Mao's first dazibao. As a result of the Lu Xun Commune's defiance, the Central Cultural Revolution Group was beginning to favor the pro-93rd Army side. Chen Boda already had ordered one of Shimen's pro-901 organizations, the Street Corps, a group of peddlers and other people who earned their living on the street, to disband, calling it "a collection of hooligans and hoodlums."

Chunfei warned us not to become complacent about our victory in Yizhen. The opposing factions had taken up guns in the provincial capital of Baoding, and armed struggle could break out any day in Shimen, he said. If guns were used, the anti-901 forces would have a direct line of supply from the 93rd Army. The pro-901 forces would be at a great disadvantage because of the Military Engineering Institute's limited access to arms. In such circumstances, our enemies could easily retake the town.

Mengzhe had taken a gamble and released our East-Is-Red Corps prisoners after only a day. His theory was that if we showed mercy, we might win some converts, and the others would be less likely to seek revenge later on. Some of his advisers disagreed with him, feeling that leniency gave the enemy more opportunity to plan retaliation. In light of Chunfei's report, even Mengzhe agreed that we should prepare for the worst.

After sending Chunfei back to Beijing to continue monitoring the discussions, the Red Rebel leadership announced plans to fortify the bell-tower courtyard to make it invulnerable to attack. In addition, we would set up an arsenal to manufacture our own explosives and firearms for defense. Mengzhe temporarily recalled the first brigade from the theater to help build the fort. We erected battlements on the roofs and new walls to block all the entrances to the courtyard except the main one, where we built a maze with an opening wide enough to admit only one person at a time. I wrote a couplet to frame the opening: "One man guards this place; ten thousand enemies cannot pass."

Our construction duties completed, we moved back to the theater and intensified our street patrols. The town was rife with rumors that the East-Is-Red Corps was planning a retaliatory strike with supporters from Shimen. When notices appeared on the streets calling for Mengzhe's death, we knew agents and saboteurs were already among us.

One market day, Sanxi, Erchou, and I saw four youths wearing bright-colored shirts and corduroy pants that identified them as city boys. We tailed them awhile before confronting them. "Where are you from?" I asked.

"Shimen," said the tallest of the four, eyeing my spear.

"What are you here for?"

"Market day."

"Let's see your identification."

"We don't have a unit."

"What faction do you belong to?"

The boy glanced at my Red Rebel armband. "Pro-901. We belong to the Street Corps."

"Fart!" shouted Sanxi. "The Street Corps has been disbanded. You must be anti-901 spies!"

The youths looked frightened. They insisted they were not spies. We took them to the theater, where Leiting conducted a preliminary interrogation. They still protested their innocence. Leiting instructed us to escort them to Yizhong for more thorough questioning. Shut up in a small room in the bell-tower courtyard, the boys finally admitted to being agents from Shimen. But they claimed to know very little about the local factional struggles. They begged us to let them go, promising they would not work for the anti-901 faction again.

Mengzhe ordered them placed in four separate rooms for

further interrogation about the East-Is-Red Corps' plan of attack. Sanxi, Erchou, and I were assigned to the youngest, a boy of fourteen. "You'd better confess before we use force," Sanxi warned, snapping his belt in the air. The terrified boy said that he and his friends were not involved with any faction. They were runaways and petty thieves, traveling around looking for pockets to pick. The boy said he had not been home for two years. He said they had admitted to being spies for fear of being punished as criminals.

Although we were disappointed to learn that our suspects were mere pickpockets, the discovery seemed to delight a group of young factory workers who had been hanging around our school. They took charge of our prisoners, stripped the tallest boy, the group's financial manager, and relieved him of all the money sewn into his pants and underwear. Then they began to whip the boys with their belts. I managed to rescue the smallest one, but they took the other three to Rear Lake, beat their bare buttocks with the rubber transmission belt from the pump house, and threw them into the water.

The pickpockets were jailed in a small room and ordered to write confessions. The older ones admitted to raping girls. After a few more beatings, they were put to work sweeping the bell-tower courtyard. When I told Sanxi that I thought the treatment was too harsh, he responded that I was too naïve about class struggle. "We have to punish these reactionaries," he said, "or they'll go out and commit more crimes against the people."

We did not find any more suspects, let alone real spies. Nonetheless, rumors of an East-Is-Red Corps comeback persisted. The Red Rebel leadership summoned the first brigade back to Yizhong for good. Sanxi, Erchou, and I left the theater and rejoined Zongwei in our small room in the bell-tower courtyard. We brought with us a 500-watt theater spotlight that lit the room up brighter than daylight.

Family Skeletons

Weihua returned from our hometown with a straw sunhat covering the scar from the rock that had struck him on his head. "I found out what Grandpa's family background is," he told me.

"I thought it was middle peasant," I said.

"Grandpa's father was a big landlord in Shuiyuan. Grandpa's status is bankrupt landlord."

"Bankrupt landlord?" I had never heard of such a category.

"That means that by the time of Land Reform, he no longer had enough farmland and farmhands to be classified as a landlord, even though his father was," Weihua explained. "Bankrupt landlord isn't as bad as landlord." I thought it sounded even worse: a good-for-nothing landlord who had lost all his money.

That was just part of the story that Weihua had unraveled during his stay in the mountain town. Grandpa's brother, the one who had killed himself, had three grandsons. Each had inherited some of their grandfather's hardwood furniture after his suicide. It was far better furniture than one would normally find in a middle peasant's home. Weihua had visited the eldest grandson, who showed him a picture of Grandpa's father, our great-grandfather, that was kept hidden behind a wardrobe. The old man had been rather rich until the Anti-Japanese War. Then he had become addicted to opium. Before long, Grandpa and Grandpa's brother were opium addicts as well.

The family fortunes had declined swiftly. By Land Reform, twelve shops, 33 hectares of farmland, and a multitude of houses had gone to the creditors. Mama had grown up in poverty, knowing only hunger until the Eighth Route Army came along and recruited her into a propaganda performance team. I vaguely remembered having seen Mama perform the part of the child heroine Liu Hulan in a play in our hometown long ago. So how had Mama, daughter of a bankrupt, opium-smoking landlord, married Papa, a Communist and guerrilla leader?

Weihua knew that story, too. After the defeat of the Japanese, Papa had been put in charge of Shuiyuan county's public security work. A campaign to rehabilitate opium addicts was under way. Grandpa was one of those Papa had ordered arrested for rehabilitation. He was weaned off the opium, until he was smoking only tobacco. One day Mama had arrived with food for Grandpa while Papa was inspecting the program. Papa was already married. Like many marriages, his had been arranged, and he spent little time with his wife. After meeting Mama, he got a divorce. Many revolutionary cadres were getting divorces at that time. When he married Mama, all he owned was two Japanese army blankets. They used bricks as pillows on their wedding night.

Weihua said the young man in Shuiyuan whom we had always called Brother An was our real stepbrother. An was now a political activist in the town. His faction supported the prefecture's 48th Army, which was at odds with the 93rd

Army. So, in a roundabout way, An and we were allies. We also had a stepsister named Nu, whom I had never heard of. She had accompanied Weihua to Yizhen and would go with him to Lingzhi to see Papa.

"Everyone in Shuiyuan knows these stories," Weihua said. "If you want to know more, you'll have to ask Mama and Papa themselves." I could not imagine myself asking Mama and Papa about such things—even if we ever got back on speaking terms. But now I understood why Mama sometimes fought with Papa when he talked about going back to visit his hometown. She often argued that sending money would be enough.

There was one more piece of news from Shuiyuan: Papa's family origin, originally poor peasant and later raised to lower-middle peasant, had been reclassified again. Now it was middle peasant. The faction opposing Brother An's faction had insisted on raising it, saying Papa's old seven-room house where An lived was too luxurious for a lower-middle peasant.

Weihua took me to meet our stepsister, Nu, who was waiting for him in his dormitory room. With her patched, coarse cotton clothes, downcast eyes, and red cheeks, she was unmistakably a country girl. Even her homespun red armband looked rustic.

"Big Sister," I said, "do you have Red Guards in Shuiyuan?"

"Every town has them," she said, looking at her hands.

"Do you use weapons like this?" I showed her the sword hanging from my belt.

"We don't use weapons to fight. I use a sword to chop firewood on the hillsides every day."

Family Skeletons

Weihua planned to take Nu to Lingzhi the next day. I went to the school clinic and, when Dr. Yang was not looking, filched a bottle of opium cough syrup for Weihua to take along to Grandpa.

Playing with Fire

Huantian came back to school looking for me. A Red Rebel guarding the perimeter of the bell-tower courtyard escorted her inside. She had quit the East-Is-Red Corps quite some time before because she felt discriminated against. She said that Nkrumah and Delta had dropped out too. These days, she was working in the fields in her home village. She had come to town with her father for market day. Instead of returning with him, she stayed and became a Red Rebel.

She went to work in our arsenal, which occupied the old music hall on one side of the bell-tower courtyard. It had an all-girl workforce, headed by a senior named Yongrui, who had received training from the Missile Engineering Institute and the County Military Department. The girls had started with bottle bombs and now were turning out mines and grenades. They produced their own gunpowder from nitrate, sulfur, and charcoal. They also made a dynamite substitute of chemical fertilizer and sawdust. Allies at a steel plant near the railroad station supplied the casings.

Huantian showed Sanxi, Erchou, and me how to assemble a grenade. Taking up a shell, she pointed out that the checkerboard pattern would break into small pieces to increase casualties. She methodically filled the shell with gunpowder, inserted a fuse, sealed the shell with clay, attached a small piece of friction paper and a wire to the fuse, screwed a wooden handle onto the shell, tied a string to the wire and a ring to the string, and fixed the ring on the handle with a paper seal. The paper seal was to prevent accidental ignition. Under her supervision, each of us made his own grenade. While we were working, some boys carried in a barrel of aluminum powder from the County Light-Industry Bureau. They said the Missile Engineering Institute would send a whole truckload of TNT the next day. Huantian let us use some of the aluminum powder in bottle bombs.

We tossed our first homemade grenades into a vegetable patch outside our room where some of the monsters and demons had grown turnips. We had barely run inside and shut the door when three bangs sounded in succession. We opened the door to find smoke rising from the garden and fragments of turnips scattered all over.

The expected East-Is-Red Corps strike had not materialized by early September, but we did not relax our vigilance. The latest messages from Chunfei, our ambassador to Beijing, urged us to prepare for more fighting. Our leadership decided to deploy an interlocked minefield around the bell-tower courtyard, rigged to be remote-controlled from the Principal's Building. For a week, we dug ditches around the courtyard to plant dynamite mines. We also put crates of grenades on the rooftops.

Our military training intensified. We spent long hours practicing spear and sword fighting and hand-to-hand combat. The first brigade still marched through town periodically. Once Leiting deliberately failed to give a left-turn order and let the whole brigade march knee-deep into a reed pond. Afterward he said it was to show off our iron discipline, for the benefit of any East-Is-Red Corps agents among the onlookers. Sanxi, Erchou, and I often went to the arsenal to make grenades. Sanxi in particular seemed to like helping Huantian. We teased him about his romance. He insisted that it was nothing more than a militant revolutionary friendship.

As the tensions mounted, some students found excuses to leave. One day, Zongwei told us he was going home because his mother was sick. Erchou, Sanxi, and I sat on our beds watching him pack. He unrolled a scroll painting of four scholars playing chess on a boat drifting down a river and handed it to me. "This is my newest painting," he said. "You can keep it here. I'll try to come back as soon as possible."

"He won't come back until peace returns," Erchou predicted after Zongwei had gone. "Cowards like him don't know how to fight," Sanxi said. "We don't need him." Saying nothing, I hung the painting on the wall.

Erchou and I had just settled down for an afternoon nap a few days later when a violent explosion rocked the ground. We jumped from our beds, grabbed our weapons, and emerged to see thick black smoke rolling through the courtyard. The smell of gunpowder filled the air. We raced to the arsenal, now a huge heap of burning debris. A figure stumbled out of the smoke and collapsed. It was Sanxi. His face was black and swollen, and his clothes had been blasted off his body. We carried him to a bed. Dr. Yang examined him and sent him to the county hospital.

We organized a bucket brigade. The flames were doused and the search for other victims got under way. Mengzhe ordered us to dig in the smoldering wreckage with our bare hands to avoid hurting anyone who might still be alive. Students first uncovered Yongrui, badly hurt but alive. Two more girls were dug out. One would survive. The other, the tomboy Huantian, was pronounced dead on arrival at the county hospital.

Sanxi had kidney injuries beyond the county hospital's ability to handle, so he was sent 160 kilometers away to the provincial hospital in Baoding. Erchou and I saw him off at the railway station. He lay limply on a stretcher, his ruddy peasant face now wan. As the train pulled away, he put his head out the window and shouted, "Don't let my sword get rusty! I'll be back soon!" The wind was blowing his hair over his face so I could not see his expression. Like most of us, he had not bothered to get a haircut in months.

The Red Rebels held a memorial meeting for Huantian, at which we recited quotations from Chairman Mao: "Whenever there is struggle, there will be sacrifice." "Tens of thousands of revolutionary martyrs died before us for the revolutionary cause." "Let us march along the path crimson with the martyrs' blood." Mengzhe made a speech exhorting us to carry on with Huantian's cause. She was buried in what had become a cemetery outside the north side of the city wall, near the graves of the drowned youth, Teacher Shen, and Vice-Principal Lin Sheng. Her tombstone was engraved with the words, "Red Rebel Revolutionary Martyr, 1949–1967."

Two hundred people, including Erchou and me, volunteered to revive the arsenal. The Red Rebel leadership selected only ten. Neither Erchou nor I was among them. The new manager was Mengzhe's general-staff secretary, Jinfeng. Manufacture resumed in a workshop near Rear Lake, a safe distance from the bell-tower courtyard. Only staff members were allowed in. All completed explosives were stored in empty rooms in Vatican City. The new arsenal went into operation around the clock to make up for our losses. By early October, it had produced more than what had been blown up.

Preparations for imminent war continued. The Red Revolutionary Rebel Headquarters of Yizhen County had drawn up an overall defense plan for the county seat. In case of attack, our main task would be to secure the road that passed by our campus and through the small north gate in the city wall, the main route between the railway station and downtown. Our leaders decided to tunnel up through the city wall and build a lookout post to guard the road. We worked in three shifts, 24 hours a day, one team digging from the top of the wall downward while another team worked upward. Erchou and I slept by day and shoveled by night for a week. Electric bulbs were installed as the tunnel deepened. One day at dawn, the two teams met. A cold drizzle descended, making the hot bulbs that had been on all night explode.

The Obstinacy of Truth

More than two months had passed since my quarrel with Papa. When Weihua was escorting our stepsister, Nu, from Lingzhi back to Shuiyuan, he stopped at Yizhong to tell me that Mama and Papa had forgiven me. The time was ripe for a reconciliation. I told Erchou that I was going home for a brief visit. Erchou also was thinking about going home. "Make sure you come back," I joked. "You, too," he replied. "Don't be a deserter like Zongwei."

Faded slogans attacking Papa could still be discerned on the walls of downtown Lingzhi, but the focus of attack had shifted to the county Party secretary, the one who had been in another county leading a Four Cleanups team when Papa first came under criticism. His tactic of putting on an army uniform to protect himself had backfired, earning him the name of "chameleon" on top of "counterrevolutionary revisionist." I felt pleased that the secretary was getting criticized instead of Papa, and even more delighted to see denunciations of Han Rong, the former Party secretary of Yizhen, who had persecuted Papa. Han Rong was now in disgrace as Party secretary of Shimen. The rebels of Lingzhi took an interest in him because he had been Party secretary of Lingzhi even before he had gone to Yizhen. They wanted him to come back to stand trial for past "counterrevolutionary revisionist activities" in Lingzhi.

I thought of a saying that Grandpa liked to quote: "Good will be rewarded with kindness and evil with punishment; it is not that evil is not punished in time, but that the time has not come yet." Perhaps it was true after all.

As I was looking over the new dazibao, a voice called, "Big Brother, how do you like this?" It was Zhihua. He and Xinghua were dressed like twins in torn blue jackets and dirty blue pants. Each had a red armband, a big Chairman Mao badge on his chest, and a little red book in his hand.

"What are you doing? Are you allowed to join the Red Guards now?" I asked.

"No, nobody wants us," Zhihua said, "so we organized our own Red Guard Brigade. I'm commander-in-chief."

"Commander-in-chief! How many troops do you command?"

"The two of us, Meiyuan, and Yiyuan, plus a few kids from the County Military Department."

"What do you do?"

"Study Chairman Mao's quotations, write dazibao against the 901, and sometimes collect garbage to sell," Xinghua said proudly.

"What do you have against the 901? They've never been to Lingzhi."

"Your 901 is different from ours," Zhihua said seriously. "Even though the 901 has never come here, Daba and his Thought Guards are 901 followers. They oppose the 93rd Army tank regiment that supports Papa. So we have to oppose them."

"Of course." I could not argue with his logic. "How are the Thought Guards doing?"

"They are doomed. They have no sympathizers left. Daba is having a terrible time. Wherever he goes, people yell at him. Yesterday, a bunch of peasants surrounded him and pushed him down. He raised his little red book high in the air and shouted 'Struggle by reason, not by force!,' but nobody listened to him. He was just like a turtle in a jar!" Zhihua's face was flushed with excitement.

Grandpa was sitting on the kang when I entered the house. He thanked me for the medicine I had sent home with Weihua and asked me how my hand was. I had almost forgotten about my chicken-claw madness. The last bit of stiffness in my hand had yielded to the summer heat.

Mama made her usual evening visit with Yiyuan. She did not even mention my fight with Papa. "It looks as if Papa's troubles are over!" she said. "The rebels made an investigation and decided to liberate him. One rebel faction has classified him as a comparatively good cadre, and another faction has classified him as a cadre who made serious mistakes, but mistakes belonging to the category of contradictions among the people. Only Daba and a handful of diehard 901 anti-army factionalists still consider him a capitalist-roader. These people are no more than mice running across the street; they have become very unpopular."

The tank regiment as well as some of the rebel organizations wanted Papa to be on the county's new Revolutionary Committee, a "three-in-one" organization with representatives from the army, the cadres, and the rebels that would replace the old county leadership. However, other people were backing Papa's second in command, Mo Yin the "wind-sailor," as the cadre representative. The army representative was going to be the head of the County Military Department; there was not much dispute over that. As for the rebel representative, some said the county government's former typist might be chosen, and others thought it would be Papa's former aide, Qin Mao. "Who knows?" Mama said. "Let them fight it out among themselves."

When I told Mama that I wanted to apologize to Papa, she said, "Don't be silly. He doesn't need your apology. Let bygones be bygones." She added that I should not visit Papa that night in any case, because rebels from Beijing were coming to interview him about a vice-minister in the central government who was under investigation. The man had fought beside Papa during the Anti-Japanese War.

The interview proved frustrating for both Papa and his visitors, according to the account Mama gave us the next day. The investigators believed that Papa's former colleague was a Kuomintang agent who had sneaked into Papa's guerrilla unit. Papa did not agree. "He did not sneak into our guerrillas," Papa said. "On the contrary, we kidnapped him and forced him to join us. He was a professor, and at the time, our party and army were struggling to win over the intellectuals. We kidnapped him to join our revolutionary troops so that he would not be forced to join the Japanese."

The visitors pressed Papa to reconsider his testimony, saying, "We know that your political career is at a crucial point. We revolutionary rebels from Beijing have a lot of influence. The rebels here have decided to liberate you, but they may change their minds."

Papa continued to insist that to the best of his knowledge the man was not a Kuomintang agent. When the rebels asked him if he was afraid of offending someone of such high rank, Papa said, "I couldn't care less about his high post. When we brought him into the guerrillas, it was to save him from being used by the Japanese. We never dreamed of becoming officials. Whether he stayed on the revolutionary road after that, I have no idea. I have not seen or heard from him since 1945. But I'm sure he was not a Kuomintang agent when he joined us in 1942."

The rebels were losing their tempers. "This is a test of your loyalty to Chairman Mao and your attitude toward the Cultural Revolution. You have flunked the test!" They said they would discuss Papa's case with the rebels in charge of him in Lingzhi and submit their recommendation on whether he deserved to be liberated. Papa merely replied, "I'm sorry. I must tell the truth."

As Mama related the conversation, I found myself wishing once more that Papa would be more flexible in dealing with such people. If he was not liberated, if he retained the label of capitalist-roader, our family would face a bleak political future. Even if my brothers and sisters and I severed relations with him, nobody would trust us. The combination of bank-rupt landlord and capitalist-roader would haunt us all our lives.

When I entered Papa's room, he was seated at the desk, his eyebrows knitted, drawing hard on his pipe. He did not mention our quarrel, and I did not complain about his stubbornness. Instead, we talked about the plans for forming the Revolutionary Committee. Papa said that, contrary to the guidelines stipulated long ago in the Sixteen Points, there would be no election. The provincial military authorities would have the final say. "This is an abnormal period," he said. "No Party, no government, not even police or courts. Everything has collapsed. Under such circumstances, the military has to be responsible for organizing things."

He seemed to be thinking hard as he puffed on his pipe. "The Cultural Revolution is supposed to broaden democracy. But as the saying goes, a thing turns into its opposite if pushed too far."

On the Run

The mid-October afternoon that I returned from Lingzhi, taking my usual shortcut from the bus station to school along the city wall, I saw clusters of people with helmets and rifles standing along the road outside the small north gate. Their bayonets gleamed in the autumn sun. Our troops had real guns! Excitedly, I began to run through the overgrowth of bushes on top of the wall. As I neared the road, I realized with horror that these were not our people. Not a Red Rebel armband was in sight.

Our lookout fort over the road was deserted. The giant searchlight we had installed was still there, but the Red Rebel flag was no longer flying. Spears and swords lay everywhere as if abandoned in haste. I descended into the tunnel and found it empty as well. What could have made our strong-willed Red Rebels give up this vital position?

Emerging from the other end of the tunnel behind Rear Lake, I ran across the campus. Scores of Red Rebel students had gathered under the willows in front of the Teachers' Building. Their faces told me that something dreadful had happened. My brigade leader, Leiting, was about to make a speech. "Comrades-in-arms," he said. "I salute you as the brave rear guards in our strategic withdrawal."

I learned the dimensions of the catastrophe from my schoolmates. At a meeting in the Great Hall of the People the previous day, Chen Boda, the head of the Central Cultural Revolution Group, had declared the pro-901 faction a "*fangeming dazahui*"—a "counterrevolutionary hodgepodge." Many of our allies in Shimen had been rounded up and killed. Some had jumped off buildings waving the Lu Xun Commune flag. The 93rd Army had blockaded the Hutuo River, cutting off all routes to Shimen. Most of the Red Rebels, under Mengzhe's command, already had retreated in the other direction to Baoding. There, the 48th Army was supporting the student rebel alliance that the Lu Xun Commune had joined, the August Fifth Storm.

"Our enemies are pouring into the city and deploying their troops," Leiting said. "We will have to escape in groups of two and three. Take off your armbands and leave all the weapons behind. They have checkpoints at every intersection. After you break through the blockade, try to go north to Baoding. That will be our base for recovery and counterattack. If you can't get there, try to hide somewhere until the tide turns. We must save our strength and await the opportunity to strike back. Comrades-in-arms, ultimate victory will be ours!"

I was bewildered that circumstances had turned against us so quickly. Had not Chen Boda been mediating between the two factions? Had he not given the pro-901 side the name Lu Xun Commune? How could he wantonly brand us a "counterrevolutionary hodgepodge"?

Suddenly, I was alone with my questions. Everyone else had adopted the last of the Thirty-Six Stratagems and run away. I headed for my room in the bell-tower courtyard. If Erchou was there, we could leave together. As I entered the courtyard, I tripped over a piece of wood. It looked like a carpenter's ruler carved from oak, but it seemed far too heavy for a ruler when I picked it up. It was a camouflaged sword, the type known as a "two-man grab" because you could let your adversary grab the sheath as you pulled out the blade to stab him. I took the sword with me.

Erchou was not in our room. Perhaps he had not returned from his visit home and was safe and sound in his village. I looked at the helmets, armor, swords, and spears hung lovingly on the wall. They would have to stay behind, with Zongwei's painting. I took the money I had found in the Army Hospital from its hiding place under my thin mattress and put it into a canvas shoulder bag, along with a homemade dagger and a new pair of pants that Mama had given me. After a moment's hesitation, I wrapped the two-man grab sword in the mattress to take along.

On the Run

As I was about to leave the room, I thought of the four grenades in my bedside drawer. Why not set a trap for the East-Is-Red Corps? I unscrewed the cap and pulled the ring out of one grenade, trying to figure out how to tie it to the door. Then it occurred to me that the wrong person might open the door. Erchou might come back. I also thought of what Grandpa would say. He would tell me not to take the initiative to harm others. I gave up the idea, replaced the ring, and rescrewed the cap. However, I did put two grenades in my bag. Then I picked up my bulky bundle and went out.

Where could I go? I doubted whether I could get out of Yizhen with my mattress under my arm. I thought of our former neighbor, Old Liu, the retired army officer who owned the dilapidated shrine where Papa had written his petition letters. I could take a route past the reed ponds and behind Democracy Street Primary School to his house. I would go there first and then decide how to get out of town.

As I approached the primary-school playground, five men carrying pistols strode by. After they had passed, I heard the shout "Halt!" They surrounded me before I could even turn around. "Open your bundle!"

"It's just a mattress," I said.

One of them grabbed the mattress and unrolled it. "You little bastard!" he said as he picked up the sword. "What's this?" I felt a blow on the side of my head. Everything spun around as I fell.

By the time I stood up again, another man had pulled the money, dagger, and grenades from my bag. The first man pointed his pistol at my forehead. I held very still.

"Where are you going and why are you carrying all these deadly weapons?" he said, shaking the pistol barrel as if it was his finger.

On the Run

"Yizhong is full of these things," I said. "I just picked them up for fun. I'm on my way to see my father's friend."

A crowd was collecting around us. I felt a little safer. The man lowered his pistol. Putting my billfold in his pocket, he said, "We're confiscating your things."

"May I have my pants back?" I asked. "Look at the ones I'm wearing; they're all worn out."

"Who knows if the pants really belong to you? Maybe you stole them."

"Fine. You keep them. May I go now?"

"Are you dreaming? Do you think we'll let you go so easily?"

The man told his partners to summon some revolutionary rebels to take care of me. They brought back Caolan, my class monitor, leading five other girls from class 85 who belonged to the East-Is-Red Corps. "Jianhua, how are you?" Caolan said, her derisive eyes looking at me from beneath her helmet. "Last time, we were your prisoners of war, and now you're ours. Did you ever think things would change so drastically?"

"Chairman Mao says that everything in the universe is constantly changing. It's a law of nature." I tried to sound casual.

Prodding and poking me, the girls escorted me to their temporary jail at the Commerce Bureau. Lushuang, the head of the Night Tiger Team, was led into the courtyard at the same time. His hands were tied behind him and blood was running down his legs. An East-Is-Red Corps student had speared him in the thigh.

My captors ushered me into a small room containing a desk and a few stools. I expected to be tied up and tortured, but nothing like that happened. They merely gave me the text of a letter that Chairman Mao had written during the War of Liberation urging a Kuomintang general to surrender, and made me read it aloud twice. Then Caolan said, "It's time for you to make a choice: either stick to your counterrevolutionary hodgepodge and remain a diehard as filthy and contemptible as dog's dung, or come over to our side and become a revolutionary."

I reviewed the Thirty-Six Stratagems in my mind, trying to find one that might apply. "Pretend to be foolish while remaining intelligent" might work. I should appear as cooperative as possible in order to gain a respite. I put on a smile and nodded agreement with whatever they said. They seemed pleased by my behavior. At dinner time, they even brought me steamed bread and fried bean sprouts. My head was throbbing and I did not feel hungry, but I tried to eat as much as possible to please them more. After dinner, they let me go.

I ran all the way to Old Liu's house. Aside from some tough-looking men patrolling the streets, almost nobody was out. The peddlers' cry of "Pot-stewed hare meat!," which had returned to the streets under the Red Rebels' reign, had disappeared once again. An unofficial curfew was in force.

Old Liu and his wife, who were 901 supporters, took me in like a son. They had sent their own son to stay with relatives in the South for fear that he would get hurt in the factional fighting. I had been with them three days when a youth wearing dark glasses and a cap showed up at the door. I immediately recognized Leiting's deep voice. He too had been hiding in town. He wanted to go to Baoding to find Mengzhe. "We can't wait for death," he said. "We mustn't admit defeat. We still have the people's support. We have to keep struggling."

Leiting's brother, a train engineer, was going to be coming through Yizhen tonight. Leiting's best chance to escape from town was to board his brother's locomotive. He wanted me to accompany him to the station so that if he was captured I could send a message to his family. "If they catch me, they'll kill me," he said matter-of-factly. "Will you help me?"

"Of course," I said. "You're my brigade leader."

After midnight, we took a twisted route through narrow lanes and across empty fields to the signal post along the railroad tracks. The signalman was a friend of Leiting's brother. At 2:00 A.M., a long freight train pulled in. A man in oily work clothes swung down from the locomotive amid the white steam. It was Leiting's brother.

"The 48th Army has sealed off Baoding to keep pro-901 people out," he said. "They dare not defy Chen Boda. You cannot go to Baoding right now. My train is going to Baotou in Inner Mongolia. From there, you can go to Urumqi to stay with our uncle." Leiting assented to the plan, looking a bit disappointed. The two brothers boarded the locomotive. I stood by the track as the train coughed away into the night.

The signalman told me to stay with him and go back to town at daybreak. But Yizhen seemed like a prison. I did not want to go back. I decided to go to Erchou's village, ten kilometers to the north. If I found him, we could try to sneak into Baoding together. I started walking through the open countryside, filling my nostrils with the smells of sweet potato and sorghum. Day was breaking when I knocked at Erchou's courtyard gate.

Erchou had a bandage around his forehead and bruises on his face. He said that he had returned to Yizhong, unaware of the drastic turn of events, the day after our withdrawal. Before he could even enter the gate, Little Bawang and some others had captured him. They tied his hands and feet, pushed him down on the cement floor of the school bathhouse, and locked the door. For a day and a half, he lay there with nothing to eat or drink. Finally his cousin, a girl who belonged to the East-Is-Red Corps, accidentally found him and released him.

"If the East-Is-Red Corps comes after me again, they'll have a hard time finding me," Erchou said as he led me to an inner room of his house. He removed a big urn and a stone slab to reveal an opening in the floor. We descended into a spacious cellar furnished with a straw mattress, quilts, a lamp, and a stack of books. The cellar was linked to a network of tunnels the villagers had dug during the war against the Japanese. "How do you like this place? Would you join me for a while?" Erchou looked at me expectantly.

"What's the use of hiding like a fugitive?" I said. "We're not defeated yet. We have a lot of supporters. I think we should go to Baoding to join our comrades."

Erchou's reservations showed on his face. "The 93rd Army is checking on travelers everywhere, and even the 48th Army no longer welcomes us because of Chen Boda's condemnation. I would rather stay home, recover from my injuries, and see what develops."

"You're just a coward, like Zongwei," I said.

I stayed at Erchou's home for the day. His mother cooked us a big peasant dinner and his father gave us a cup of hard liquor apiece. After dark, I said goodbye and set out. I evaded the guards at the local railway station and boarded a train at the far end of the platform. The cars were full of peasants with big bundles of produce, taking advantage of the political chaos to do some speculating.

A stir among the passengers woke me from sleep a few hours later. We had reached a small station a few stops before Baoding. Soldiers were making their way through the car, inspecting tickets. Their leader said they were acting on instructions from the Central Cultural Revolution Group. They were to turn back anyone going to Beijing to appeal to the central authorities or going to Baoding from Shimen. They questioned all the people holding tickets for Beijing or Baoding and put most of them off the train. Those of us without tickets were put off too.

The soldiers brought us to a nearby building, read us Chairman Mao's quotations on revolutionary discipline, and told us that everyone would get a free ride home the next day. These soldiers were neither fierce nor vigilant, and I easily slipped away as they were escorting us to a southbound train the next morning. By noon, after walking to the next station, I was bound for Baoding on another train. I had crossed the blockade.

I scanned the notices posted on the walls of the Baoding railway station until I found the one I wanted: "Red Rebels of Yizhen Number One Middle School, please join your comrades-in-arms at Struggle Road Primary School!" A hundred Red Rebels were living in a classroom there, under the protection of the 48th Army, which was not forcing out those who had already reached Baoding. Seeing the familiar faces, especially Mengzhe, I felt like a child coming home.

Factional fighting in Baoding had reached such proportions that gunshots rang out all day and all night. Most of us remained in the school, in an atmosphere of uncertainty and confusion. Every day, Mengzhe and his secretary, Jinfeng, went out to discuss our situation with 48th Army people and came back with encouraging words to boost our morale. We looked forward to getting out of this state of exile, although nobody knew exactly how we would stage our comeback.

Among the exiles was a senior named Qiqi, daughter of the former Party secretary who had persecuted Papa, Han

Rong. I had never bothered to talk to her because of the grudge I bore against her father. I discovered that she did not like her father either, because he had abandoned her mother and married another woman several years back. I became good friends with Qiqi and her classmate Songying, an optimistic country girl. Songying had been the Youth League secretary of her class and knew quite a bit about Marxist dialectical materialism. "Our defeat may seem like a bad thing, but it can be turned into a good thing," she would tell me. "It has hardened us and purified our ranks."

I had been in Baoding a week when Mengzhe brought me news of Sanxi. Officials at the provincial hospital had said they could no longer treat Sanxi because his kidneys were damaged beyond repair. Mengzhe suspected the real reason was that the dominant faction at the hospital sided with the Provincial Military District, which was feuding with the 48th Army and supporting the 93rd.

"How can they be so inhuman?" I said. "Chairman Mao says that medical workers should heal the wounded, rescue the dying, and practice revolutionary humanitarianism." "The highest principle now is factionalism," Mengzhe said. "I argued with them, but they didn't listen. Only after I got a 48th Army officer to help me out did they agree to let Sanxi stay for the time being."

That evening, I borrowed a bicycle and rode across the city to visit Sanxi. The dimly lit streets teemed with people involved in arguments, fistfights, and chases. Nobody even paid attention to the sporadic sound of gunfire. Some boys ran right in front of me, forcing me to brake so suddenly that I fell off the bike, and a bus stopped just short of rolling over me. Passengers looked out of the windows with annoyed expressions. The driver cursed me.

On the Run

Sanxi was sleeping in his hospital bed. He shared a room with seven other patients. He was hooked up to some complicated devices and looked much thinner. I took his hand. He opened his eyes. "Jianhua," he said. "Is it true that we have been defeated?"

"No, we have just entered a new stage of the struggle. We will win in the end, because we represent Chairman Mao's revolutionary line."

"Jianhua, I've missed you and our comrades so much." He squeezed my hand. "When I lie here, feeling so lonely, I comfort myself by thinking of those great battles. I can't stand being here. I want to go back with you and continue the fight."

"Sanxi, you lie here fighting your injuries, and we are out there fighting our enemies. We are fighting for the same purpose, to defend Chairman Mao's revolutionary line. The best thing you can do is to rest and recover so that you can come back to join us. Don't you remember what Chairman Mao said when he was in the hospital?"

"Might as well stay and make the best of it," Sanxi said with a faint smile.

As I told Sanxi my latest adventures, a bit of red returned to his pale cheeks. We talked until a nurse intervened and said that I was tiring him. I promised to visit him every day as long as I was in Baoding. I kept my promise. Every evening, I would buy some fruit and go to the hospital. He and I would talk and joke as we ate the fruit.

Meanwhile, the position of the Red Rebels in Baoding was becoming even more precarious. Friends in the 48th Army had let Mengzhe know that, because of pressure from the Central Cultural Revolution Group and from Chen Boda himself, they could no longer shelter us. Factions supported by the 48th Army began to urge us and our allies who had fled Shimen to leave. They even marched through the streets shouting, "Warmly send off our comrades-in-arms from the Lu Xun Commune to return to Shimen to make revolution!" We knew that we would have to leave.

Mengzhe moderated a long, emotional discussion about what to do next. Some people said we should go to the Taihang Mountains to wage guerrilla warfare. Xiangsheng advocated this course, saying, "They have killed many of our comrades. We should cherish no illusions that they would let us survive." Others said we should return to Yizhen and do underground work. Songying enthusiastically endorsed this course. She said she had hidden a mimeograph machine, ink, and paper under the rafters in her dormitory room; these could be used for propaganda to mobilize the masses to rise up. "This is exactly what our Communist forefathers did under Chiang Kai-shek's reactionary rule. We can learn from them." Eventually, we reached a compromise: the Red Rebel leaders would go to the mountains with a small team to evade capture by the East-Is-Red Corps, while the rest of us would return to Yizhen to do underground work. The leaders would continue to direct us from a revolutionary base in the mountains.

Xiangsheng wanted to go to the mountains but was not allowed to because his clubfoot would limit the mobility of our headquarters. He was very unhappy. When Mengzhe took back a pistol that Xiangsheng had received before the retreat and gave it to his secretary, Jinfeng, Xiangsheng cried like a child.

The 48th Army bought us train tickets back to Yizhen. We were ready to leave for the station when Erchou appeared at the primary school. "What the hell are you doing here?" I asked. "We're going home." He looked at me with a guilty expression. "I decided I should rejoin my comrades." I immediately thought of Sanxi. He would be miserable when we left. I took Erchou to the hospital to visit him.

When we got to Sanxi's room, he was just being moved onto a gurney. I asked where he was going. A nurse told me in a stern voice that he was going to the operating room for more surgery. Sanxi stretched out a trembling hand toward Erchou. His weak smile disappeared entirely when we told him that we had to return to Yizhen. We tried to comfort him by saying we would come back to see him when the situation improved. He just shook his head. Through the tears blurring my eyes, I watched the gurney roll down the hall and disappear through a set of double doors.

From Victors to
Vanquished

Once our train crossed the Shimen prefectural limits, we began to see armed soldiers and militiamen on every railway platform. The nearer we got to the city of Shimen, the more there were. As the train clattered along through the darkness, Erchou, Qiqi, Songying, and I complained about how unfair life had become. The current policy called for a grand revolutionary alliance. But Chen Boda had labeled our side a counterrevolutionary hodgepodge, the 93rd Army was suppressing us, and even the 48th Army was discriminating against us. What kind of grand revolutionary alliance was that? We talked until the train neared Yizhen, when we all fell silent.

Several hundred militiamen carrying rifles and machine guns were waiting on the Yizhen railway platform. It must have just rained, for the ground was wet and the mass of steel helmets and bayonets glistened with reflected light. The militiamen came aboard in groups to inspect tickets. They took away anyone bound for Shimen who was suspected of being a Lu Xun Commune member. Then they ordered all passengers with tickets for Yizhen off the train. As we stepped onto the platform, we saw the Lu Xun Commune people lined up at gunpoint. Facing the bayonets bravely, they began to sing the way revolutionary heroes did in the movies:

> Once the gun sounds,
> We go to the battleground.
> I've made my mind up,
> I'm ready to die on the battleground today.
> If we're finished,
> So be it.

Everyone knew this song. It was a quotation from the invincible general Lin Biao. You were not supposed to sing it unless you faced a last-ditch battle. It was a song of desperation. Inspired by this heroic group of young people, my companions and I joined in. We sang the song again and again. I felt my heart beating in time to each note.

The militiamen herded our comrades from Shimen onto several open trucks, which drove away. They also took away some comrades from Yizhen. They did not seem to care about us. We marched back to school singing militant songs. A few menacing-looking guards walked alongside us, but when we turned off at Yizhong they kept walking toward downtown.

From Victors to Vanquished

We continued to sing at the top of our lungs as we entered the school gate. Our underground mission no longer seemed relevant. I felt defiant. I expected the enemy to come charging out at the sound of our defiant song, and I wanted to fight them. However, the enemy hordes were nowhere to be seen.

Songying said she was going to her room to recover her mimeograph machine. She and two other girls had just left when a small group of East-Is-Red Corps students appeared and ordered the rest of us to stop singing. A shouting match ensued.

"It's our right!"

"You have no rights! Don't you know the situation?"

"What situation? Don't bully us!"

"You've been thoroughly defeated!"

"We'll win ultimate victory!"

"Chen Boda says that you are a counterrevolutionary hodgepodge!"

"You're the counterrevolutionary hodgepodge!"

"If you don't conduct yourselves properly, we'll let you feel the iron fist of the dictatorship of the proletariat!"

"He who laughs last laughs best!"

In the midst of our argument, someone whispered in my ear, "They've called in the army. We must leave right away." As the message circulated through our group, we turned back toward the main gate. We were too late. The steel grates had been pulled shut. Several soldiers with machine guns stood inside the gate. When we tried to open a grate, a soldier stopped us and said nobody was allowed to go out.

We retreated to the third floor of the Principal's Building to discuss tactics. The building was still stocked with broken bricks that we had piled there when we controlled the campus. Bricks were of little use to us now. Reminding ourselves of the saying "Ten years is not too long for a gentleman to wait for revenge on his enemy," we decided that composure and patience were our best weapons under the circumstances.

Footsteps sounded on the stairs. Five soldiers with submachine guns came in. They said they were from the 73rd Army and had orders to search us. I had never heard of the 73rd Army. They directed us into an empty room at the east end of the building, made each of us come into the hallway to be patted for weapons, and then sent us down the hall to another room at the west end. Having found nothing, they told us not to leave the building and went away.

The night was half over. We sat on the floor disconsolately, too tired to talk, too worried to sleep. Screams rising from the direction of the bell-tower courtyard brought us to our feet. Standing on the back porch of the Principal's Building, we could see that one room in the far corner of the darkened courtyard was brightly lit. People were gathered by the door. Some waved flashlights. An argument was going on.

"Counterrevolutionary whore! How dare you try to murder our comrade!"

"I was defending myself! Don't you dare touch me, you counterrevolutionary savages!"

Qiqi, Erchou, and I all recognized Songying's voice at the same time and rushed downstairs to rescue her. At the foot of the staircase, a group of East-Is-Red Corps students brandishing spears, swords, rifles, and clubs confronted us. Little Bawang, Shuanggen, Xiangyun, Caolan, and Congfang were all there. Little Bawang had three grenades tied to his belt. "Jianhua, I thought you were through with this sort of heroic work," Caolan chided. "Don't expect us to be lenient again."

From Victors to Vanquished

"We need to see Songying," I said.

"Sorry, you can't go. Commander Fangpu has instructed us that nobody is to leave this building."

"I beg you, let us go," I entreated.

"She injured one of our comrades with a stencil board," Caolan said. "She is too wild. She must be punished."

"Please, please, don't beat her," Qiqi said. "If you want to punish her, let me substitute for her."

Little Bawang pointed a samurai sword at us and said, "Go back upstairs, you stinking counterrevolutionaries! You are now turtles in a jar. We will make no deals."

The two girls who had been with Songying were marched in at spearpoint. They came upstairs with us and told us how East-Is-Red Corps students had surprised them in Songying's room, searched the room, and found the mimeograph machine. An East-Is-Red Corps girl had given Songying a slap in the face. Songying had picked up the steel stencil board and hit her on the head. "We have to rescue her," one of her companions said. "They might beat her to death!"

Qiqi began to sing mournfully—the song the East-Is-Red Corps students had sung on the first night of their hunger strike in the County Military Department courtyard:

> Lifting my head, I see the Big Dipper,
> Deep in my heart, I miss Mao Zedong;
> In the black night when I think of you,
> Brightness floods into my heart;
> When I feel at a loss, I think of you,
> You illuminate my way like a beacon.

The solo became a chorus, loud, stirring, full of resolve. We went out on the back porch overlooking the courtyard. Tears rolled down our cheeks. We broke into the "Internationale."

From Victors to Vanquished

Our singing resonated over the dark campus. I picked up a loudspeaker horn that was lying on the porch and put it to my lips as I sang.

Some of the shadows roaming around below shouted at us to stop. More shadows raced across the courtyard and around the building. We changed our song to Chairman Mao's poem "Moon Over the West River," describing a battle with the Kuomintang in the Jinggang Mountains:

> Besieged by thousands of circles of enemy troops,
> We stand lofty and firm like a towering mountain.

Footsteps pounded on the stairs like rain. We hurriedly retreated to the room at the east end of the hall and linked arms. If they wanted to seize anyone, they would have to take us all. Arm in arm, we continued singing. Qiqi was on my left. Yuanxiao, a member of the Night Tiger Team, was on my right. Erchou was across the room. When my eyes met his, I saw a trace of fear. I gave him an encouraging look. He nodded back.

The enemy's footsteps pounded down the corridor. Fangpu appeared at the doorway, Little Mihu just behind him. Looking at us scornfully, Fangpu took a piece of paper from his pocket and began to read. It was a blacklist. The first name was Weizhong, the leader of the Red Rebels' third brigade. Fangpu waved his hand. A score of his followers surged through the door to seize Weizhong. We tightened our circle. Our enemies tugged at us. We held fast. Fangpu ordered more people in. They descended like wolves, pounding our backs, pulling our hair, hitting us with spear handles. We tried desperately to keep our arms locked.

A violent pull made me lose hold. I was shoved, punched, kicked, and cursed down the corridor to the room at the west

From Victors to Vanquished

end. Qiqi, Erchou, and other comrades were there, but Yuanxiao, the boy from the Night Tiger Team, and Weizhong, the head of the third brigade, were not.

Little Bawang marched in. "Erchou, why did you run away without our permission?" he demanded. "If I had not run away, I would have starved to death," Erchou said coldly. "Fart!" Little Bawang slapped him across the face. Blood trickled from his lips.

Little Bawang eyed me like a leopard assessing its prey. "Your little trick didn't save you either," he said. "Diehard counterrevolutionary!" "Who's the counterrevolutionary? We're the true revolutionaries!" I said. "Take him away!" Little Bawang ordered. Two boys stepped forward and grabbed me by the arms.

Fangpu and Little Mihu appeared again. Little Mihu tried to avoid my gaze. Fangpu was smiling at me. "Jianhua," he said, "it's not too late to reconsider your position and come over to the true revolutionary side." He turned to Little Bawang and said, "Give him another chance." The two boys holding my arms let me go. "Think it over," Fangpu said. He led his followers out. Fangpu's show of mercy disgusted me. Never had I hated him so much. I cursed myself for not finding my tongue fast enough to rebuke him.

We counted our ranks and found thirteen comrades missing. We had lost those on Fangpu's list in the scuffle. The rest of us, scraped, bruised, and aching, stood silently on the back porch. Somewhere in that dark courtyard, our comrades were being interrogated and tortured.

I had to piss. I went downstairs. My classmate Xiangyun halted me with a spear. "You're not allowed to leave the building," she said.

"I have to piss."

From Victors to Vanquished

288

"Can you hold it?"

"No, I'm going to wet my pants."

"In that case, you can go. You know we pay attention to revolutionary humanitarianism." Xiangyun and another sentry followed me to the nearest lavatory, pointing their spears at my back. "Don't worry. I won't try to escape," I said. "I can't leave while you're holding our comrades and torturing them."

"They're just receiving some education."

"I hope your revolutionary humanitarianism extends to them."

"We know how to take care of them."

They waited outside while I relieved myself, escorted me back, and took a few more people to the lavatory, one at a time.

The chill of late autumn forced most of us inside, but Qiqi stayed out on the porch all night. None of us slept. At dawn, Qiqi came in and told us the sentries had left. We went downstairs into the bell-tower courtyard. The atmosphere seemed as calm as if nothing had happened. The only movement was somebody crawling on the ground at the far side of the courtyard. It was Yuanxiao. His face was bloodied and swollen almost beyond recognition. "They beat me for quite a long time," he said. "My legs hurt so much that I can't stand up."

We found the others, each in a different room. Some lay on the floor bound with ropes. Some were strung from beams. Weizhong had been tied to a chair and gagged. The discovery of Songying was the biggest shock. She lay unconscious on the floor in a pool of blood. Her pants had been stripped off. Her blouse was torn, revealing her breasts. She had been beaten so badly that her whole body was purple.

Qiqi took off her jacket and wrapped it around Songying.

From Victors to Vanquished

We moved her onto a bedboard and carried her to the county hospital at a near-run. Fortunately, we had many sympathizers there. They promised to do their best to save her. We waited at the hospital until midmorning, when a doctor informed us that Songying had regained consciousness. He said her tormentors had pushed dirty socks and twigs into her vagina, causing heavy bleeding and shock.

The next task was to send our other injured comrades home. We bandaged them up and took them to the railway and bus stations in a slow-moving procession. The able-bodied supported the wounded, carrying the weakest on their backs. Qiqi was helping Yuanxiao, her arm around his waist and his arm over her neck. She did not seem the least self-conscious about helping a boy in such an intimate way.

The rest of us decided to withdraw from Yizhen once again. Only Qiqi would stay, to watch over Songying until the hospital released her. Several of us went to say good-bye to Songying. She was wrapped in bandages from head to toe, with only her swollen eyes showing. When I asked if she was in pain, she murmured, "No, not much." She added, "Our generation, growing up in peace and happiness, never experienced torture. When I read *Red Crag*, I could not imagine how human beings could be such brutes. Now I know." She told us to be confident and persevere in our struggle. Qiqi finally had to tell her to stop talking in order to conserve her strength.

Erchou invited me to go home with him. His village did not welcome an outsider. The pro-93rd Army faction there, once small but now swollen with the pride of victory, discovered me. Its leader, a village schoolteacher, accused Erchou's family of harboring a diehard counterrevolutionary. Erchou's father, a timid peasant who knew his place, did not want trouble. He found it hard to ask me to my face to leave, so he yelled at Erchou instead. I understood the message and left on my own. Erchou saw me off, apologizing profusely. I said that I understood his family's situation and bore his father no grudge. We parted in the fields.

Living in Limbo

I spent two weeks at home in Lingzhi, helping Zhihua cook for the family. Grandpa's illness had worsened with the on-set of winter. He coughed incessantly, and we had to empty his cuspidor several times a day. Papa spent his days receiving investigators and revising his self-criticism. We waited anxiously for news of his official rehabilitation. Try as I might to concentrate on family affairs, I could not get the Red Rebels' unfinished cause off my mind. I missed my comrades terribly. I had an irresistible urge to return to Yizhong, the dungeon from which I had so recently escaped. Finally, I did go back.

The room I had shared with my three classmates looked bare and dusty. All my belongings except a dirty quilt had disappeared. I moved into an office with a few older Red Rebels who had also returned. We held occasional secret meetings in town and furtively scattered leaflets at night. We also tried, without success, to contact our leaders in exile. We refused to believe the rumor that they had been captured. The war might go on for several more years, but someday Mengzhe would march triumphantly down from the mountains to re-take the campus.

How wrong we were. The East-Is-Red Corps had tracked down Mengzhe, Jinfeng, and the others, arrested them, and imprisoned them at the Commerce Bureau. I overheard East-Is-Red Corps students bragging about how they had marched Mengzhe into the courtyard and knocked him unconscious with one blow of a club.

Our dreams of a comeback shattered, we abandoned our secret activities and found other ways to pass the time. Some of my roommates composed poetry and practiced calligraphy; others carved woodcuts of Chairman Mao's head. I resumed my old hobby of building radios. I went downtown every few days to buy components and study circuit diagrams in the electronics section of the bookstores.

Most of the East-Is-Red Corps members moved from the Commerce Bureau back to school, confident that the Red Rebels had been quashed for good. I did my best to avoid my enemy classmates. Except for an occasional sneer across the dining hall, they did not bother me.

The 73rd Army sent two officers to Yizhong to help consolidate the victory of the East-Is-Red Corps. By then, I had learned that this unfamiliar unit was an antiaircraft artillery unit just back from Vietnam. It was based in Shimen with the 93rd Army. The two representatives, both army doctors, were an odd pair. One was tall and thin, with the pale face of a scholar, the other stocky and bearded. All they seemed to do was to walk the campus with pistols at their hips.

More Red Rebel students returned toward the end of November. Many of them put up statements declaring their withdrawal from the Red Rebels. Some referred to our organization as "the hodgepodge Red Rebels." Some applied to join the East-Is-Red Corps. I began to hate these opportunists even more than the East-Is-Red Corps people, although I knew they were sailing with the wind in order to survive.

I ran into Shuanggen under the willows one afternoon. He put on a smile that did not seem malicious, so I tentatively smiled back. "Jianhua, what are you waiting for?" he said, gesturing to the withdrawal statements on the walls. "He who understands the temper of the times is a great man."

I phrased my reply with care. "I'm concentrating on my semiconductor studies right now. I'll consider your advice."

"Sooner or later, you'll have to do it. Sooner would be better than later."

"I'll consider it."

"Don't think the impregnable pass is ironclad; today we stride through it and start anew," he said, quoting one of Chairman Mao's poems.

Shuanggen approached me several more times with the same suggestion. At first, he seemed to be acting in good faith. Then he began to sound threatening. His attitude made me all the more stubborn, although I never refused him outright.

I was still in bed one morning, immersed in a radio manual, when a knock came on the door. I rose and opened it to find Papa standing outside with Caolan. "Thanks to this nice girl, I finally found you," Papa said. "Your school's in such disorder, it's hard to find anyone."

Caolan left without a word as Papa stepped in. He was wearing a black overcoat with a fox collar, the same coat he had worn every winter since he was county head of Shuiyuan fifteen years before. He looked frail. His eyes were misty and his hair was streaked with white. Nonetheless, he seemed to be in good spirits. "I'm on my way to Shimen to attend a Mao

Zedong Thought study class," he said. "I thought it might be a good idea to check on you."

"I'm fine," I said. "I have a lot of radio books to read."

Papa's eyebrows descended into a frown. "I think you had better read Chairman Mao's works and other useful things. Have you read the *Red Flag* editorial on realizing a grand revolutionary alliance?"

"Who wants an alliance? The head of the Central Cultural Revolution Group gave us a death sentence, and our opponents mercilessly suppressed us."

"I'm not criticizing you." Papa's voice was stern. "But I told you long ago not to oppose the People's Liberation Army. You didn't listen to me."

I did not answer. He continued, "You should examine your petty-bourgeois thinking. One moment, you're a fanatic for struggle by force. The next, you're totally disillusioned and avoid politics altogether. That's not the right attitude. I think you should approach your classmates, admit your mistakes, and reconcile with them. They'll treat you decently."

"How do you know?"

"The girl who came with me was very nice. She promised me that they wouldn't treat you harshly if you would only withdraw from the Red Rebels."

Papa was lobbying for the East-Is-Red Corps! I looked him straight in the eye and said, "Papa, I can't give up my principles. I don't believe that those people represent Chairman Mao's revolutionary line. Would you give up your principles? I know that you wouldn't. In fact, you never have. That's why Yizhen's city wall still stands."

"I acted on behalf of the majority then," Papa said. "I understand that only four or five of you in your whole class stood on the losing side. You never gained majority support."

"Our side has a majority in the school as a whole and in Yizhen as a whole."

"Yizhen is a complicated place. The People's Liberation Army had to wrest it by force from the Kuomintang. There are still a lot of bad elements here. They like to fish in troubled waters. A majority in Yizhen means nothing. What about the prefecture? Are you in the majority in all of Shimen prefecture? I doubt it."

"Truth sometimes rests with the minority."

"The Central Cultural Revolution Group has declared who is right. Comrade Chen Boda was Chairman Mao's personal secretary for a long time and understands Mao Zedong Thought better than you. You should obey."

As Papa continued to lecture me, I asked myself if this was the same man who had always fought for truth and often paid dearly for his principles. Was this the man like a sword, who would rather break than bend? The sword seemed to have lost its edge. Papa wanted me to obey, to swim with the tide. He droned on. I nodded mechanically from time to time, having lost track of what he was saying. I did not want to argue with him anymore.

Eventually, he finished his lecture, and I found a chance to ask him if his attendance at the study class meant that his final liberation was near. He said that he did not know. He was looking forward to getting liberated, for he missed work very much. After all, he said, writing self-criticisms was not a very productive way to earn your salary.

Class Brothers Take Revenge

East-Is-Red Corps people ordered my roommates and me out of our office and turned it into a darkroom. They said they were preparing a photography exhibit on the two-line struggle—between Chairman Mao's revolutionary line and the bourgeois reactionary line. We moved to another room three rows away from my old dormitory.

Little Bawang and his followers had occupied our old room. The door was always shut and the windows were covered by blankets. It did not take long for their secret to leak out: the East-Is-Red Corps had set up torture chambers to punish students who had played a prominent role in the Red Rebels or who refused to defect. I began to notice former Red Rebels limping around campus as if they had been injured. When I tried to talk to them, they evaded me.

I reported the matter to the army representatives. They told me that this was a mass movement and they were not in a position to stop it; all they could do was to reiterate the Party's opposition to violence. For some reason, I felt in no danger myself. When my turn came, early one morning, I was totally unprepared.

A voice woke me. Little Mihu was looking at me with his sweet, puppylike smile. Had he come to make amends? "Come with me. We have to talk with you," he said softly. My roommates did not wake up.

I put on my padded jacket and followed him outside. It was

barely dawn, and nobody else was out. I asked him where we were going. "You'll know when we get there," he said. He led me to our old dormitory room. "Please, you first," he said.

I pushed the door open. It was black inside. My eyes had not yet adjusted to the dark when someone came up behind me and blindfolded me with a smelly rag. I was shoved forward. I felt the presence of people around me, although they did not speak.

Little Bawang ordered me to sit down. My hands were pulled backward and tied behind the back of the chair. "Do you know why you're here?" Little Bawang said. He seemed to be sitting across from me.

"You are going to torture me," I said, trying to control the trembling in my voice. "Why else would you blindfold me and tie me up?"

"Comrade Shuanggen has pointed you toward the bright and glorious road several times. You refuse to come to your senses. We've decided to give you a little help."

"I'm considering his advice."

"Considering? How long have you been considering?" Little Bawang's voice got louder. "A whole month. You don't know how to appreciate favors. Look how many Red Rebels have made their statements. Just a handful of you diehards have not. All of your leaders have been arrested. Are you still dreaming of a restoration?"

"With our leaders arrested and the Red Rebels disbanded, what need is there for a withdrawal statement?" I said. "I'm not interested in factional politics anymore. I'm just building radios."

Little Bawang's voice grew even angrier. "Nonsense! It's true that the Red Rebels have been wiped out, but you must make a clean break, both ideologically and organizationally."

Class Brothers Take Revenge

"It takes time for one to change one's views . . . " I was interrupted by a heavy blow on the leg. I wondered what kind of club they were using. It felt like a chair leg.

"How was that? Are your brains a little clearer?" Little Bawang spoke purposefully from his spot in front of me, as if he wanted me to know that he had been sitting there all the time.

"You can't do this to me. We're classmates. We're all class brothers . . . "

"Classmates? Class brothers?" Little Bawang roared. "Why didn't you say so when you were waving your spear and sword at us? Now you must confess your crimes in opposing us and the People's Liberation Army!"

"I did oppose you, but I never opposed the People's Liberation Army. Why should I oppose the People's Liberation Army? You know that my father is a veteran guerrilla leader who fought side by side with the People's Liberation Army during the war years."

"Let me remind you of something. You must recall shouting 'Down with Li Tongmao!' Li is a commander of the 93rd Army. How do you explain your act?"

"It's true that I shouted that slogan. But Li is Li. He doesn't represent the whole army. If I don't remember wrongly, your people shouted 'Down with Cui Tian!' Cui was commander of the missile troops and the 901."

Little Bawang lowered his voice again. "Let's not discuss these unimportant slogans," he said. "We are interested in your serious crimes. Did you participate in beating a nurse at the Army Hospital?"

"No, I'm against beating. It was I who released that army nurse."

Class Brothers Take Revenge

"Did you participate in the fighting against our comrades?"

"Mainly I followed along as a reporter for our newspaper."

A series of blows fell on my leg. I twisted in the chair, making the rope cut into my wrists. My torturers continued striking me. Gradually, my legs became numb. Then the numbness subsided and was replaced by sharp pain. I thought they were beating me again. In fact, they had stopped.

Little Bawang resumed his interrogation from his spot in front of me. "How was that? I believe you are ready to confess now."

I felt cold. My padded jacket was wet with sweat. "I have answered all your questions," I said.

"Who are the members of the Night Tiger Team? Speak!"

"You know them all: Sanxi, Erchou . . . " I recited the names of people who had not returned to school.

"Don't play tricks with us! We want the names of those who are here. We know who they are; we just want to see if you want to reform."

"If you know, why ask me?"

Two strokes fell on my knees. I cried out for the first time.

"Stop pretending; it doesn't hurt that much. Name just one Night Tiger Team member who is on the campus right now, and we'll spare you. Otherwise, you'll have to suffer in his stead."

"I really don't know."

The clubs fell on my thighs, knees, and shins. I struggled in the chair. A blow landed on my nose. Gold sparkles danced under my blindfold. The chair fell sideways with a thump. For a second, I thought my skull had split open and I was going to die. "Grandpa!" I cried out. A hot stream of blood came out of my nose and flowed down my cheek. Minutes

Class Brothers Take Revenge

passed before my torturers righted the chair. I could taste the blood in my mouth.

"Tell us who of the Night Tiger Team is here."

My head was spinning. "Du . . . su . . . ," I murmured, hardly knowing what I was saying.

"In view of your father's prestige, I will spare you the rest of the course that other Red Rebel diehards must go through," Little Bawang said. "Send off the guest!"

Somebody untied me, and two others helped me to my feet. My legs went limp and I sat down again. They hauled me up and dragged me toward the door. Little Bawang had some final instructions. "Write a statement declaring your withdrawal and post it within three days, do you understand? Don't breathe a word about this morning, do you hear? Otherwise, you'll suffer the consequences." My eyes were uncovered in the open doorway. The daylight was dazzling. A push sent me sprawling on the ground. The door slammed shut.

Not until that evening did I recall that I had given Dusu's name to Little Bawang. I forced myself to get out of bed and limped to Dusu's room to tell him to hide. I was too late. Dusu's roommate told me that a little fellow had just led Dusu away. I berated myself: Coward! Renegade! Traitor! I had broken under torture, like the traitor in the novel *Red Crag*. I had betrayed a comrade. I hated myself for not being stronger or smarter.

The next morning, I went back to Dusu's room. He was lying in bed, sunshine falling on his face. Before I could say anything, he smiled and said, "Jianhua, I rode a helicopter last night. They hung me on a beam and beat me. They even applied their physics lessons; they saved labor by using pulleys to lift me off the floor."

I grasped his hand and said, "Dusu, I was the cause of all

Class Brothers Take Revenge

your pain." I explained, expecting him to call me a traitor and slap my face. Instead, a guilty expression swept over his face. He held my hand tight and said, "I can't blame you. I know how one feels under torture. It's enough to drive a sane person mad. When they threatened to leave me strung up for the whole night, I told them some names, too."

After leaving Dusu, I understood why Papa had grown more compliant over the years. I had yielded after an hour of interrogation and torture. I had even betrayed a comrade. Papa had experienced wave after wave of both mental and physical torture. No wonder he had made some adjustments.

I thought of Yulan, who had jumped out of the Public Security Bureau building with her red flag, and Songying, who had cursed her torturers, and all the noble Communists who had endured torture in the novel *Red Crag*. Were they made of some special material?

My legs began to hurt so much that I had to spend the next week in bed. My roommates brought me food and helped me to relieve myself in a jar. As for the statement, I postponed it until the last minute, when Little Mihu came to get it. I never bothered to find out where it was posted.

When I could move around again, my enemy classmates made me join their discussions in our old classroom. They wanted me to criticize myself, but I talked as little as possible. The two army officers sometimes joined us and talked about their experiences in Vietnam. They let students play with their pistols until one went off in Little Mihu's hands and just missed Caolan's head. My classmates also assigned me to physical labor. Working alone, I dug a pit in the frozen earth for disposing of dirty wash water.

As the weather turned colder and colder, more and more Red Rebels renounced their allegiance. Four or five torture chambers were working around the clock. Some of the torturers were using methods as brutal as those of the Kuomintang and U.S. imperialists. A girl whom Mengzhe had planted as a spy in the East-Is-Red Corps had bamboo splints driven under her fingernails.

Great Snow—midwinter by the traditional peasant almanac—arrived at the end of December with the heaviest snowfall yet. The sky was leaden, the ground white, the leafless trees swaying with their burden. I was sitting in my room, reading by the stove, when the door opened and Weihua appeared. He came in and shook the snow off his padded coat. The snow on his eyebrows melted and dripped over his face. Had my brother gone crazy? "Why did you come back?" I said. "Don't you know what has happened?"

"Of course. News of Chen Boda's speech reached our home village quite a while ago. Stepbrother An had to go into hiding because his rebel organization sided with the 48th Army faction. There's armed struggle going on in the mountains now. It's not safe there either. I thought I might as well come back and try to help our faction."

"What the hell can you do now?" I said. "We're all finished. They're beating people right and left. They've been asking for you. You can't stay here."

"Is the situation that serious? Some East-Is-Red Corps people greeted me when I came in the gate. They didn't bother me."

"That's terrible! They know you're here. You have to leave, immediately!"

"Where can I go?"

"Anywhere. Go see Old Liu and his wife. They'll help you hide."

Just then, a group of East-Is-Red Corps students came in.

Class Brothers Take Revenge

Leading them were Weihua's classmate Hezui, "harelip," and a senior nicknamed Huahuagongzi, "playboy." Hezui's father was a Long March veteran who had lectured to our politics class several times, always telling the same story about eating leather belts while crossing the grasslands. Huahuagongzi's father had once been a petty official in charge of the Medicinal Herbs Department of Yizhen county. Papa had removed him for embezzlement. I knew the two boys were running a torture chamber in Ding Yi's old office. Both had ropes hanging from their leather army belts. A pair of glistening handcuffs dangled on Huahuagongzi's hip.

"Weihua, come with us," Hezui said. "We have something to discuss with you."

"You can't take him!" I said. "He's sick." I grabbed Weihua's sleeve. "Brother, they want to beat you!"

"Nonsense!" Hezui snapped. "We only want to talk. How could we beat a classmate?" He turned to Weihua again. "Let's go."

"Don't believe them! Don't go!" I begged Weihua. Weihua moved toward the door. "I've never harmed them. I don't think they would harm me," he said. He and the other students went back out into the snow.

Following them to the Teachers' Building, I grabbed Weihua's arm again and entreated him to stay with me. "I'm not afraid," he said. "Let's see what they'll do to me." I hung onto his arm until two boys pulled me away and held me back. "You can't beat my brother, you can't beat my brother!" I shouted as Weihua faded into the snow. The two boys holding me knocked me down and ran to catch up. Frantically, I went looking for an older Red Rebel who could intervene on my brother's behalf. Nobody would do it. My roommates appealed to the army officers. They would not help either.

Class Brothers Take Revenge

I paced my room in anxiety and despair until a dull thump sounded outside the door. I opened it to find Weihua lying facedown in the snow. His cotton-padded jacket had been slashed into strips. The cotton stuffing and the snow were turning red with his blood. My roommates helped me lift him onto a bed and went to find a doctor. Weihua's face was covered with cuts and bruises. I began to remove his blood-stained clothes. There were welts on his back and legs. He regained consciousness and looked at me. "Those bandits robbed me of my Parker pen," he said.

Failing to find Dr. Yang, my roommates brought back the two army officers. Hearing that the case was serious, they had agreed to come with their first-aid kit. Perhaps the 73rd Army had sent doctors on purpose, knowing their medical skills might be needed. They did not ask how the injuries had occurred or who was responsible. They listened to Weihua's heart, took his blood pressure, examined his limbs, dressed his cuts, and said he would be fine.

Weihua could not stand for several days. Hezui and Hua-huagongzi had beaten him with leather belts, bricks, clubs, and door springs. They had not asked him any questions; nor had they bothered to cover his eyes.

The snow fell gently for another few days. By the time it had stopped, Weihua was able to get up. I persuaded him to go home. At three o'clock one morning, I helped him trudge through the knee-deep snow to the rear of the campus, where I gave him a boost onto the top of the city wall. He set out for the early bus to Lingzhi.

Class Brothers Take Revenge

The Radiance of the
Setting Sun

As 1967 drew to a close, Yizhong's dormitories were nearly full again for the first time in a year. Almost all the students had returned. Most of the former Red Rebels seemed resigned to the East-Is-Red Corps' victory. Moreover, people believed that the Party's call for a grand revolutionary alliance signaled an end to the movement. Students began to talk about resuming classes, graduating, and going to college.

The East-Is-Red Corps leaders became our administrators. They ordered all teachers, most of whom had spent a leisurely summer and autumn at home, back to school with the threat that otherwise they would be deemed to have resigned of their own accord. Not wanting to lose their "iron rice bowl" of lifetime tenure, the teachers all came back. Those who had taken no sides in the factional fighting were welcome to join the East-Is-Red Corps. The ox ghosts and snake spirits were asked to clean the old recreation building and move into its small, cell-like rooms. As for those who had sided with the Red Rebels, many became guests of the torture house. I heard that our homeroom teacher, Wen Xiu, had been beaten for helping us run our newspaper.

The unluckiest was Ding Yi. He belonged to neither faction, but was still the school's number-one capitalist-roader and counterrevolutionary revisionist. Once again, the former Party secretary mounted the auditorium stage to take airplane rides. This time, he had some young companions: Mengzhe and other Red Rebel leaders rode the jet with him. The East-Is-Red Corps branded Mengzhe an "active counterrevolutionary" and accused him of diverting the general orientation of the Cultural Revolution, as well as of harboring the number-one capitalist-roader, Ding Yi, and the ox ghosts and snake spirits. Mengzhe also had to shoulder responsibility for the Red Rebels' supposed "atrocities." Mengzhe's secretary, Jinfeng, was called his "concubine." Lushuang, head of the Night Tiger Team, was reviled as "chief executioner."

We hardly ever saw our leaders between meetings, for they were kept under lock and key and guarded around the clock. We knew they were being tortured. When they appeared on-stage, they looked more like ghosts than human beings. Mengzhe, his head shaven, his face covered with cuts and bruises, a week's growth of whiskers on his chin, showed no emotion as his captors held him in the jet-plane position. Even when renegade Red Rebels mounted the stage to denounce him, his face remained blank. I could scarcely remember the commander-in-chief whose calm, gentle confidence could inspire the winds and clouds to do his bidding. The East-Is-Red Corps required everyone to attend these meetings. I sat as far back in the auditorium as I could and tried to imagine that Fangpu and Little Bawang were up there riding the jet plane instead.

I felt very much alone during this period. I had not seen Zongwei for more than two months. Erchou had not returned either. Sanxi still languished in the hospital in Baoding. News of his condition was bad: the hospital could not evict him but barely gave him any treatment. I appealed to the army representatives at Yizhong for help, but they said it was not their affair.

Fangpu was maneuvering to consolidate his power. In line with instructions from Beijing, a three-in-one revolutionary committee would be formed to run the school. First, a preparatory committee was set up. Rather than seek the top position, Fangpu invited Yizhong's old principal, Wu Du, back from Beijing's Central Party School to head the committee. Fangpu became vice-chairman. The two army doctors became the army representatives. Everyone said that Wu Du was merely a decoration and that the two army men could not stay on the campus forever. Therefore, the future of Yizhong rested in Fangpu's hands.

One afternoon during a struggle meeting, as I leaned on a windowsill at the rear of the auditorium, Little Mihu came up outside the open window and told me in a flat voice, "You had better come with me to see your comrade-in-arms."

"Who?" I asked, wondering whether it was an auspicious or an ominous message.

"You'll see when you get there."

I climbed out of the window and walked with Little Mihu toward our old dormitory. He ushered me into the room next to the one in which I had been tortured. Two of my enemy classmates were there. Upturned chairs and some rope lay on the floor. "He's over there," Little Mihu said, directing me to a bunk bed in the corner.

It was Zongwei. He lay on his back on the bare wood of the lower bed, his eyes half-closed, his face ashen. His padded jacket was draped over the bedpost. The new red cotton sweatshirt he had worn underneath was torn. His pants, once blue, were dark with blood. His belt was missing and his fly was open, revealing red sweatpants that matched his shirt. He was barefoot.

"Zongwei, your comrade-in-arms is here!" Little Mihu

The Radiance of the Setting Sun

shouted sarcastically as I stood there like a wooden statue. "Open your eyes to look at your comrade-in-arms!" Zongwei opened his eyes and gave me a vacant stare. I searched for a sign of warmth, or just an appeal for help. Instead, I thought I saw disappointment, disgust, even hatred. Did he think that I had betrayed him? Did he think that I had come to persuade him to surrender? Otherwise, why would I be walking around healthy and unharmed? I felt ashamed. I wanted him to forgive me. I wanted him to know I was not a renegade. His tired lids slid back down over his eyes.

"Zongwei!" one of my enemy classmates yelled. "Confess your crimes right now!"

Zongwei opened his eyes and said in a weak voice, "I'm too tired." His eyes closed again.

"Stop pretending!" the other boy bellowed. "If you don't hand in your confession today, it means that you don't want to leave!" The two boys continued to yell at Zongwei but got no response.

"Let me go fetch Dr. Yang," I begged the students.

"He is not going to die," said Little Bawang, who had just entered the room. "He's pretending. Don't be taken in. Let him confess."

Zongwei was breathing hard. His lips were white and cracked. He opened his eyes again and said in a barely audible voice, "Water, I want water . . . " His dry lips moved clumsily. "Please, let me get some water," I said. "He can't confess in this condition." Little Bawang said nothing, perhaps a sign that he did not object. I grabbed a bowl and ran all the way to the boiler room by the dining hall. I filled the bowl with water from the boiler and walked back as fast as I could, trying not to spill it.

The two boys were still yelling at Zongwei to confess when

I knelt down by the bed. The water was too hot. I blew on it for a while. I put my arm under Zongwei's shoulders, lifted him up, and put the bowl to his lips. Grasping the bowl with both hands as I held it, he drank like a person dying of thirst. I asked him to stop. He did not listen. He gulped down the whole bowlful without a pause. I asked him if he felt any better. He did not answer. I laid him back down and draped his jacket over his upper body.

His appearance did not improve. I went outside and found Little Bawang talking with Caolan and Congfang. I begged him to let me get Dr. Yang. He bluntly refused. When I returned to Zongwei's bedside, I found him gasping for breath. His face was gray. I ran out again in a panic. Little Bawang was gone. I found Shuanggen and persuaded him to come look at Zongwei. He was scared too, and agreed to let me get Dr. Yang.

I ran to the clinic. When I told Dr. Yang about Zongwei, she looked uncomfortable. She said the East-Is-Red Corps had been harassing her for treating some injured Red Rebels, and she was afraid to go too far. Nearly in tears, I pleaded with her, "Dr. Yang, you can't just sit by when he needs you; you have to go save him!" At last, she picked up her first-aid kit. I thanked her and ran back to the dormitory.

The enemy classmates had left. Zongwei was breathing a bit easier now. He looked at me and moved his lips, but I could not understand what he was saying. Dr. Yang came in. She tried to roll up Zongwei's pants, but they were stuck to his legs with dried blood. As she slit open the pant legs with scissors, she flinched. When I looked at Zongwei's bare legs, I knew why. They were riddled with holes the diameter of a pencil, surrounded by strings of loose flesh the consistency of shredded pork. Blood and pus oozed from the wounds.

The Radiance of the Setting Sun

"What in hell did they use on him?" Dr. Yang muttered. Looking around the room, I found the answer to her question: the pokers used to tend the stove. My classmates had flailed Zongwei with those steel hooks. I did not tell Dr. Yang, for fear that she might faint.

I began to feel relieved as Dr. Yang cleaned and dressed Zongwei's injuries. All of a sudden, she stopped working. Zongwei was panting hard again. With each breath, he seemed to expel more air than he was taking in. Dr. Yang took his wrist and felt his pulse. She stood up and went out, saying only, "I have to talk to them." In a few minutes, she came back in. "His pulse is very weak," she said. "We're going to send him to the hospital. Your classmates have gone to find a cart."

Little Bawang, Shuanggen, Little Mihu, and some other East-Is-Red Corps students came in. They pushed me aside and started to lift Zongwei. He gave a cry of pain and threw his head back. His eyes rolled up until only the whites were showing. My comrade was dying. I had heard that dying people recovered consciousness just before death, and then their eyeballs rolled up. "The last radiance of the setting sun," it was called.

"Be quick, or he won't make it!" I cried out.

"Who are you ordering about?" Little Bawang said. "Get out of our way." I had to step aside as they carried Zongwei outside.

A two-wheeled cart, its shafts tied to the rear rack of a bicycle, was waiting at the door. A dirty quilt lay in the cart. Zongwei's head hung backward as they set him down. His eyes were still open. He seemed to be gazing at the hazy winter sky, but I knew he was seeing nothing. It was said that people who died with unfulfilled wishes or as victims of injustice never shut their eyes. Zongwei might fit into both categories.

Dusk was falling. The struggle meeting in the auditorium had ended, and students were going back to their dormitories. Little Bawang and his followers pulled the cart onto the path. Little Bawang swung himself onto the bike. The others ran along on both sides. The crowds of students hardly gave them a glance. For several hours, I clung to the belief that Zongwei would return. After dinner, the loudspeakers summoned the East-Is-Red Corps leadership to an emergency meeting. Then I knew I would never see my friend again.

The official explanation for Zongwei's death that emerged over the next few days was this: Zongwei had come to town on market day to do some shopping and had stopped by the school. He got into an argument with some girl classmates and insulted them with foul language. The girls called the boys. Zongwei resisted. The boys took him away and were subduing him when he suddenly died of heart failure caused by an old disease.

I knew the only ailment Zongwei had suffered from was something the locals called "sheep-hair nails." Tiny white bristles would appear on his back from time to time, causing an unbearable itch. When he got an attack, Teacher Wen would bring him home, where her ugly old mother rubbed buckwheat dough on his back to pull out the bristles. How ridiculous to claim that his old disease had led to heart failure!

Zongwei had died a violent, unjust death. I had seen the blindfold, the ropes, the instruments of torture, the wounds, the blood with my own eyes. But the East-Is-Red Corps and its allies at the Public Security Bureau would never let anyone see the body. Absurd as their fabricated story was, nobody

The Radiance of the Setting Sun

would ever question it. I could not challenge it either. All I could do was curse my foes to myself.

Thus we entered the year 1968. We marked new year's day with yet another struggle meeting against the Red Rebel leaders.

Zongwei's mother, a widow, came to town on an oxcart driven by her nephew to take her son home. The East-Is-Red Corps did not let me talk to Zongwei's family for fear that my story might differ from the official version. I watched the cart roll off with the closed coffin containing Zongwei's frozen body. Zongwei's mother was weeping. Loose wisps of her white hair drifted in the cold north wind.

A few days later, a boy from my class named Qinghai, who had gone home during the factional fighting and had joined the East-Is-Red Corps after returning to school, handed me a piece of folded paper as he passed me on the path. Opening the paper, I found a message asking me to meet him that evening by Rear Lake. My heart began to race at the thought that he might be setting a trap on behalf of Little Bawang.

I went despite my fears. It was a moonless night. Qinghai was wearing a heavy hooded coat. Putting a cold hand in mine, he said, "Jianhua, I know that you may suspect me, but you'll get to know me in time." We began to walk, hand in hand, to keep warm.

"I want to talk with you because I can't talk to anyone else," Qinghai said.

"Why not?"

"I can't trust anyone else."

"Even your East-Is-Red Corps comrades?"

"If I tell them what I really think, they'll expel me or brand me as politically suspect."

"If you can't trust them, why should you trust me?"

"There's something I must tell you." His words tumbled out in a rush. "Jianhua, I don't like terror and violence. I could understand why the two sides fought. But I don't understand why one side still beats people, even after its complete triumph. I had nightmares about Zongwei's death for several nights. Then came Teacher Wen's rape . . ."

"What are you talking about?" I stopped abruptly and stared at him.

"Little Bawang and some of his followers gang-raped Teacher Wen. After Zongwei died, Little Bawang ordered Teacher Wen to write an affidavit about Zongwei's serious disease. She wrote about the sheep-hair nails and described how her mother had helped treat it. This wasn't satisfactory. Little Bawang wanted her to write that Zongwei had gone into shock several times. Teacher Wen told him she couldn't deceive the people and the Party. They beat her and then they raped her."

"She was our teacher for more than two years. She treated us like her own children. How could Little Bawang do that?"

"He has become a beast!"

We resumed walking. "Do you know how Zongwei was beaten?" I asked.

"I was in the room. Zongwei was on his way to the market. He didn't know that things had changed so much. He thought that struggle by force was over, and that we were back to the days of great debate. When Caolan and Congfang saw him and asked him to surrender, he said, 'You're the ones who should surrender. Don't go around with your noses in the air.' The girls got angry and called the boys, who tied him up."

I knew that Caolan had disliked Zongwei even before the Cultural Revolution. One day during class, Zongwei had

The Radiance of the Setting Sun

313

loudly pronounced the first syllable of her name with a falling tone instead of a low and rising tone, making it sound like "fuck." Everyone had burst into laughter. Even though Zongwei's slip of the tongue was not deliberate, Caolan had held a grudge against him ever since.

"Twenty students joined the beating," Qinghai continued. "Even Caolan and Congfang and a few other girls took part. They used chair legs, door springs, and pokers. They kicked him all over. Little Bawang demanded to know how much money he had stolen to buy his new sweat suit. Zongwei said his mother had bought the suit with her earnings from several months' work on her loom. Little Bawang demanded that he take the suit off. He held onto it, and they beat him more fiercely. I couldn't stand his screaming and moaning anymore, so I left the room."

For a few minutes, we trudged along the lake without speaking. The only sound was our feet crunching through the crusted snow.

"The East-Is-Red Corps leaders called that emergency meeting to plot their cover-up. They passed a four-point resolution: one, Zongwei provoked the beating; two, Zongwei died of heart failure due to an old disease; three, all beatings from now on will be restricted to the lower part of the body, below the hips; four, any efforts to take advantage of the incident to oppose the East-Is-Red Corps will be suppressed."

Qinghai told me he was keeping a diary in code. He added, "I saved the blindfold and ropes they used to bind Zongwei. In a socialist country like ours, murderers shouldn't go unpunished. We can't let them get away with murder." A few days later, he gave me the bloodstained relics. I hid them in the rafters above the ceiling in my room.

The Radiance of the Setting Sun

Three Loyalties
and Four Boundless Loves

"Chaos after prolonged unity and unity after prolonged chaos are eternal rules under heaven." Grandpa had often cited this opening sentence of the *Romance of the Three Kingdoms*. It seemed to apply to the situation at Yizhong. After a long period of disorder, a new order was coalescing.

Yizhong's Revolutionary Committee was formally installed with fanfare and celebration in January. It had taken exactly a year for Fangpu to realize his dream of wresting power from the school's Party Committee. He was now called Vice-Chairman Fangpu. Principal Wu Du was the chairman, representing revolutionary cadres. The former head of the school's Financial Department represented faculty and staff, since he was the only staff or faculty member who had actively sided with the East-Is-Red Corps. The other members were East-Is-Red Corps students; it went without saying that no Red Rebels could serve. The two army officers served as supervisors. They brought in a whole 73rd Army platoon to bolster what *Battlefield News* called the "newborn red revolutionary power." *Battlefield News* had a press monopoly now; *Red Rebels* was long since defunct.

Aside from Yuling, who was not expected, Huantian and Zongwei, who would never return, Sanxi, who was still in the hospital in Baoding, and Yuanchao, whom nobody had seen since the Red Rebel triumph at the Army Hospital, everyone in class 85 had returned to school. Erchou and I reluctantly moved into the room next to Little Bawang's torture chamber, for the Revolutionary Committee wanted us together in class groups. I took the blindfold and ropes with me. Erchou and I buried them under the brick-paved floor, beneath the spot where Zongwei had fallen.

Maybe Little Bawang wanted to put on a milder façade, or maybe he craved sun and fresh air. For whatever reason, he and his followers took the blankets down from the windows of the torture chamber and replaced them with paper. However, they did not stop tormenting people. Almost every night, Erchou and I were awakened by screams and moans coming from the next room. Erchou was afraid they would come to get him for escaping from the bathhouse, but they never did.

One night, the screams became so terrible that we got up to look through a rip in the paper. Our enemy classmates were interrogating a senior Red Rebel as he crouched on the floor with his hands tied behind him. A pulley swayed on a beam. They pressed him to confess how much money he had stolen during the factional fighting. He said none. They beat and kicked him until he said twenty yuan. Not satisfied, they beat and kicked him some more. The figure kept rising until it was 800 yuan. At this they became openly skeptical and asked him to declare once and for all how much he had taken. He said he had taken nothing and had made up the figure because he could not stand the torture.

Erchou and I were glad when the torturers suspended their operations to concentrate on a new campaign. Called Three Loyalties and Four Boundless Loves, it was said to have originated at an air base near Shimen, but nobody really knew for sure. The Three Loyalties were loyalty to Chairman Mao, loyalty to Mao Zedong Thought, and loyalty to Chairman Mao's proletarian revolutionary line. The Four Boundless Loves were boundless love for Chairman Mao, boundless love for Mao Zedong Thought, boundless love for Chairman Mao's proletarian revolutionary line, and boundless love for the proletarian revolutionary headquarters headed by Chairman Mao.

The campaign consisted of decorating our classrooms, reciting Chairman Mao's quotations and three most-read articles, and declaring our love and loyalty. Class 85 put a poster of Chairman Mao in an army uniform on the back wall. Underneath, we painted ocean waves and ships, and a radiant red sun rising on the horizon. Under that, we wrote the inscription "Sailing the seas depends on the helmsman," imitating Lin Biao's calligraphy. Above the picture, we wrote "Respectfully wish our great leader, great teacher, great supreme commander, and Great Helmsman Chairman Mao an infinitely long life," in the handwriting of the scholar Guo Moruo, who was so revolutionary that during the campaign to smash the Four Olds, he had declared all his previous writings to be trash.

Every morning, we assembled before Chairman Mao, raised our little red books above our heads, and chanted "Wishing our great leader Chairman Mao an infinitely long life, and his close comrade-in-arms good health forever!" We would sing the song "Sailing the Seas Depends on the Helmsman." Then we would read quotations in accordance with the day's agenda. If we were going to study with the 73rd Army people, we would recite "With the army and people united as one, who under heaven can match us?" If we were going to attend a struggle meeting against Mengzhe and Ding Yi, we recited "Everything reactionary is the same; if you don't hit it, it won't fall." Every evening before bedtime, we assembled again to sing, chant, wave our red books, and report to Chairman Mao about what we had done during the day. These routines at the start and end of the day were called "asking for instructions in the morning and reporting back in the evening."

The campaign grew more creative and varied. Chairman Mao quotation contests became popular. Caolan recited all 270 pages of the red book without missing a word. Xiangyun could recite any quotation as soon as you gave her the page number and category. I did not do very well at quotations, but impressed people with my flawless recitation of all 37 of Chairman Mao's published poems. Little Bawang did everything he could to avoid these contests.

Dances were another way to express our loyalty. The most popular one was set to a Tibetan tune, "On the Golden Hill of Beijing." To carry out Chairman Mao's instruction to "fight selfishness and repudiate revisionism," we adopted the People's Liberation Army system of "red pairs." Erchou and I naturally formed a red pair. Our classmates called us the "black pair." Maybe they were right, for we never did mutual criticism and self-criticism the way we were supposed to. Instead, when the two of us were alone, we cursed the East-Is-Red Corps.

The campaign led to a movement to "revolutionize daily life." It consisted of replacing daily talk with quotations from Chairman Mao. When you got out of bed in the morning, instead of saying, "Let's get up," you said, "Carry the revolution through to the end." When you went to bed, you said, "Never forget class struggle." People greeted each other with, "Serve the people." If you bought anything, be it a movie ticket, pencil, or bottle of soy sauce, you had to initiate the transaction with a quotation. This was troublesome for older people with poor memories, but nobody protested. One had to sacrifice some personal convenience for the sake of making revolution.

Chairman Mao quotations were useful in many situations. In the marketplace one day, I heard a housewife and a sales-woman trading quotations at a vegetable stall. The housewife was choosing tomatoes with great care, examining each one, since they were expensive in the winter. The displeased sales-clerk said, "Fight selfishness and repudiate revisionism." The housewife replied, "We Communists pay great attention to conscientiousness." They quoted back and forth until they were ready for a fight. Onlookers used quotations to stop them.

The Three Loyalties and Four Boundless Loves campaign was a positive development as far as Erchou and I were con-cerned. Carrying it out took precedence over the antagonisms between us and our East-Is-Red Corps classmates. The ces-sation of torture next door allowed us much more sleep. We no longer had to be on the defensive every minute of the day and night.

The news of Papa's liberation lifted my spirits even more. The central radio station broadcast a story about the Mao Zedong Thought study workshop that Papa had attended in Shimen, and mentioned Gao Shangui as an example of a rev-olutionary cadre who had gone among the masses to seek forgiveness and had joined the new organ of revolutionary power. Erchou congratulated me, saying, "Now you can trade your dog-cub-of-a-capitalist-roader cap for your son-of-a-revolutionary-cadre cap." The story also appeared in the *People's Daily*. I went downtown to buy my own copy, which I posted on the wall of my room. I invited several East-Is-Red Corps classmates in to see my latest radio project just so they would see the newspaper.

Good tidings were followed by bad. Sanxi returned to school dead. Little Mihu, a look of derision on his face, brought Erchou and me the news. A number of East-Is-Red Corps students were standing outside the room where Sanxi lay. One said, "Look, the foxes have come to mourn the death of the hare." Sanxi was stretched out on two desks pushed together, his eyes closed, his mouth slightly open as if he wanted to say something. His round, ruddy peasant face had shrunk to a bony, yellow mask. I lifted one of his skeletal hands and felt the calloused palm.

Erchou and I stayed by Sanxi's side the whole afternoon, unaware of time passing. Neither of us had an appetite for dinner. We went to bed early without talking but unable to sleep. My mind was full of memories of Sanxi, his earthy jokes, his brawny peasant strength, his zest for battle. I had never once heard him complain. I heard Erchou tossing in his bed and knew that he was thinking of the same things.

Sanxi stayed in that room for two days until his father came to take him to their village for burial. Erchou and I did not talk with his father. We lacked the courage to face him. We felt responsible for Sanxi's death. If only the Red Rebels had defeated the East-Is-Red Corps, the hospital would not have let Sanxi die.

I went to Lingzhi a few days later to spend Spring Festival with my family. Chairman Mao quotations in fresh red paint and pictures of Chairman Mao captioned with the character for "loyalty" on a red heart adorned the walls of the villages along the road. As the bus entered the Lingzhi county limits, a row of roadside guardians, some built of mud, others of snow, came into view. Local peasants had sculpted them to mock the capitalist-roaders. The figures were hard to recognize, but signs made their identities clear. Head of State Liu Shaoqi was there, and so were the provincial and county Party secretaries, and even the former county Party secretary, Han Rong. I was glad to see that Papa was not included.

Enthusiasm for the Three Loyalties and Four Boundless Loves was even higher in Lingzhi than in Yizhen. Almost everyone in the streets was wearing a Chairman Mao portrait on a necklace, and some of the older people held the portrait up in front of their chests as they walked.

Not a poster against Papa remained. He was now vice-chairman of the county's new Revolutionary Committee, having prevailed over Mo Yin the wind-sailor. I was happy about the outcome until I learned that Papa was but a figurehead. True power rested with a group of military men, led by the head of the County Military Department, who was chairman of the committee. Papa was in charge of agricultural production and had virtually no say in political decision-making. This did not bother Papa, however. When I got home, he had already left for his model brigade, Tile Terrace. He would spend Spring Festival with the peasants there.

Last year's Spring Festival was no more than a grim memory now. An air of exuberance permeated our little mud-brick house. Though still bedridden, Grandpa was directing preparations for the feast from the kang. "Jianhua, what did I tell you last year when your Papa was in trouble?" he asked. "Did Grandpa predict wrong?" "Of course not," I said, "because you'd mastered Marxist dialectical materialism." Grandpa's laughing turned into choking coughs. I pounded him on the back and insisted that he rest.

Mama had bought us a quarter of a pig this year. When she came on Spring Festival morning to eat jiaozi, she also brought gifts from the tank regiment that supported Papa: a bag of exquisite Chairman Mao quotation books, half the size of the regular ones, and some large Chairman Mao badges, one as big as a soup bowl. The metal used to make the badges reputedly came from B-52's shot down in Vietnam. My sisters, brothers, and I were so happy that we capered around to the dance called "On the Golden Hill of Beijing."

Weihua returned to Yizhong with me. As we left the house, Mama told us that Papa had written to Fangpu asking him to ensure our safety. With Papa fully rehabilitated, Fangpu could not take such a request lightly. When we walked in the school gate, we saw that our statue of Chairman Mao had arrived. The giant figure was lying in front of the Principal's Building, partly covered by a tarpaulin. All over the country, people were erecting such statues to express loyalty and love for Chairman Mao. Our Revolutionary Committee had ordered ours from a factory in Tianjin that was working around the clock to meet the demand.

I pulled back the tarpaulin to better admire the figure. Chairman Mao was five times as large as life. He was wearing an overcoat and an army cap with a star. His right hand was uplifted, exhorting us to carry on the revolution. The concrete was colored and textured to resemble light pink marble.

Chairman Mao was lying on the ground because his base was not complete. An old tree had been chopped down and a concrete base poured on the spot, but Fangpu did not think it good enough. He had ordered some marble slabs to cover the concrete. Only Fangpu could make Chairman Mao wait without causing a political crisis.

When the marble slabs arrived, they were far too big, so Fangpu assigned a group of teachers to cut them to the proper size. Out of curiosity, I stopped by the workshop where they were working. The air was filled with dust. My physics teacher, the Yankee Feng, and my geology teacher, the rightist Liu, were cutting the stone. My Chinese teacher, the Kuomintang officer Li, was polishing the cut pieces at a grinding machine. A cotton mask covered his mouth and pink particles clung to his sweaty forehead, making him look like a Beijing opera clown.

I watched him for quite a while. I had the urge to address him as Teacher, but felt it would be out of place. "That looks like an interesting job," I finally said. Teacher Li looked at me. His eyes smiled above his mask. "I'm glad to have the opportunity to reform myself through such significant work," he said.

"May I help?" I said.

"Thank you, no. It's too dusty here. You'd better leave."

"Let me try just one," I insisted.

Teacher Li yielded. He found me a mask and let me help him hold the marble slabs against the polishing wheel. We did not talk much. We did not need to talk. It seemed like the old days before the Cultural Revolution, when teachers and students got along. I felt so content among these ox ghosts and snake spirits that I went back to the workshop and helped Teacher Li for several days. Erchou complained that I was not spending enough time with him.

At last, Chairman Mao was righted upon his glistening pink base. It was a grand sight. A white marble plaque

Three Loyalties and Four Boundless Loves

commemorated the event: "Greatest leader, greatest teacher, greatest supreme commander, and greatest helmsman Chairman Mao, erected by the Revolutionary Committee of the East-Is-Red Middle School of Yizhen and all Red Guards of the East-Is-Red Corps, February 1968." Our school henceforth would be known as the East-Is-Red Middle School, Fangpu announced. Teachers Feng, Liu, and Li were not at the ceremony, for all ox ghosts and snake spirits had been confined to their rooms.

Hostage for a Hobby

The ardor of our Three Loyalties and Four Boundless Loves cooled after Spring Festival. My East-Is-Red Corps classmates looked for new diversions. They plundered the school warehouse and found some musical instruments. Now a screeching violin and weak trumpet notes disturbed our rest. They got hold of pistols and shot bullets into the classroom roof. When they tired of that, they tossed grenades into Rear Lake.

I took advantage of this period to work on a five-transistor radio. Just as I finished the job and was tuning in the central broadcasting station, several explosions went off outside. Little Bawang and Shuanggen were standing there laughing while smoke rolled out of the pit I had dug for disposing of wash water. "It's getting warm," Shuanggen said. "We don't need it anymore. This is easier than filling it in."

Another explosion went off. I went outside again. Little Bawang, Shuanggen, and Little Mihu were picking themselves up off the ground before another demolished pit. "That's dangerous," I said. "You shouldn't stay so close."

"Nonsense!" Little Bawang said. "We're experimenting to find the safe spot."

"The soldiers told us that there's always a safe spot," said Shuanggen. "If you lie down at the right place in time, you'll always be safe."

Little Bawang turned to Shuanggen and said with a sneer, "You two wouldn't have done it if not for my dare."

"We accepted it, didn't we?" Little Mihu said.

"Look at your frightened face!" Little Bawang said. "Don't pretend to be so brave!"

No sooner had I gone inside again than the three of them came in and fixed their eyes on my radio. Little Bawang picked it up and fumbled with the knobs. "Let me borrow this for a few days," he said. Before I could reply, he took a handful of bullets out of his pocket and tossed them into the stove. Erchou and I ducked as the bullets exploded. Little Bawang did not even flinch. "So you agree," he said. He departed with the radio, his two companions following.

I had spent two weeks making this radio, skimping in the dining hall even more than usual to buy the components. I wanted to appeal to Wu Du, chairman of the Revolutionary Committee, but Erchou dissuaded me, saying that it would only invite more trouble. Erchou and Weihua lent me money to build another radio. This one was even better. It had eight transistors and received many more stations. We even listened to Radio Moscow attacking the Cultural Revolution—secretly, because "listening to enemy radio" was a serious crime.

Hostage for a Hobby

Little Bawang heard about my new project. He came by with the five-transistor radio and said he wanted to trade it for the eight-transistor one. I knew that if I refused, he would take both anyway, so I had to agree. "If you like radios so much, why don't you learn to build them, instead of borrowing mine?" I said. He replied that he would start right away.

He started that afternoon by breaking into the physics laboratory to steal materials and tools. He and his followers turned their torture chamber into a radio workshop. I taught them the rudiments of transistors and drew them two- and four-transistor circuit diagrams. However, Little Bawang had neither the talent nor the patience to assemble a radio. His finished product was a mute tangle of electronic parts. He was so angry that he smashed it with a pistol butt. His followers did not do much better. Only Shuanggen succeeded in building a working radio, and his sounded like a mosquito.

Little Mihu appeared in my room early one morning and asked me to go next door, assuring me that there was nothing to fear. A jumbled mass of radio components and wires was spread over several desks. Musical instruments lay on the floor. Enemy classmates sat staring at me from the bunk beds lining the walls. "Jianhua," Little Bawang said in a friendly voice, "I have invited you here to serve as our engineer. You will help us build radios. If you perform well, we'll accept you into the East-Is-Red Corps."

He told me the rules. I could not leave their dormitory room. Erchou would deliver my meals. I must not divulge the source of parts and tools. I must work fast but maintain high quality. I would be expected to bring their nonfunctioning radios to life and to build an eight-transistor radio for Little Bawang, a seven-transistor one for Shuanggen, and five five-

Hostage for a Hobby

transistor ones for other East-Is-Red Corps activists. Little Mihu qualified for a five-transistor radio because of his excellent service as Fangpu's courier. After I finished this first batch of radios, I could start on the next batch—a radio for every East-Is-Red Corps member in class 85.

With no right to refuse this great honor, I became their slave. Erchou was pressed into service as my butler. Under duress, he also resumed his role as class barber. I immersed myself in my new job. The smell of tin solder drove my cares from my mind. My skills improved rapidly, and each radio took less time to assemble than the last. I obeyed all the rules and added a few of my own: I was entitled, for instance, to sneak some of the best transistors into my pocket.

Meanwhile, my captors resumed playing with guns and grenades. This led to the first casualty among my enemy classmates. A grenade exploded in Little Mihu's hand. The county hospital saved his life but not his arm. When Erchou and I heard about it, we agreed that it served him right.

The day after the accident, Little Bawang relieved Erchou and me of our duties while he attended to Little Mihu's case. We were lying in our own beds, relishing our newfound freedom, when the former editor of *Red Rebel*, Qiude, came in. Looking around conspiratorially, he unwrapped a small paper bundle and held up an object resembling a small stick.

"Do you know what this is?" he asked. Erchou and I shook our heads. "This is your classmate Little Mihu's little finger!" Qiude burst into laughter. "I found it in the bell-tower courtyard. Other Red Rebels found pieces of his arm and threw them into Rear Lake to feed the fish!" Qiude's expression turned from delight to anger as he added, "This bloody finger

Hostage for a Hobby

is small payment for the blood of our comrades." He tossed the finger into our stove. The fire flared and sizzled, and a foul smell filled the room.

Little Mihu did not return to school until early March. By that time, eight of our East-Is-Red Corps classmates were about to leave for the army. Ordinarily, the People's Liberation Army took in new recruits at the beginning of the year. In 1967, when making Cultural Revolution was taking precedence over everything, the army had skipped the annual recruitment. In 1968, we expected the same. However, with the growing tensions on the Sino-Soviet border, the army had abruptly announced a recruitment drive.

Yizhong's Revolutionary Committee said that anyone except the main Red Rebel leaders could apply. Erchou, Weihua, and I all registered. Erchou had always wanted to be a military man. I had never contemplated an army career, but with all the universities closed, I could not think of anything better.

Although all three of us passed the physical examination, none of us was chosen. Several former Red Rebels were accepted, so we could not claim that the school Revolutionary Committee had discriminated against us because of our factional affiliation. Everyone knew, however, that the committee had given East-Is-Red Corps students the best recommendations. More than a hundred of them would be inducted. Rumor had it that Fangpu's top strategist, Jinian, known to the Red Rebels as the "dog-headed military adviser," had recommended that any members with blood on their hands escape this way. Fangpu was staying, but Jinian had enlisted. Little Bawang, Shuanggen, and the other boys who had beaten Zongwei to death would be leaving their bloodstained reputations behind. My new friend Qinghai was going too. He told me he could no longer bear life at school.

The campus emptied as students accompanied the new recruits to the railroad station. Little Bawang and Shuanggen took along the radios I had made. Erchou and I boycotted the procession. Little Mihu also stayed behind.

Little Mihu could not have returned to school at a worse time. The enthusiasm of the new recruits only made him more depressed. He had just turned seventeen. But for his accident, he might have been going into the army too. The school Revolutionary Committee had paid all his medical expenses and awarded him a monthly allowance for "sustaining wounds while implementing tasks for the public." But nothing could compensate for the loss of his arm.

The sarcasm and arrogance that Little Mihu had displayed in the service of his East-Is-Red Corps masters had vanished. He looked at me now with a mournful expression that begged for sympathy. I reminded myself of the crimes he had committed against me and my comrades. Nonetheless, I could not hate him as much as before.

Soon after our schoolmates went off to the army, the provincial capital was moved from Baoding to Shimen. People who were fond of interpreting political events said that Chen Boda had engineered the change to strengthen his position. He had never really trusted the 48th Army in Baoding. In Shimen, however, he had the 93rd and 73rd armies on his side.

When the provincial Revolutionary Committee was set up, the *People's Daily* hailed the event with an editorial headlined, "The sons and daughters of the kingdoms of Yan and Zhao have lofty ideals!" Yan and Zhao were the two states that had occupied what was now a single province during the Warring States period more than two thousand years earlier. People who were adept at reading things into the newspapers said that Yan and Zhao also were allusions to the pro-93rd and pro-901 factions, and that the factional struggle was not over yet.

The Twelve-Force Typhoon

Grandpa's philosophy of conflict was, "The loser is bandit, the victor king." The rightist scholar Hu Shi had once said, "History is like a little girl, for people to dress up as they fancy." The victors at what was now called the East-Is-Red Middle School demonstrated the truth of these statements. In the spring of 1968, they totally rewrote the history of the previous year and a half.

The school Revolutionary Committee called an assembly to officially proclaim Yulan, who had plunged to her death from a window at the Public Security Bureau, a revolutionary martyr. At the same meeting, the committee invalidated the declaration naming Heping, who had died as a prisoner in a jeep, a revolutionary martyr. The East-Is-Red Corps unveiled its "two-line struggle" exhibition of faked and doctored photographs. Pictures of Red Rebel leaders had been airbrushed so they would look like criminals. Some of my enemy classmates were glorified as "long-marchers" in a caption to a picture of them walking along the top of the city wall.

The future was as uncertain as the past was elastic. My

classmates and I would have entered the senior division of school the previous summer. Now Erchou was talking about dropping out and returning to his village to earn work points in the fields. I urged him to wait a little longer and see if classes resumed. "Let those ox ghosts and snake spirits teach us?" he replied.

Our hopes were revived in late March, when Lin Biao arrested the acting chief of staff of the People's Liberation Army, Yang Chengwu, and two other generals. It happened right on the stage of the Great Hall of the People, with thousands of high army officers looking on. Yang had written an article in the *People's Daily* entitled "Establish the Absolute Authority of Mao Zedong Thought in a Big Way and a Special Way." It was said that Chairman Mao had ordered Yang's arrest because he did not like the idea of "absolute authority" and "big way." The reason that Erchou and I were happy with Yang's downfall had nothing to do with this philosophical debate, however, or with other crimes Yang was said to have committed in Beijing. We were happy because Yang was a former commander of the 93rd Army. The East-Is-Red Corps and other pro–93rd organizations had often boasted of being linked to Beijing's "proletarian revolutionary headquarters" through Yang. Yang was said to have championed the pro–93rd Army cause at the negotiations called by Chen Boda. The enemy had lost its most powerful spokesman.

Once again, Red Rebels began to dream of a reversal. Our undisguised pleasure put the East-Is-Red Corps people on guard. One day, some of them overheard me quoting two lines from a Tang poem to a former Red Rebel brigade leader:

Even raging wildfire cannot burn it out;
When the spring wind blows, it springs up again.

The Twelve-Force Typhoon

331

They put up a dazibao citing my words as evidence that the Red Rebels were plotting a "counterrevolutionary counterattack," and calling on East-Is-Red Corps members to beat us back. That evening, as I stood with my classmates before Chairman Mao's portrait, Caolan demanded that I confess my "ideological circumstances" to Chairman Mao.

I tried to humor my classmates by saying that I now felt content with East-Is-Red Corps rule. They did not believe me. They made me stand right in front of Chairman Mao and formed a semicircle around me. They even let Erchou stand with them. Little Mihu was there too, a distant look in his eyes.

"Speak!" Caolan ordered. "Why did you recite that poem to Shuhua?"

"Because he likes poetry."

"Don't you know that he's a Red Rebel leader?"

"People can change. If Kuomintang war criminals can be reformed, a student certainly can."

"Don't play your stupid games," Congfang said. "Why did you choose that poem?"

"Because this is early spring and the grass is growing."

"Are you dreaming of a restoration?"

"I'm telling the truth."

"You bastards still haven't learned how to behave!" said a boy we called Zhubajie, the name of the pig deity in *Journey to the West*. Zhubajie had been small potatoes in the enemy ranks until Little Bawang's departure. Lately, he had taken command of the remaining boys. "You won't tell the truth until we use force!" he said, giving me a kick behind the knees.

As I fell to the floor, Caolan restrained Zhubajie from kicking me again. "Apparently, you need some Mao Zedong Thought to help you reform," she said. "Recite the quotation on page ten, paragraph two."

I could not find the words.

"No wonder you're such a reactionary; you don't even know Chairman Mao's works," said Zhubajie. "We're not going to let you stand up until you recite the quotation."

"Maybe we're being too strict," Caolan said. "I'll tell you the first few words, and then there should be no problem. Listen: 'Everything reactionary . . .' "

"Everything reactionary . . . Everything reactionary . . ." I could not go on.

"Think again. It should be easy for a man of letters like you."

"Everything reactionary . . ." I still could not think of the rest of the quotation. Erchou gave me a reassuring look. Little Mihu was no longer there. Some of the others started taunting, "Stupid! Reactionary!" I glanced around in confusion. I could see between my classmates' legs to the brooms resting in the corner of the classroom. The quotation jumped into my mind. "Everything reactionary is the same; if you don't hit it, it won't fall. As a rule, where the broom does not reach, the dust will not vanish of itself," I recited.

"That's not quite right. Try again," Caolan said.

After several more tries, I remembered the phrase that I had left out: "Everything reactionary is the same; if you don't hit it, it won't fall. This is also like sweeping the floor; as a rule, where the broom does not reach, the dust will not vanish of itself."

"Now recite it ten times." I repeated it ten times. "Now make your confession."

The Twelve-Force Typhoon

"I have nothing to confess. I withdrew from the Red Rebels long ago, and the Red Rebels organization does not exist anymore."

"Did you not take pleasure in the arrest of Yang Cheng-wu?" Zhubajie inquired. "Did you not think his arrest might pave the way for your comeback?"

"No, I didn't."

"I must warn you that if you have any unrealistic illusions, you'd better give them up," Zhubajie said. "The revolutionary red power will not change."

I could not convince my classmates of my innocence. At last, they let me get up from my knees and ordered me to submit a written confession. I wrote that when my father had led a guerrilla unit against the Japanese he had known Yang, then a district military commander; that I had heard many stories about Yang's service as commander of the advance force on the Long March; and that I felt sorry for Yang and hoped for his reinstatement. I knew this feigned sympathy totally contradicted Chairman Mao's revolutionary line, for Chairman Mao himself had ordered Yang arrested. Nonetheless, it satisfied my classmates.

The reversal that we Red Rebels yearned for did not occur. By the time the shrubbery atop the city wall was turning green again, the pro–93rd Army side had taken over Yizhen county's new administration. The deputy political commissar of the County Military Department, who had fled to Shimen to seek refuge when the other department officials sided with the 901, had returned to become chairman of the County Revolutionary Committee. Fangpu was vice-chairman. Wei-hua's classmate Hezui could strut about even more proudly because his Red Army veteran father was a committee member. By contrast, my classmate Yuanchao's father, also a Red

Army veteran, had been forced to resign as head of the Army Hospital because he had leaned toward the 901. He was planning to retire to his hometown in Jiangxi province. Yuanchao and his sister Kangmei had gone ahead to look for a house.

Fangpu also became a member of the standing committee of Shimen prefecture's Revolutionary Committee. My former editor Qiude assured me, "The higher the helicopter rises, the harder it will plunge to the ground." But Fangpu's political career seemed to be on an ever-rising trajectory.

By the time the lilac bushes burst into purple blossom, we were involved in a new campaign. Chairman Mao had made a speech saying that factionalism was not completely bad. Proletarian factions should fight bourgeois factions, and proletarian factions could unite with one another, but not with bourgeois factions. This inspired the Twelve-Force Typhoon campaign, intended to defend the newborn proletarian revolutionary committees against class enemies. The time was still not ripe for a grand revolutionary alliance.

The Twelve-Force Typhoon made a broad sweep across Yizhen, targeting landlords, reactionaries, counterrevolutionaries, capitalist-roaders, "diehard madmen," and "anti-army elements." All the villains accumulated since Liberation, plus the leaders, activists, and unrepentant members of the losing faction, had to put on white armbands with black characters identifying their crimes.

Ding Yi, still "number-one capitalist-roader and counter-revolutionary revisionist," Mengzhe, "black chieftain of the madman's hodgepodge," and Jinfeng, "tramp and concubine of the black chieftain," took countless more jet-plane rides on the stage of the school auditorium. The disgraced teachers were also dragged out again. I saw Zhubajie knock Teacher Li down in a rice paddy and submerge his head under the

The Twelve-Force Typhoon

muddy water. On another occasion, I saw him drumming on Teacher Liu's bald head with a stick. Not long afterward, Teacher Liu went to the Army Hospital with bleeding ulcers and had three-fourths of his stomach removed.

East-Is-Red Corps students made Red Rebel students put on white armbands and kneel down before Chairman Mao morning, noon, and night. The noontime sessions were often held outside for other students to see on their way to lunch. Although the weather had turned warm, some of the Red Rebels still wore their thick padded winter clothes for protection. Once-proud warriors like Xiangsheng, now labeled the "black cripple general," and Chunfei, "black madman ambassador," crouched and kowtowed submissively while their classmates kicked their buttocks.

Their submissiveness may have saved their lives. One who did not submit was Yongrui, former director of our arsenal. Her classmates harassed her in countless ways, making it impossible for her to eat or sleep. One day, I saw her washing her bowl over and over again at the sink in the dining hall. The bowl was covered with ink. A few days later, I watched her struggle to stand upright while her classmates pulled her hair to force her head down. When she had weakened, the students threw her onto the classroom floor and kicked her unconscious. She revived and asked to go to the toilet. She could not stand up. Many onlookers had gathered, but neither I nor anybody else dared to help her. She dragged herself outside toward the lavatory. Later in the day, Red Rebel students found her body on the path. She was buried outside the north city wall with the others who had died ingloriously.

Perhaps my classmates had decided that I posed no threat, or perhaps they respected Papa's status, for even Zhubajie left me alone. Erchou escaped the dragnet too. Nonetheless, we

The Twelve-Force Typhoon

took precautions. One night, we dug up the blindfold and ropes that had bound Zongwei and threw them down the well in the bell-tower courtyard.

Weihua was not so lucky. At first, his classmates merely made him apologize to Chairman Mao, without even making him kneel down. Late one night, however, a group of students beat him up again. One of Weihua's friends woke me early the next morning to tell me. He said that Weihua had disappeared. I finally found him lying on a bench at the bus station waiting for the next bus home. His jacket was torn and his face was covered with cuts. Hezui and Huahuagongzi had laid another trap, enlisting the aid of younger students to throw Weihua off guard. When the bus came, I helped Weihua to a seat and told him to see a doctor as soon as he got to Lingzhi. He nodded absently. I later learned that he had fainted the moment he stepped into the house. He stayed in the local hospital for a week recovering from internal injuries.

The struggle meetings continued at school, and the white armbands proliferated. I was surprised when the former head of the school's Financial Department appeared with one. "The only revolutionary among the entire faculty and staff" had become a "color-changing chameleon." His former student allies, having kicked him off the school Revolutionary Committee, had locked him in a room and were feeding him nothing but bread made of sweet-potato flour. I encountered him once in the lavatory, straining with constipation as he squatted over the pit.

On market days, all the victorious organizations in the county paraded their Twelve-Force Typhoon victims through the streets of Yizhen. The County Revolutionary Committee enlarged the marketplace and built a permanent stage for struggle meetings. The movement reached its height in mid-

June, with a rally attended by ten thousand people. Mengzhe and other top leaders of pro-901 factions stood on the stage, held by armed police. Several hundred "special guests" with white armbands knelt on the ground between the stage and the audience. The authorities were "killing the chicken to scare the monkey," as the old saying goes. They sentenced some of their captives to jail terms and others, including Mengzhe, to labor reform. A policeman kicked Mengzhe behind the knees to make him fall, pulled his arms behind his back, and snapped a pair of shining handcuffs on his wrists.

After the rally, the typhoon subsided. Some former Red Rebels were dispatched with the ox ghosts and snake spirits to grow vegetables by Rear Lake. Others were allowed to take off their white armbands and rejoin their classmates. The East-Is-Red Corps even absorbed some of its old adversaries into its organization by creating a new class of members. The original members were now called Red Guards and had the right to wear red armbands. The new ones were Fighters and could not wear red armbands. Although Erchou and I never applied, we were named Fighters anyway. Now we could mix with our classmates and attend most of their meetings. We remained in our own room but could enter the room next door at will.

I resumed reading radio manuals and experimenting with new circuits. Erchou made woodcuts of Chairman Mao on the tops of broken desks. Meanwhile, for the boys next door life had become aimless and boring. From time to time, they brought in a couple of teachers and made them slap each other or crawl on the floor. At night, they would light campfires outside the dormitory to attract cicadas and eat those that plunged into the flames. One day at noon, I stepped into their room to find them engaged in collective masturbation.

The Twelve-Force Typhoon

Lying in bed stark naked, their penises displayed like a row of antiaircraft guns, they were competing to see who could shoot the highest.

The school Revolutionary Committee declared that we would have a two-month summer vacation, the first since the summer of 1965. Weihua had returned to school. Fearful that his old enemies would beat him a third time, I persuaded him to go home early. On the last day before vacation, I faced his enemies instead.

Hezui and Huahuagongzi had one of their flunkies summon me to a room in the Teachers' Building. When I told them that Weihua had left, Huahuagongzi grabbed the front of my shirt and said, "You brothers are playing tricks!" Letting go of my shirt, he opened a folding fan with the flick of a wrist, closed it again, and used the folded fan to poke me in the chest. I backed up a few steps. He kept poking me until I had backed up all the way across the room. He struck me on the head with the fan and yelled, "Halt!"

I had stopped beneath a portrait of Chairman Mao. Pointing to the picture, Huahuagongzi ordered, "Confess your crimes!" Just as I had seen my comrades do during the Twelve-Force Typhoon, I bowed three times to Chairman Mao and said, "Great leader Chairman Mao, I apologize to you, for I did not study your works well, and I took the wrong side in the great winds and waves of class struggle . . ."

I went on and on until Huahuagonzi ordered me to stop. He ordered me to sweep the cement floor. I did so. He ordered me to sprinkle the floor with water to keep the dust down. I went to the dining hall and brought back a bucket of cold water. I sprinkled the floor. As long as they did not beat me, I did not mind humoring them.

When I had finished my tasks, Hezui pointed to a washbasin and said, "Drink a basin of cold water to refresh your-self, and then you can go." He laughed as he filled the basin from the bucket and placed it on a desk in front of me. I drank a third of the water and put the basin back on the desk. Hua-huagongzi rapped me on the head with his fan. I picked up the basin again and drank some more, very slowly. My stom-ach was starting to ache. I put it down again and said, "I can't take anymore."

"Stop pretending," Hezui said. "I know you can finish." I forced down some more, letting as much as possible flow down my chin and inside my shirt. When the basin was two-thirds empty, Huahuagongzi got impatient and dumped the rest on my head.

"Now," he said, "go get the worst person at school and bring him back here."

"How do I know who the worst person is?" I said. "You have to tell me. If I don't satisfy you, you'll be angry."

"It doesn't matter; just get the one you think is the worst."

I walked slowly out of the building as I contemplated this demand. It would be a difficult decision, for whoever I sent them would be their next amusement. I went to the recreation building and found Eclectic Zhu. No sooner had he trotted off to the Teachers' Building like a goat than I regretted my choice. Eclectic Zhu might be an ox ghost and snake spirit, but he had never harmed me. I chased after him. My bloated stomach slowed me down. Eclectic Zhu got to the room be-fore me. I put my ear to the door and heard Huahuagongzi say, "Why are you here?"

"A student said you wanted me."

"You motherfucker, who wants an ox ghost and snake spirit like you? You've been struggled against so much that you stink! We want those madmen! Go away, you motherfucker!" My guilt assuaged, I retreated to my room, collected my things, and set out for the bus station.

As I passed Rear Lake on my way to the small north gate, I saw Mengzhe's secretary, Jinfeng, working in a tomato patch. She was barefoot, with her pant legs rolled up to the knee. The back of her blue jacket was wet with sweat, and her hair clung to her sunburned face. She still wore her white armband. Nobody was guarding her. She was working all alone and could easily have run away. "Sister Jinfeng, why don't you flee?" I said.

She turned to me. "Thank you, but I don't want to leave. I want to be near Mengzhe," she said. "Anyway, where could I go? I don't have food coupons or money. People would know what kind of person I am. They would pick me up right away and send me back." She was right. She looked shabby and beaten-down. With one look, anybody in the county could guess that she was from the defeated faction.

"Sister Jinfeng, take care of yourself," I said. "The clouds will pass and the sky will clear." I shook her hand, and left without looking back.

The Irretrievable Past

Grandpa and my younger brothers and sisters had moved out of their crumbling mud house and into a sturdy brick one across town. Grandpa was on his feet cooking again. He walked unsteadily and stood hunched over, but his hands were nimble as ever with the cleaver. Classes had resumed in the schools of Lingzhi. Xinghua, Meiyuan, and Yiyuan were attending primary school in their new neighborhood, and Zhihua had entered the middle school. The curriculum consisted mainly of reading Chairman Mao's works.

The house seemed crowded after Weihua and I had moved in for the summer. Worried about his future, Weihua alternately brooded and raged. In one outburst of anger, he smashed Xinghua's rabbit hutch, making Xinghua cry the whole afternoon.

Papa decided to send Weihua and me to his favorite production brigade deep in the Taihang Mountains. He said that working at Tile Terrace would help to reform our outlook on the world as well as to build up our strength. Weihua and I set out for the brigade one day in late July, taking a bus into the mountains and trudging another ten miles through a valley, using a meandering river as our guide. The valley narrowed as we walked, and the river was only a few meters wide when we reached our destination—twelve villages nestled against the slopes, their terraced fields ascending like staircases to the tops of the hills.

After a month of farm labor, Weihua decided that he had worked enough. He hitched a ride out on a visitor's truck. I was worn out too. In the evening when I joined the villagers in Mao Zedong Thought study sessions, I could hardly keep my eyes open. The brigade leaders assigned me to lighter work at brigade headquarters, helping five girls embroider a tapestry of their socialist mountain brigade. They wanted to send the tapestry to Chairman Mao for the upcoming Ninth Party Congress.

It was mid-September when I returned to Yizhen. Heavy ears of rice were nodding in the yellow paddy fields. In spite of battles, campaigns, and typhoons, a good harvest was in sight. The peasants would reap, eat, and live on, as they had for thousands of years. But the place we now called the East-Is-Red Middle School would never be the same. Earth-moving machines still rattled, and trucks shuttled back and forth among the hills of rocks and cement on the sports ground. The classrooms were dilapidated, the walls thick with layers of paper, dirty glue, and faded ink. Desks and chairs had been smashed and used for firewood. The science laboratories had been plundered. The music hall had been blown up. Above all, the faculty had been demolished. The dead were dead, and the survivors were no longer themselves. Desks, chairs, and microscopes could be replaced, run-down buildings rebuilt, but the loss of our teachers was irretrievable. With our own hands, we had destroyed the heart of our school.

Shortly after I moved back into my dormitory room with Erchou, our classmate Yuanchao showed up at the door. He wanted to have a last glimpse of the school before moving to the South. His father had been edged out by young upstarts at the Army Hospital and was looking forward to retirement. Yuanchao had found him a quiet place to settle down. When I asked about his sister Kangmei, Yuanchao said she was in Jiangxi province with her husband. "She met a young guy in a restaurant who belonged to a local gang of ruffians, and in three days they were married," he said. "There's nothing you can do after the rice is cooked. My parents didn't agree at first, but since she'd slept with him they had no choice."

After Yuanchao left, I pondered how unpredictable life could be. Who would have thought that Kangmei, the pretty schoolgirl, daughter of a Red Army veteran, would marry a hooligan at the age of seventeen? I felt even more perplexed about my own future.

Our immediate fate was soon determined: everyone who

The Irretrievable Past

343

was still at school would graduate. The County Revolutionary Committee made the decision shortly after the Central Committee convened an enlarged plenary session in Beijing and declared Liu Shaoqi a "renegade, hidden traitor, and scab."

Chairman Mao had called on students to "go up the mountains and down into the countryside to receive re-education from the poor and lower-middle peasants." Most of my schoolmates, especially those who came from the countryside, preferred to stay in town. Within a few days of graduation, all the Red Guards of the East-Is-Red Corps were assigned urban jobs in county organizations and businesses. Zhubajie went to the Commerce Bureau and Caolan to the Light-Industry Bureau. Congfang went to work at the cinema. Little Mihu became the gateman for the County Revolutionary Committee. A few less active East-Is-Red Corps members in my class became waiters and waitresses in restaurants, which they considered much better than returning to their villages to "repair the globe."

Former Red Rebels fared differently, of course. Those from peasant families returned to their villages with their useless diplomas. Those from the town of Yizhen were assigned to a suburban commune. I said goodbye to Erchou, who was going home to till the earth. Weihua and I went back to Lingzhi. We felt indignant at the East-Is-Red Corps' abuse of power, but there was nothing we could do.

Neither Weihua nor I wanted to go back to work with the peasants. When Papa asked me to make a speech at a rally for local middle-school graduates about my determination to "go up the mountains and down into the countryside," I declined. If I made such a speech, I would have to live up to it, and then I would not be able to do anything else. Weihua declined the invitation too, saying that if all our East-Is-Red Corps schoolmates had gotten real jobs, why should we go to the countryside?

Not that we had high aspirations. Weihua now said he would be satisfied to become a postman delivering mail by bicycle. I thought that I would like to get a factory job. Sometimes Zhihua joined our discussions; he would like to be a cook, he said, so he could eat to make up for what he had lost during the Three Difficult Years.

In the meantime, Weihua worked as a volunteer at the county bookstore. Every day, he brought home outdated picture books that he had rescued from the trash heap—children's versions of *The Romance of the Three Kingdoms* and other vestiges of the Four Olds. I attended to Grandpa, whose bronchitis had worsened again as the cold weather set in. He stayed on the kang all day, choking and sputtering. I made him tea, which he drank right from the spout of a small porcelain teapot. Sometimes he would ask me to go out and buy him cigarettes to make him cough so he could clear his throat, despite doctor's orders not to smoke.

One day, Grandpa broke the spout of his teapot. I could not find another of that kind in the local department store, so I went to Shimen to buy him a new one. Shimen was much quieter than a year ago—no dazibao, no loudspeaker debates, no fighting in the streets. The Madman's Commune was a thing of the past. Now the power of the new revolutionary committees prevailed. Nobody knew what was happening behind the high walls of the Missile Engineering Institute, but rumor had it that the 901 cadets were going to Vietnam for real battle and that the academy would close. I found a pot for Grandpa in a porcelain shop and boarded the train. It was already dark when I got off at Yizhen, too late to catch the last bus to Lingzhi. I decided to visit my old school.

The campus lay lifeless under the moonlight. I went from dormitory to dormitory. All were empty and dark, and smelled of mildew. Reluctant to stay in this ghostly place, I considered going to Old Liu's house in town. Then I saw a dimly lit window in a corner of the bell-tower courtyard. Getting up my courage, I went to the door and knocked.

Teacher Li opened the door wide. "Come in!" he said in a jovial voice. His cheeks were flushed. I smelled hard liquor. "Tonight is new year's eve!" he said. I had not realized that this was the last day of 1968. "Let me wish you a prosperous new year, Teacher Li," I said as I stepped from the cold night air into the warm room. The only furnishings were a coal stove, a table, and a bed.

"Happy new year to you too. We should all feel happy," Teacher Li said. "Sit down, Jianhua. Tonight, we two, an old teacher and a young student, should drink to our hearts' content." I sat on the edge of the bed. Teacher Li put a plate of rabbit meat on the table and said, "Freshly pot-stewed. I got it this afternoon in town." He poured some clear liquor into a bowl, handed it to me, and toasted, "Bottoms up!"

"Bottoms up, Teacher Li!" The fiery liquid burned my throat and made my eyes water. I began to cough. "Quick, have some hare meat and you'll feel better!" Teacher Li said. I followed his instructions and did indeed feel better.

Teacher Li looked at me, his eyes moist. "It makes me feel good to be called Teacher again. Nobody has called me Teacher for a long time. But let's not mention those old mat-

The Irretrievable Past

346

ters tonight. Let's talk about new things and look forward to the new year. Jianhua, do you remember Bai Juyi's poem about drinking wine? That fits my mood tonight."

He recited it, his body swaying back and forth, his glistening bald head describing circles in the air, as in the old days when he had recited poems in the classroom:

> A jug of newly brewed green foamy wine
> Sits on the small red earthen stove;
> Evening approaches with snow on the way.
> Do stay to drink a cup with me.

Teacher Li's happiness was infectious. We sat up half the night at the creaky table, drinking, eating hare meat, and reciting Tang dynasty poems. Finally, he cleared the table and said, "It must be past midnight. We have entered the new year. We should rest. Let's go next door and get you a bed."

"Why take the trouble to move it?" I asked. "I can sleep there, if you'll lend me a blanket."

"It gets very cold at night. You must sleep in here with the stove."

We moved another bed into the small room. My head was dizzy with drink. Teacher Li talked on for a while. The last thing I heard before I fell asleep was that the East-Is-Red Corps students who had gotten jobs in town would have to return to their villages or settle in the countryside after all.

We got up late on the first morning of 1969. Teacher Li was still cheerful as he saw me to the gate. Such a man would welcome anybody, even Little Bawang, out of the cold for food and drink.

At the bus station, I encountered Little Mihu and his brother, who had served with an antiaircraft artillery unit in

Vietnam and had been wounded and demobilized. Little Mihu was going back to his village after losing his job as gateman for the County Revolutionary Committee. His brother had come to help him collect his things. "Fangpu tried to get me special treatment, but it didn't work out," Little Mihu said.

I looked at his empty sleeve and then at his face. He looked back at me sadly. Then he looked down at the front of his cotton-padded coat. His remaining hand played with a button. "Is everything all right with you?" I said. "How are things at your home? How about your mother? I haven't seen her for so long." I had gone home with Little Mihu for the weekend just once. His mother had instructed him to fetch a cabbage from the production team's collective fields. When I had told Little Mihu that it was wrong to rob the collective for personal use, he had said he could not disobey his mother. I had vowed never to visit Little Mihu's home again.

"Mama is fine," Little Mihu said. "She often asks me why you never visited again. What can I tell her? It was all my fault. As for me, I'm fine too, except sometimes I feel lonely. Our classmates do not keep in touch with me."

"Forget about the past. Let bygones be bygones. We should look into the future." I could not think of anything to say to someone who had lost an arm. Little Mihu lifted his head and looked at me again, gratitude in his eyes. I saw the sweet, naïve Little Mihu I had once known. I shook his left hand to say good-bye and boarded my bus. On the way home, I decided to build him a radio.

The Irretrievable Past

The Way Out

As the saying goes, "When the cart comes to the foot of the hill, it will find its way up." Weihua and I had been waiting at the foot of the hill for months. We found our way up when the People's Liberation Army came to Lingzhi to recruit new servicemen.

It was called "compulsory service," performed by citizens as a duty without pay, but in fact nobody needed to be compelled to serve in the People's Liberation Army. Peasant lads eager to leave the countryside had always vied for the privilege. With the universities closed, middle-school graduates like ourselves were joining the competition in multitudes. Weihua was enthusiastic about joining the army, believing it far better than returning to Tile Terrace, and even preferable to the postal service. To me, it seemed the only way out.

We signed up at the recruiting station for Lingzhi and surrounding villages, along with thousands of other young men. Since I was three months short of seventeen, I registered as a year older to meet the minimum age requirement of eighteen. A preliminary visual inspection eliminated half of the applicants. The inspectors' penetrating eyes gave me gooseflesh, but both Weihua and I passed this first test.

The next day, we returned to fill out political background forms. This stage of the process would weed out half the candidates again. I was worried that Mama's bankrupt-landlord status might ruin our chances, so I suggested that we declare her middle peasant, as we had in the past. Weihua said we would be in terrible trouble if our lie was discovered. Mama turned pale when she heard my idea and told me to tell the truth. "Your father's background as a lifelong revolutionary will offset it," she assured me. I did as she said. When I handed in my form, I saw that the others going into the pile all claimed poor- and lower-middle-peasant origin. I slipped mine into the middle of the pile, too embarrassed to lay it on top.

Despite my fears, Weihua and I passed the political evaluation. The next step was a physical examination, which would halve the number of candidates once more. Everything from heartbeat to testicles came under scrutiny. We had three chances to pass the blood-pressure test. After flunking twice, I took a pill and passed.

As our army prospects grew brighter, Grandpa grew more and more subdued. One night as we lay on the kang, he said to me, "Child, joining the army may be one choice, but I think you should go back to our hometown to till the soil. Get a wife and settle down. Shuiyuan is a lovely place."

"Grandpa, I want to join the army to continue the revolution," I said. "I don't want to be a peasant for the rest of my life."

"What's so great about joining the army and continuing the revolution? Your father has devoted his whole life to the revolution, and look what has happened to him. Officialdom is not so enviable. Being a peasant is better than anything." He continued, "It's fine if your big brother wants to join the army. His temperament suits it. You're the reflective, scholarly type. You don't belong in uniform."

"Grandpa, I know what you mean," I said. "I won't stay in the army for long. If I get the chance to go to university, I

The Way Out

will go. But right now, all the universities are shut. I'll join the army for a couple of years, and I'll still be young when I get out."

Grandpa was quiet for a while. Finally, he said, "Child, Grandpa can't prevent you from going. This time, though, I may not get up. After you leave, I won't see you again."

"Grandpa, I'll be back to see you!" I pulled the covers over my head. My eyes overflowed with tears, wetting my pillow and quilt.

While Weihua and I were waiting for final notification, we learned that recruits would be divided among three types of service. Top candidates would go to nuclear-missile bases, second-class to the navy, and the remainder to regular army logistics units. We did not even dream of being assigned to a missile base. The political standards were too strict; recruiters investigated family histories going back three generations and disqualified people for the slightest question. So we began to hope for the navy.

Just at this time, Mama became the target of a new campaign, motivated by Chairman Mao's instruction to "get rid of the stale and take in the fresh" in the ranks of the Party. Any capitalist-roader, revisionist, devil, ghost, traitor, or spy who somehow had retained Party membership was expelled immediately. Members who were not considered Party activists were being "persuaded to withdraw." Mama fell into the latter category. The slogan "Clean the daughter of bankrupt-landlord Fu out of the Party!" appeared in the County Revolutionary Committee courtyard.

Weihua and I suspected that the Lingzhi County Military Department had engineered the criticism of Mama to embarrass Papa and keep us out of the army. We decided to make a personal appeal to the recruiters, taking advantage of Papa's influence as vice-chairman of the County Revolutionary Committee. We invited the recruiters to come to our house, hoping that once they saw our shabby home, they would realize that Papa was a good official, and that therefore his sons would make good soldiers. Whatever the reason, the officer representing the logistics troops agreed to accept us.

Even as third-rate recruits, we felt especially happy as Spring Festival approached. I made fresh pork sausages in preparation for the holiday. I also made two radios, one for Grandpa, the other for Little Mihu. I wrote Little Mihu a letter asking him to come to Lingzhi.

Little Mihu came on the eve of the lunar new year. He had ridden a bicycle one-handed all the way from his village. He looked envious when I told him I was leaving for the army, so I did not mention it again. I asked him about his village, and he said that nothing had changed, and that probably he would live the same way for the rest of his life. At lunchtime, I cooked him a big bowl of noodles and presented him with his radio. He turned it on, twirled the dials, and stroked the wood cabinet with his one hand. In the afternoon, he carried the radio while I walked him and his bicycle to the hilltop east of town. He fixed the radio on his bike rack, mounted the seat clumsily, and rode away, his left hand on the left handlebar, his right sleeve flapping uselessly.

Five days after Spring Festival, Weihua and I reported for army duty at the county guest house. We lined up according to height in the courtyard, where bundles of crisp new uniforms were broken open and distributed. We were led to the public bath house, where we jumped into the big hot pool like dumplings dropping into a steaming pot. We had one last physical checkup. Then we put on our new khaki suits. They were winter uniforms, made up of quite a few layers, all of the best cotton. I admired myself in a big mirror. Never had I had such fine clothes. Now, short of a red star, I was a true soldier.

I caught sight of a few former Red Rebels from Lingzhi among the throngs of new recruits and their parents in the guest house courtyard. We looked at each other and laughed. An officer dragged me onto a hillock as a prize exhibit, showing the different parts of my uniform, layer by layer, to a crowd of captivated peasants. "Rest assured," he cried out, "your sons will not be cold!"

We spent three days at the guest house, studying Chairman Mao's quotations. The last afternoon, I was able to go home to say good-bye to Grandpa. When I walked up to the kang in my khaki uniform, he looked at me through his spectacles for a good while before saying, "Child, you have grown wings! Now you can fly! Fly away, fly away!" As he spoke, tears ran from his eyes and down into his wispy beard.

"Grandpa, don't be sad," I said, tasting my own salty tears. "I'll write to you. I'll come back to see you."

Grandpa turned away from me and lay on his side facing the wall, his shoulders quivering.

The next morning, the new recruits marched across town to the cheers of friends and family who lined the streets. Canvas-covered trucks were waiting for us at the foot of the hill on the east side of town. From my spot on the back of a truck, I found Mama and my younger brothers and sisters in the crowd. They were waving at me. Zhihua was wearing the clothes that I had discarded three days before.

We boarded a freight train that evening. The doors to the boxcars slid shut. The clatter of steel against steel filled our ears as the train carried us northward.

The Way Out

Postscript

Hours before Papa died of cancer in 1978, he sang "Song of the Taihang Mountain Guerrillas" and asked us to scatter his ashes over the mountains of Lingzhi county.

Six years later, the people of Lingzhi dedicated a monument to former County Head Gao Shangui. They set a slab of white Taihang marble on a hilltop overlooking a panorama that Papa himself had designed: terraced plots of corn and fruit trees up the sides of the valleys, yielding to pine woods on the heights, in accordance with Papa's afforestation plan of "capping the mountains with pines, belting them with fruit orchards, and binding their feet with terraced fields."

When Papa died, I still did not know him well. But I continued to hear stories about his past that illustrated how bold he had been before successive political movements gradually wore him down. He faced the first severe consequences of his obstinacy in 1952, the year of my birth. He was head of Shui-yuan county, and the Three Antis Campaign against corruption, waste, and bureaucracy was under way. The provincial party authorities assigned him a quota of five "tigers"— meaning he had to find five corrupt officials who had embezzled more than 50,000 yuan each. He refused to comply, stating that total government revenue in his poor county was less than five tigers' worth. So the authorities named Papa a "big tiger" and jailed him for four months. I did not learn this story until eight years after his death.

Papa worked in Shimen for the last three years of his life, as chief of the prefectural Afforestation Bureau. He was in the countryside until then. He had left Lingzhi to work in an even more remote county in the mountains after Weihua and I joined the army in 1969. The chairman of the new Provincial Revolutionary Committee had transferred him as punishment for his lack of enthusiasm in the movement to "get rid of the stale and take in the fresh" in the Party ranks.

Grandpa was not as lucky as Papa; Papa's soul found its final resting place, but Grandpa's is still wandering around. Grandpa died two months after Weihua and I left for the army. He had always insisted that he wanted to go home when he died, saying, "Falling leaves return to their roots." Mama and Zhihua hired a truck to take his body to the ancestral burial ground in Shuiyuan. Near Baoding, where the pro–48th Army faction was fighting with supporters of the Provincial Military District, they ran into gunfire. The truck driver refused to go on. Grandpa finally was buried in the Fu family cemetery near Lingzhi. Mama said it was the same Fu family anyway. Zhihua carved Grandpa's name on a brick and buried it by the grave. When we looked for the grave years later, hoping to take the remains to Shuiyuan, we found it had been covered by a factory.

Weihua became a career soldier. After several years on patrol along the border between Inner and Outer Mongolia, he attended an army academy and became a teacher there. I took a different route, changing careers several times. I drove an army truck for two years, delivering stone and cement to build military fortifications in the suburbs of Beijing in preparation for war with the Soviets. When colleges and universities reopened to accept "worker-peasant-soldier students," I went to engineering school. Ultimately, I became a journalist. Weihua married a nurse and settled in Shimen. I married an American while attending postgraduate school in Beijing and followed her to the United States.

The changes that occurred in my country during those years are well known. In 1971, the "invincible general" Lin Biao was publicly proclaimed a traitor when he died in a plane crash after his plot to assassinate Chairman Mao and seize state power had failed. Chen Boda, who had doomed the Red Rebels with one casual remark, was arrested for complicity in Lin Biao's conspiracy.

In 1976, Premier Zhou and Chairman Mao died; meteorites and earthquakes hit; and the Gang of Four were arrested. The Gang included Chairman Mao's widow, Jiang Qing, who had come to our attention early in the Cultural Revolution for her statement "attack by reason and defend by force." The other members were Yao Wenyuan, whose critique of the historical play "Hai Rui Dismissed from Office" had foreshadowed the attack on the Three Family Village and whose caustic writing style students had tried to emulate; Zhang Chunqiao, a Shanghai Party propagandist; and Wang Hongwen, a factory security officer who had risen to national prominence in the Shanghai "January Storm" by leading rebel workers in a takeover of the municipal government.

Deng Xiaoping, who reemerged from disgrace in 1973 and resumed work as a vice premier only to fall again in 1976, rose once more in 1977. The arch-capitalist-roader Liu Shaoqi was posthumously rehabilitated in 1980. In 1981, the Party formally proclaimed the Cultural Revolution a catastrophe. The truth of the old saying, "A thing turns into its opposite if pushed too far," had been proved once again.

When I left China in 1982, another kind of revolution was sweeping through the countryside—the revolution of private

Postscript

357

enterprise. When I returned for a visit in 1984, it had captured the cities as well. Mama and my brothers and sisters were still eating out of the common pot of socialism in Shimen, but Zhihua was thinking of throwing away his iron rice bowl to start a photography studio.

In Yizhen, people were talking about rebuilding the city wall and turning the town into a tourist attraction with streets representing the Tang, Song, and Ming dynasties. Renovation and new construction were under way everywhere. Two of the four dilapidated pagodas were being rebuilt. The four Celestial Kings of Dafo Temple had magically reappeared. The plaza where we had attended struggle meetings against capitalist-roaders was a giant free market. Although one occasionally came across a faded slogan from the Cultural Revolution, there was a new saying: "Time is money, efficiency is life; talented people are capital and knowledge is power!" Young people walked through town in tight blue jeans, and high heels were not a rarity. Instead of dazibao, signs advertising public dances were posted in the street.

Our school, closed for a decade, had been resurrected— and its Cultural Revolution name, the East-Is-Red Middle School, was quite forgotten. The Chairman Mao statue inside the gate was gone, replaced by a rockery and a fountain. The workshop where Teacher Li and others had cut the marble slabs for the statue's base was now a general store run by teachers to make extra money.

Teacher Li had died. He, Teacher Shen, and Principal Lin Sheng had been posthumously rehabilitated. Other monsters and demons were scattered around the province. My homeroom teacher, Wen Xiu, had transferred to Shimen's best middle school. Teacher Liu had given up teaching geography to become chairman of the Political Consultative Conference in a neighboring county. The Yankee Feng and his wife had returned to Tianjin. Guo Pei had gone to Beijing. The former Party secretary, Ding Yi, had retired and was confined to a wheelchair.

I was eager to find some of my old comrades, but I encountered an old enemy first. I had talked to no one from the enemy camp for sixteen years. When I saw Caolan on the street, I surprised myself by calling out to her. She invited me home for dinner. She was now a mother of two and worked as a middle-level manager in a tractor factory. Her husband, a former classmate who had secretly sent our side information about Little Bawang's torture chamber, had become an army doctor. We talked not about the Cultural Revolution, but about our lives since. Caolan insisted that I stay overnight, and furthermore that I sleep in the main bedroom while she and her husband joined the two children in the other room. She insisted on moving the electric fan into my room.

My only surviving comrade-in-arms among my classmates, Erchou, was working in a cooperative shop in his township and tilling farmland contracted to him under the new system of household responsibility. We spent a day talking over beer and watermelon while his ten-year-old son sat in the marketplace with the load of watermelons they had hauled into town behind their new tractor.

I learned that Yuling had married an army officer and was teaching English in a middle school in Xinjiang, in the far northwest corner of China. Her parents had been cleared and reinstated in their former jobs.

Little Bawang had gone to work in a trucking company after being demobilized. But as the result of an investigation into Zongwei's death conducted as part of a campaign to get rid of the "three kinds of people"—followers of the Gang of Four, diehard factionalists, and those who engaged in beating, smashing, and looting during the Cultural Revolution—he had been expelled from the Party and sentenced to two years' probation.

Shuanggen had gone to college and was working at a fodder-research institute. Because of his involvement in the death of Zongwei, he too had been expelled from the Party.

Little Mihu was an elementary-school teacher in his village. Over the years, he had learned to do everything as well with one hand as others do with two.

Xiangyun had married an overseas Chinese and gone away with her husband to pursue the good life.

Zhubajie had gone to business college, gotten a job at the Provincial Statistics Bureau, and won the heart of the bureau chief's daughter—a marriage sure to advance his career. He was slated for promotion to vice-director of the bureau when his involvement in Zongwei's death caught up with him. He too had been expelled from the Party and demoted to ordinary office worker.

Most of my other classmates from the enemy faction were doing fine in various jobs—except for one who had died in an accident, another who had died of illness, and a third who had gone crazy and burned himself to death while yelling, "I want to go to university!"

As for the leaders of Yizhong's two Red Guard factions, East-Is-Red Corps Commander Fangpu had lost all his power, while Red Rebel Commander Mengzhe had become a successful businessman.

Fangpu had been deprived of his high-ranking titles one by one, until he was merely director of the County Propaganda Department. Then he had been named one of the "three kinds of people," stripped of his remaining post, and expelled from the Party. He is now working as a salesman for a state-run wholesale company.

Mengzhe was well on his way to becoming a "red capitalist," one of China's first batch of self-made millionaires. After early release from labor reform, he had returned to his village and worked in the fields for several years. Then he had started a television and radio repair service. His instincts and timing were perfect; the Party was just beginning to encourage entrepreneurship, and television sets were proliferating in the villages. His next step was to set up a private school for television technicians, drawing students from all over the country. Within a couple of years, he had a six-figure income. After more than a decade in ignominy, he had become the talk of the town.

It is said that one difference between a peasant and an entrepreneur is in their treatment of money: the peasant buries his in the ground, while the entrepreneur uses his to make more money. Mengzhe put his earnings into an all-purpose company that he named the Rising Force Industrial Corporation. He was president, and his board of directors included some experienced old capitalists and a newly retired provincial government official. When I visited my former commander-in-chief in his new ten-room house, he was contemplating whether to buy a bankrupt state-owned factory.

Mengzhe said that nothing was beyond his consideration; his corporation would deal with everything from import and export to canning, chemicals, and garment manufacture. He had spent a great deal of money on advertising, enticed technicians with high wages, recruited expert advisers, and even met with the provincial governor to discuss joint ventures with foreigners in the seaport city of Qinhuangdao.

Postscript

361

As a businessman, Mengzhe had the same charisma and easy manner that had won the loyalty of his Red Rebel troops. I told him that if he had been able to develop the nine-member Lu Xun Commune into the seven-hundred-strong Red Rebel Headquarters, he certainly should do well with his corporation. He laughed and said that he had been doomed to fail in those circumstances since he had no control over the political situation, but that now he was in firm command. I asked him what he would do if policy changed. "Let's back off ten thousand steps and assume such a change is possible," he said. "By the time the government might consider such a change, my corporation would already have thousands of employees. Who would feed them if the corporation were disbanded?"

Mengzhe saw the economic reforms as a continuation of our nation's efforts to find the most suitable road into the future. He said the reforms, like the Cultural Revolution, represented a struggle to reshape people's thinking, to shake off outmoded ideas and move into the modern age. Although this new revolution lacked the fury of the Cultural Revolution, it touched people's souls far more deeply and would have greater effects on the development of the society.

As I left Mengzhe's house, he told me that if I wanted to start a private newspaper in China, he would fund it. "Come back soon or you'll be left behind!" were his parting words.

Appendixes

Appendix A
Biographical Notes

BETHUNE, NORMAN (1890–1939)
A Canadian surgeon who went to China in 1938 to aid the resistance against Japan. Bethune worked with the Eighth Route Army in the Taihang Mountains, tending wounded soldiers. He died of blood poisoning from an infected cut after operating without gloves. He became a frequently cited example of "revolutionary humanitarianism."

CHEN BODA (b. 1904)
Mao Zedong's long-time personal secretary, who headed the Central Cultural Revolution Group. His political career ended at the Tenth Party Congress in 1973, when he was implicated in Lin Biao's conspiracy to seize state power. He was tried as a member of the "Lin Biao anti-Party clique" in 1980 and sentenced to 18 years' imprisonment.

CHEN YI (1898–1971)
Famed commander of the New Fourth Army during the Anti-Japanese War. Rebels ousted him from his post as foreign minister at the beginning of the Cultural Revolution. He died of cancer, and his funeral was the only state funeral to be attended by Mao Zedong after 1966.

CHIANG CHING-KUO (b. 1909)
Chiang Kai-shek's eldest son, now president of the Kuomintang regime on Taiwan.

CHIANG KAI-SHEK (1887–1975)
Kuomintang leader who came to power in a coup d'état in 1927. On the eve of the Communist victory in 1949, he fled from the Chinese mainland to Taiwan, where he remained president of the Kuomintang regime until his death.

DENG XIAOPING (b. 1904)
Secretary-general of the Secretariat of the Chinese Communist Party at the start of the Cultural Revolution. Deng became a main target of criticism but emerged as the key architect of the subsequent economic and political reforms. He is currently chairman of the Central Advisory Commission to the Central Committee and chairman of the Central Military Commission.

HAI RUI (1514–87)
Minister of revenue during the Ming dynasty. He was dismissed from office several times and was once jailed for criticizing the emperor. His name has become synonymous with honesty and uprightness.

HU YAOBANG (b. 1915)
Secretary-general of the Youth League at the beginning of the Cultural Revolution. Recruited into the Red Army as a boy in the 1930's, Hu was still in his teens when he finished the Long March. He is now secretary-general of the Chinese Communist Party.

JIANG QING (b. 1913)
Mao Zedong's widow. *See* Glossary, "Gang of Four."

LAOZI (6th century B.C.)
A shadowy figure credited with writing the text on which Daoism (Taoism) was built. There is some question whether the text, the *Dao De Jing*, was the work of one man.

LEI FENG (1940–62)
A soldier who dedicated himself to helping others. After his death

in an accident, his diaries and good deeds were publicized, and a nationwide movement to learn from his selflessness was launched among schoolchildren.

LIN BIAO (1907–71)
A Red Army general by the time he was in his twenties, Lin won a reputation as invincible after his field army swept across the whole of China on the eve of Liberation. Named defense minister in 1959, Lin had a great deal to do with the personality cult that developed around Mao Zedong. At the Ninth Party Congress in 1969 he was officially named Mao's heir. He is said to have won every battle but his last: he and his wife and son died in a plane crash in Mongolia, allegedly trying to flee to the Soviet Union after his plot to assassinate Mao failed.

LIU HULAN (1932–47)
A dedicated Communist and land-reform activist, this fifteen-year-old girl was hacked to death with a haycutter by the troops of the warlord Yan Xishan when she refused to cooperate with them. She is honored as a revolutionary heroine.

LIU SHAOQI (1898–1969)
A career revolutionary who led underground work in Kuomintang-controlled areas before Liberation and replaced Mao as head of state after the Great Leap Forward failed. He became the main target of the Cultural Revolution and died in custody. He was posthumously rehabilitated in 1980.

LU XUN (1881–1936)
A physician-turned-writer, considered modern China's greatest man of letters. An activist in the antifeudal May Fourth Movement of 1919 and leader of the left-wing writers' union in Shanghai in the 1930's, he was an outspoken opponent of Kuomintang rule.

MAO ZEDONG (1893–1976)
A founder of the Chinese Communist Party, chairman of the Party

from midway through the Long March until his death, and mastermind of the peasant revolution that culminated in the People's Republic, Mao dominated Chinese politics for some 40 years.

MENCIUS (372 B.C.–289 B.C.)
Philosopher of the Warring States period whose idealistic theories greatly influenced the subsequent development of Confucianism.

STUART, JOHN LEIGHTON (1876–1962)
American diplomat, born in China of missionary parents, who served as president of Yenching University in Beijing and as the last U.S. ambassador to China before Liberation. His staunch support of the Kuomintang inspired Mao Zedong to write an essay entitled "Farewell, Leighton Stuart."

SUN YAT-SEN (1866–1925)
Sun, a Western-trained physician, mobilized the sentiments of Chinese around the world against the Qing dynasty. His efforts culminated in the Republican Revolution of 1911. He served as provisional president for a brief time, then ceded the presidency to the military commander Yuan Shikai.

TAO ZHU (1906–69)
A Party official who rose suddenly to vice-premiership at the beginning of the Cultural Revolution, only to become a target of the Red Guards, together with Liu Shaoqi and Deng Xiaoping. Tao died in disgrace after being denied the medical treatment he needed. He was posthumously rehabilitated in December 1978.

WANG GUANGMEI (b. 1922)
The daughter of a Chinese capitalist, Wang was born in the United States and went to China as a child. She joined the Chinese revolutionary movement in the 1930's and married the activist Liu Shaoqi in 1948. She became well known as the head of a rural work team in the Four Cleanups Movement. During the Cultural Revolution, she was attacked along with her husband. She was rehabili-

tated in 1979 and currently serves on the standing committee of the Chinese People's Political Consultative Conference.

WANG HONGWEN (b. 1932), *see* Glossary, "Gang of Four."

XU XIANGQIAN (1902–85)
One of the famed "Ten Marshals" of the People's Liberation Army, Xu was retired from the Central Committee Politburo just before his death.

YAO WENYUAN (b. 1931), *see* Glossary, "Gang of Four."

ZHANG CHUNQIAO (b. 1915), *see* Glossary, "Gang of Four."

ZHOU ENLAI (1898–1976)
Premier of the People's Republic of China from Liberation until his death. A veteran military commander, Zhou served as the chief Communist negotiator with the Kuomintang during the war against Japan. He is credited with holding together the Chinese economy and protecting many officials and intellectuals from Red Guard attacks during the Cultural Revolution. Efforts to prevent public displays of mourning after his death from cancer led to the Tiananmen riots of April 1976, which in turn led to the downfall of the Gang of Four (*on which see* Glossary).

ZHU DE (1886–1976)
Commander-in-chief of the Red Army and the Eighth Route Army, and foremost among the famed "Ten Marshals" of the People's Liberation Army. Zhu was also vice-chairman of the People's Republic in the 1950's and chairman of the National People's Congress from 1959 until his death.

ZHUGE LIANG (A.D. 181–234)
Ingenious statesman and strategist who served as prime minister of the state of Shu during the Three Kingdoms period.

Appendix B
Glossary

Anti-Japanese War; also called the War of Resistance Against Japan. The part of the Second World War fought in China. For the Chinese, the war began July 7, 1937, when the Japanese attacked the Marco Polo Bridge southwest of Beijing, and ended September 3, 1945, when Japan surrendered to the Allies.

Beida. Short for Beijing University.

Black Categories. Six types of undesirable family background: landlords, rich peasants, counterrevolutionaries, bad elements, rightists, and capitalists. *Compare* Red Categories.

Boxer Rebellion. A movement against the Western powers that developed among secret societies of peasants in North China in the late 19th century. The rebellion reached its climax in 1900, when the Boxers and Chinese imperial troops besieged foreign embassies in Beijing. The troops of the Western powers retaliated, driving the Qing court out of the capital and looting and burning the famed Summer Palace. The Qing court was forced to sign the Treaty of 1901, which guaranteed the Western powers compensation of 980 million taels of silver, allowed foreign troops to be stationed in Beijing, and dismantled North China's coastal defense.

Cadre. Originally, a Communist Party official, but now extended to include all kinds of civil servants, from administrators to office workers.

Central Committee. The central leadership group of the Communist Party. The current committee is made up of about 210 full members and 140 alternates.

Central Cultural Revolution Group. An ad hoc leadership group

Mao Zedong organized at the beginning of the Cultural Revolution to bypass the Central Committee.

Chuanlian, literally, "joining the great circuit." A term used during the Cultural Revolution to refer to the Red Guards' travels around the country, ostensibly to exchange revolutionary experiences but more often to sightsee.

Communist base area. A region where the Communist Party established control before its nationwide victory. In these areas, the Party set up new local governments, carried out land reform, and maintained sanctuaries from which to conduct guerrilla warfare against the Japanese and the Kuomintang.

Comrade, *tongzhi*, literally, "people of the same ideal." The term initially was adopted among Communists, but after Liberation it came into widespread use as a replacement for "Mr.," "Mrs.," or "Miss." It became particularly significant during the Cultural Revolution, when people who came under criticism lost the right to be addressed as comrade.

Comrade-in-arms, *zhanyou*, literally, "fighting friends." Though originally restricted to the army, the term took on a broader sense during the Cultural Revolution, when it came to mean people of the same political faction.

Daqing oilfield. An oilfield in Northeast China, discovered and opened up in the early 1960's, that became a symbol of the policy of economic self-reliance. It still produces the bulk of China's crude oil.

Dazibao, literally, "big-character poster." Such posters became the major vehicle of debate and criticism during the Cultural Revolution. The right to write *dazibao* was one of the "four bigs" written into the Chinese constitution during the Cultural Revolution. The other three were the rights to speak out freely, air views fully, and hold great debates. The National People's Congress removed the "four bigs" from the constitution in 1982.

Dream of Red Mansions. A Chinese literary masterpiece, written by Cao Xueqin in the mid-18th century, that chronicles the decline of a feudal clan. More than 400 characters figure in this 120-chapter novel.

Drum Tower. A tower in central Beijing where, in ancient times, the striking of a drum sounded the hour.

Dynasty. China has been ruled by 37 dynasties, spanning more than 4,000 years, as follows:

Xia, 21st to 16th centuries B.C.
Shang, 16th to 11th centuries B.C.
Western Zhou, 11th century B.C.–771 B.C.
Eastern Zhou, 770 B.C.–256 B.C.
    Spring and Autumn period, 770 B.C.–476 B.C.
    Warring States period, 475 B.C.–221 B.C.
Qin, 221 B.C.–207 B.C.
Western Han, 206 B.C.–A.D. 24
Xin, A.D. 9–23
Eastern Han, A.D. 25–220
Three Kingdoms (Wei, Shu, Wu), 220–80
Western Jin, 265–316
Eastern Jin, 317–420
Northern Dynasties and Southern Dynasties (Song, Qi, Liang, Chen, Northern Wei, Eastern Wei, Western Wei, Northern Zhou), 386–581
Sui, 581–618
Tang, 618–907
Five Dynasties era (Later Liang, Later Tang, Later Jin, Later Han, Later Zhou), 907–60
Northern Song, 960–1127
Southern Song, 1127–1279
Northern Conquest dynasties, 916–1234
    Liao, 916–1125
    Jin, 1115–1234
Yuan, 1271–1368
Ming, 1368–1644
Qing, 1644–1911

Encirclement and Annihilation campaigns. Chiang Kai-shek launched five campaigns against the Communist base area in Jiangxi province between November 1930 and December 1933.

Appendix B

The first four were defeated, but the last one inflicted great losses on the Red Army and drove it to the epic Long March (q.v.).

Fen. The Chinese penny, i.e., 1/100 of a *yuan* (q.v.).

Forbidden City. The imperial palace in the center of Beijing, now open to tourists as the Palace Museum.

Foreign concessions. Extraterritorial enclaves in China's coastal cities imposed on the Qing court by the Western powers in the second half of the 19th century.

Four Cleanups. The first post-Liberation political campaign to emphasize the idea of class struggle. It was launched in early 1963 to get rid of corruption and malfeasance in politics, economy, organization, and ideology.

Four Olds. Old ideology, old culture, old customs, and old habits, the targets of a campaign conducted early in the Cultural Revolution.

Friendship Pass. A pass on the Sino-Vietnamese border. Originally called Suppress-the-South Pass, its name was changed to Harmonize-the-South Pass in 1953, and to Friendship Pass in 1965, reflecting the history of the two countries' relations. Though it has retained that name, the pass has witnessed constant border clashes between China and Vietnam since 1979.

Gang of Four. Mao's widow Jiang Qing, the rebel leader Wang Hongwen, the writer Yao Wenyuan, and the Party propagandist Zhang Chunqiao. All four rose to political prominence during the Cultural Revolution. They were arrested in October 1976 and charged with responsibility for ten years of lawlessness. They were tried in late 1980 and convicted and sentenced to prison terms in January 1981.

Great Hall of the People. An immense hall on one side of Beijing's Tiananmen Square (q.v.), built in ten months in 1959. Its main auditorium holds 30,000 people and its banquet hall seats 5,000.

Great Helmsman. One of the four titles bestowed on Mao Zedong by Lin Biao. The other three were "great leader," "great teacher," and "great commander."

Great Leap Forward. A movement for accelerated industrialization based on grass-roots efforts launched in 1957–58. This period saw the large-scale collectivization of agriculture and produced

Glossary

373

important achievements in water conservation and control. However, the program proved unrealistically ambitious and led to great economic setbacks.

Han. The majority nationality of China, accounting for 94 percent of the country's population.

Hui. A Moslem minority group in China, numbering about four million.

January Storm. A movement that originated in Shanghai in January 1967, in which rebel groups seized power from already paralyzed Party and government organizations.

Jiaozi. Dumplings with meat and vegetable filling, a traditional holiday dish in North China.

Jin. Basic unit of weight, equal to half a kilogram.

Kang. Brick bed that can be heated in winter by a coal fire underneath.

Key school. One of a limited number of schools in each province and municipality that have priority in the allocation of money, materials, and faculty. The key-school system, abolished during the Cultural Revolution, has been revived.

Kuomintang. The Nationalist Party, founded by Dr. Sun Yat-sen in 1912. The Kuomintang twice joined in a united front with the Chinese Communist Party against warlords and the Japanese invaders. It is still the ruling party of Taiwan.

Land Reform. The Chinese Communist Party pioneered land reform in the base areas, and extended it nationwide after Liberation. Between mid-1950 and late 1952, about 47 million hectares of farmland were redistributed among 300 million peasants.

Lantern Festival. A holiday falling on the 15th of the first month on the lunar calendar that is celebrated by setting out lanterns.

Liberation. The victory of the Chinese Revolution and founding of the People's Republic in 1949.

Long March. Driven from Jiangxi by Chiang Kai-shek's Fifth Encirclement and Annihilation Campaign in October 1934, the Red Army made a 7,800-mile march to Northwest China, where the Central Committee set up its new headquarters in Yanan. Only one-tenth of the more than 30,000 soldiers who started the year-long march survived.

Appendix B

A Madman's Diary. A novelette by Lu Xun, published in 1918 in the magazine *New Youth*, which Lu edited. Written in the form of the diary of a persecuted youth, it portrayed a "madman" in rebellion against feudal society. It was the first major literary work written in the vernacular rather than in classical language.

Mao or jiao. The Chinese dime, i.e., 1/10 of a *yuan* (q.v.).

McMahon Line. A boundary line created in 1914 by the British official Arthur Henry McMahon through a secret exchange of notes with Tibetan authorities, which put 90,000 square kilometers of Tibet under British-ruled India. The line was never recognized by China and was disputed during the Sino-Indian border war of 1962.

Monkey King. The hero of *Journey to the West*, a 100-chapter novel about the adventures of a Tang dynasty monk and his entourage traveling to India to obtain Buddhist scriptures.

Nine open letters. Nine theoretical tracts published as open letters from the Central Committee of the Communist Party of China to the Central Committee of the Communist Party of the Soviet Union after the Sino-Soviet rift in 1960. The letters accused the Soviet Union of betraying Marxism-Leninism.

Official's cap. A symbol of power and status in feudal China. Different types of caps indicated different official ranks. To "lose one's cap" was to be removed from office.

Opera. Every region of China has its own traditional operatic form, incorporating song, dance, recitation, acting, acrobatics, and martial arts.

Party committee. Generic term for the Communist Party leadership group in localities and organizations at all levels, from national units down to schools, factories, and neighborhoods.

Party secretary. Head of a Party committee.

People's communes. The rural communes that integrated government administration and economic management in the countryside. Organized in 1958 during the Great Leap Forward on the basis of farming cooperatives, each commune was composed of production brigades, often encompassing a village, and each brigade was in turn composed of production teams. The land and other chief means of production were collectively owned by the three levels of commune, production brigade, and production team, with the production team as the basic accounting unit. Distribution was based on the socialist principle, "To each according to his work." The communes have been disbanded under Deng Xiaoping's leadership, on the grounds that the system dampened peasants' enthusiasm for production.

People's Daily. The official newspaper of the Central Committee of the Chinese Communist Party.

People's Liberation Army. The armed forces of the People's Republic of China. Today's army evolved from the Chinese Workers' and Peasants' Red Army founded in 1927, which became the Eighth Route and New Fourth armies in 1937 and the PLA in 1946.

Poor and lower-middle peasants. Elements of a classification system developed to govern the redistribution of land during Land Reform (q.v.). The three major categories of peasant were poor, middle, and rich, with middle further subdivided into lower-middle, middle, and upper-middle. On the theory that the poorer one was, the more one welcomed revolution, poor and lower-middle peasants were considered the closest allies of the proletariat. Middle and upper-middle peasants were seen as potential sympathizers, and rich peasants, together with landlords, as enemies. These classifications were inheritable. They have been abolished since Deng Xiaoping came to power.

Production brigade, *see* People's communes.

Production team, *see* People's communes.

Public Security Bureau. An all-purpose police agency whose responsibilities range from traffic control and firefighting to criminal investigations and maintaining the peace.

Qinghua. Short for Qinghua University, China's premier university of science and engineering, located in Beijing.

Qipao. A close-fitting, traditional dress with a high collar.

Rationing. Introduced after the Great Leap Forward, when grain and other daily necessities were in short supply, to ensure equitable distribution. Citizens received coupons for rationed items, whose prices were fixed at low levels. Grain is still rationed in China, although several years of good harvest have led to ample supplies, and grain can be bought on the free market at higher prices without ration coupons.

Red Categories. Five classifications of revolutionary family background: workers, poor and lower-middle peasants, soldiers, revolutionary cadres, and revolutionary martyrs.

Red Crag. A novel about an infamous political prison run by the Kuomintang with American assistance in Chongqing, written by two survivors of the prison, Luo Guangbin and Yang Yiyan.

Red and expert. A slogan put forth in 1958 as the goal of Chinese education. One who was red and expert had acquired both proletarian political consciousness and specialized skills.

Red Flag. The Central Committee's journal of political theory.

Red Guards. Students who rebelled against authority during the Cultural Revolution. The first Red Guard organizations were formed in Beijing, but with Mao Zedong's approval the movement quickly spread throughout China.

Rehabilitation. The reversal of unjust or mistaken verdicts; to have one's name cleared.

Republican Revolution of 1911. The bourgeois democratic revolution led by Dr. Sun Yat-sen that overthrew China's last imperial dynasty, the Qing.

Revolutionary committees. Originally set up during the Cultural Revolution as temporary administrative organs after rebels had disrupted the workings of local governments, these committees were not abolished until the late 1970's.

Revolutionary martyr. Posthumous title bestowed on a person who died in service to the revolution during the war years prior to Liberation; sometimes awarded also for unusual heroism during peacetime.

Rightist. A label applied to hundreds of thousands of people, mainly intellectuals, during the Antirightist Movement of late 1957—a backlash that followed the Hundred Flowers Campaign, in which the Central Committee had called for criticism of its work. Many rightists were jailed or exiled to remote areas. Most were officially rehabilitated after 1978.

Romance of the Three Kingdoms. A historical novel, written in the

14th century by Luo Guanzhong, describing the wars and intrigues of the Three Kingdoms period (A.D. 220–80).

Self-criticism. A method of self-examination used by the Communist Party to solve conflicts within the Party or among the people. During the Cultural Revolution, self-criticism became tantamount to confession under duress.

Shaolin boxing. A martial art developed by the monks of Shaolin Temple, a Buddhist monastery built in the 5th century in Henan province.

Sixteen-Point Resolution. The charter of the Cultural Revolution, issued in August 1966. The document's full title was "Decision on the Great Proletarian Cultural Revolution by the Central Committee of the Communist Party of China."

Spring Festival. The lunar new year, celebrated throughout East and Southeast Asia.

Struggle meeting. The first struggle meetings were held during Land Reform, when peasants aired their grievances and denounced the landlords. They became commonplace during the Cultural Revolution as forums for the denunciation of overthrown authority figures.

Thirty-Six Stratagems. In ancient China, the number 36 was often used in an abstract sense to mean numerous; so the term originally referred to an unspecified number of military strategies. Later, scholars actually wrote down 36, using four-character sayings.

Three Difficult Years. A period of economic difficulties in the years 1960–62, now attributed to mistakes of the leadership combined with widespread natural disasters and the Soviet Union's sudden withdrawal of economic and technical aid.

Three Family Village. The joint authors of a satirical newspaper column that became the first target of criticism in the Cultural Revolution. The three authors were Deng Tuo, Wu Han, and Liao Moshao.

Three-goods student. Title awarded to students for good political thinking, good schoolwork, and good health.

Three-in-one organization. Common description of the revolutionary committees set up during the Cultural Revolution, which were supposed to include representatives from three sectors of society: government officials whose names had been cleared, the army, and the rebel groups.

Three Kingdoms, *see under* Dynasty.

Tiananmen Gate, literally, "The Gate of Heavenly Peace." Built in 1417, it stands at the entrance to the Forbidden City (q.v.).

Tiananmen Square. A 40-hectare square, the largest public plaza in the world, in front of Tiananmen Gate.

Two-line struggle. The standard description for internal political debate in the Communist Party. Party history was divided into a succession of two-line struggles, starting in the 1920's with the conflict between Mao Zedong's revolutionary line and Chen Duxiu's "right deviationist" line, and leading to the Cultural Revolution struggle between Mao's revolutionary line and Liu Shaoqi's "bourgeois line." The notion of two-line struggle was abandoned in the late 1970's.

Warring States period, *see under* Dynasty.

Water Margin. A historical novel written in the 14th century about the 12th-century peasant rebellion against the Northern Song dynasty. Also translated as *All Men Are Brothers* and *Outlaws of the Marsh*.

Work team. Probably a creation of the Land Reform movement, when the Communist Party sent task forces of Party officials and intellectuals to the countryside to mobilize the peasants. The authorities sent similar teams to localities to help initiate and guide subsequent political movements, such as the Four Cleanups (q.v.).

Wotou. Steamed cornbread, shaped like a cone with a hole underneath.

Xiaozibao, literally, "small-character poster." A condensed version of *dazibao* (q.v.).

Yanan Forum on Art and Literature. A discussion of the role of art and literature in revolution, conducted by Communists in the revolutionary base of Yanan in May 1942. Mao Zedong laid out the view that culture should serve the workers, peasants, and soldiers.

Young Pioneers. A Chinese children's organization that accepts al-

Glossary

most all schoolchildren aged 7–14. Founded in 1949, its main principle is the "five loves": love of the motherland, the people, labor, science, and public property.

Youth League. Membership in the Chinese Communist Youth League, which evolved from the Chinese Socialist Youth League established in 1922, is a prelude to membership in the Communist Party. The Youth League organizes political and recreational activities.

Yuan. The Chinese dollar, equivalent in the late 1960's to about $U.S. 0.40 and in 1986 to $U.S. 0.30.